SCHOOL SOCIAL WORK WORLDWIDE

Marion Huxtable and Eric Blyth, Editors

NASW PRESS

National Association of Social Workers
Washington, DC

Terry Mizrahi, MSW, PhD, *President*
Elizabeth J. Clark, PhD, ACSW, MPH, *Executive Director*

Cheryl Y. Bradley, *Director, Member Services and Publications*
Paula L. Delo, *Executive Editor*
Susan Fisher, *Staff Editor*
January Layman-Wood, *Acquisitions Editor*
Christina Bromley, *Editorial Assistant*
William F. Schroeder, *Translator*
Jodi Bergeman Glasscock, *Copy Editor*
Leonard S. Rosenbaum, *Indexer*

Cover by Anne Masters Design, Inc., Washington, DC
Typeset by Corinne Hsu, CLH Design, Silver Spring, MD
Printed and bound by Victor Graphics,Inc., Baltimore, MD

© 2002 by NASW Press

Library of Congress Cataloging-in-Publication Data

School social work worldwide / Marion Huxtable and Eric Blyth, editors.
    p. cm.
  Includes bibliographical references (p.) and index.
  ISBN 0-87101-348-7
  1. School social work—Cross-cultural studies. I. Huxtable, Marion. II. Blyth, Eric.

LB3013.4 .S732 2002
371.7—dc21

2001059090

CONTENTS

FOREWORD

This book opens the boundaries of international school social work. Within these pages is the story of international school social work. This book presents all school social workers with an opportunity to expand their horizons and to learn from the various descriptions of the school social work programs.

Before the mid-1990s, there had been little contact between the strong school social work program found in the United States and school social workers in other nations. Marion Huxtable was slowly developing an international network for school social work. Isadora Hare had participated in some international social work conferences representing the National Association of Social Workers and found school social workers in other nations. A few school social workers from overseas attended the NASW School Social Work Speciality Conferences (1978, 1981, and 1985) and a number of Midwest School Social Work Conferences. In 1997, a group of Koreans came to Illinois to learn more about American school social work. Marion Huxtable and I travelled to Japan to speak about school social work. However, overall, there had been limited sharing of perspectives within the international school social work community.

That has now changed forever because of one conference and this book. The School Social Work Association of America sponsored the First International School Social Work Conference, held in Chicago in the spring of 1999. That conference was a catalyst for greater international contacts between school social workers around the world. Now, this book provides for the first time a collection of articles describing school social work practice around the world. We can broaden our perspectives and learn more about our profession. This publication presents the reader with the chance to look at school social work in his or her own country and then to compare and contrast it with service delivery models from a diverse group of nations. This experience will enhance the practice of school social work.

Within these pages, we have a chance to explore in detail the practice of school social work in different countries. There are tremendous differences in the sophistication of the programs described in these chapters. However, readers will also find many similarities. Schools, students, and families face many of the same problems. Here we have a chance to learn what is being done not next door but continents away from our practice. The stories contained here are the stories of the practitioner. Some are attempts to justify the introduction of the service in their country, others show the new development of school social work, and others exhibit the maturity of the profession.

I have come away with a new perspective of my profession. Never have I had so much pride in the school social work practitioner. Read and learn about your colleagues, your profession, and yourself.

Randy A. Fisher
Executive Director
School Social Work Association of America

EDITORS

Marion Huxtable, MSW, has worked as a school social worker for Tucson Unified School District in Arizona for 27 years. She is President of the Western Alliance of School Social Work Organizations and Past President of the School Social Work Association of Arizona. In 1990 she started the International Network by researching the existence of school social work around the world and contacting school social work professional associations. She sends the information twice a year in a newsletter to school social work associations in 30 countries. She has published several articles on social work with children and school social work. She was a Consulting Editor of *Social Work in Education* (now called *Children and Schools: A Journal of Social Work Practice*) for 15 years and serves on the Editorial Board of the new *Journal of School Social Work.*

Eric Blyth, MA, CQSW, is Professor of Social Work at the University of Huddersfield, England. He has been employed in social work since 1971, spending 12 years as a social worker and manager in a social work agency in England and working in social work education since 1983. His research interests in disaffection from school include school attendance and exclusion from school. He has also undertaken research with "young carers" (children participating in the care of ill or disabled family members). He has authored numerous papers in academic and professional journals, undertaken curriculum development work on the training of education social workers for the United Kingdom's Central Council for Education and Training in Social Work, and has provided in-service training and consultancy for social work agencies. He is a member of the editorial board of the *British Journal of Social Work.* With Judith Milner, he has co-authored *Coping with Child Sexual Abuse: A Guide for Teachers* (Longman, 1988); *Social Work with Children: The Educational Perspective* (Addison Wesley Longman, 1997) and co-edited *Exclusion from School: Inter-professional Issues for Policy and Practice* (Routledge, 1996) and *Improving School Attendance* (Routledge, 1999).

CONTRIBUTORS

Paula Allen-Meares, PhD, is Dean and Professor of the University of Michigan School of Social Work. Her research interests include: the tasks and functions of social workers employed in educational settings and the organizational variables that influence service delivery; repeat births among adolescents and young adults, health care utilization, and social integration factors that influence sexual behavior and parenthood; and maternal psychiatric disorders and their direct and indirect effects on parenting skills and developmental outcomes of offspring. Professor Allen-Meares has published widely, including *Intervention with Children and Adolescents* (Longman), and *Social Work Services in Schools* (Allyn & Bacon). She is principal investigator of a W.K. Kellogg Foundation Grant, "Global Program for Youth," and co-principal investigator of the NIMH Center on Poverty, Risk, and Mental Health. She is currently editor-in-chief of the *Journal of Social Work Education*.

Gun Ros Maj Andersson, BSocSc, has been a school social worker in the compulsory school in Karis, Finland, since 1980 and is a family therapist and supervisor. She is vice president of Koulukuraattorit-Skolkuratorer Ry (The School Social Work Association of Finland).

Theresa Daniel is one of the leaders in education welfare in Ghana. Following a long career as a teacher and head teacher, she obtained the Diploma in Social Administration to become a school social worker in the Accra District. She has pioneered links between school social workers in Ghana and overseas since 1991, and has represented Ghanaian school social work at international conferences.

Sammy W. S. Chiu, PhD, is Associate Professor in the Department of Social Work, Hong Kong Baptist University. His teaching interests include social policy, youth work, and youth studies at undergraduate and postgraduate levels, and he has conducted research in the area of youth and welfare state issues. His recent research projects include youth unemployment in Hong Kong, career prospects among young new arrivals, and antisocial behavior among young people in Hong Kong. He is co-editor with Victor Wong of *Youth and Empowerment: Theory and Practice* (Hong Kong Policy Viewers) and his published work has appeared in *International Social Work, Youth and Policy, Australia Youth Studies,* and the *Asia-Pacific Journal of Social Work.*

Helen Cooper, MA, is employed by the University of Huddersfield and the Open University in the United Kingdom as a social work lecturer, where she specializes in personal development tutoring and leads student seminars on developing social work practice skills. She was an education social worker for eight years, has conducted research on professional workers who abuse children, and worked on an anti-bullying project in schools. Her previous publications include "Schools and Child Protection," co-written with Eric Blyth, in *Children, Child Abuse and Child Protection: Placing Children Centrally* (John Wiley & Sons).

Randy A. Fisher, MSW, is a school social worker in his 27th year at Mannheim Middle School in Franklin Park, Illinois. He is also the Executive Director of the School Social Work Association of America and was President of the Association from 1994 to 2000. He is the compiler of *Fisher's Descriptive Bibliography of School Social Work,* author of a number of articles on school social work, former editor of the *School Social Work Journal,* and was the first elected President of the Midwest School Social Work Council. He has presented workshops and spoken about school social work at state, regional, national, and international meetings.

Isadora Hare, MSW, formerly worked as a school social worker outside of Washington, D.C., and for many years managed the school social work program at the National Association of Social Workers in the United States of America. She is a consultant to the International Federation of Social Workers and has traveled widely in the USA and abroad. Born and educated in South Africa, she has delivered papers and published widely on children's issues, education policy, and school social work practice. Currently she is with the Office of Adolescent Health, Health Resources and Services Administration, U.S. Department of Health and Human Services.

Debra M. Hernandez Jozefowicz, MSW, received her post-MSW clinical training at the University Center for the Child and Family, Ann Arbor, Michigan. She has taught in the schools of social work at Wayne State University and The University of Michigan. She is currently a candidate in the joint doctoral program in social work and social science at the University of Michigan, and is completing her dissertation on junior high school predictors and young adult outcomes of high school dropout and low achievement.

Ki Whan Kim, PhD, MSW, is a professor in the Department of Social Welfare, Yonsei University, Seoul, Korea. He is co-author of *School and Social Welfare: Theories and Practice of School Social Work* (Hakmoonsa, Seoul) and has published numerous articles on school social work in Korea. He is co-principal investigator of "School Social Work Pilot Projects in Seoul" and is general secretary of the Korean Society of School Social Work.

Jane Loughborough, MSW, CSW, is a school social worker with the Toronto District School Board, Ontario, Canada. She has worked for more than 20 years in Canada's largest school board. She is the author of several articles on the effectiveness of school-based social work. Her particular interest is in special needs students with physical disabilities. She is currently representing the social work profession on two Ministry of Education committees and is past chair of the School Social Work Committee of the Ontario Association of Social Workers.

Godwin Pace, Diploma of Applied Social Studies (Social Work), Certificate in Social Work Management, is a school social worker at the Education Welfare Section in Floriana, Malta. He has undertaken practice and research relating to school absenteeism over a number of years and is the author of a procedural manual for the Education Welfare Section in Malta. He is also a fieldwork teacher for social work students at the University of Malta and a tutor for university students preparing for their dissertations and theses.

Mariann A. Piro-Lupinacci, BA, RST, has been a stay-at-home mother and a hospital chaplain. In August 1994, she began working as the School Pastoral Counselor for St. Valentine School, in Redford, Michigan. In June 1996 she obtained her certification as a Trauma and Loss Consultant and School Specialist from the Institute for Trauma and Loss, Detroit, Michigan. Immersed in her passion for school counseling and social work, Mariann began her graduate studies at the University of Michigan Ann Arbor, Michigan School of Social Work, and graduated in December 1999. Currently, Mariann continues to work as a school counselor/social worker for a parochial school in the Archdiocese of Detroit.

Tarja Pösö, PhD, is Professor in Social Work in the Department of Social Policy and Social Work at University of Tampere, Finland. Her publications include several texts about child protection and social work in different organizational settings (in Finnish) and she has also co-edited the books *Constructing Social Work Practices* (Ashgate) and *Reconstructing Social Work Research* (SoPhi).

Wes Shera, PhD, is Dean of the Faculty of Social Work at the University of Toronto. He has undertaken research and published widely in the areas of mental health, community development, social policy, evaluation research, and multicultural and international social work. More recently his work has focused on operationalizing and testing concepts of empowerment with individuals and communities. He has worked as a consultant/educator for the Ontario Association of Social Workers, conducted research on community and school-based initiatives to improve youth outcomes, and completed a study of educational evaluation in elementary and secondary schools in Shanghai.

Marie-Antoinette Sossou, lecturer and Head of the Social Work program at the University of Ghana, is currently a doctoral student at the Graduate School of Social Work, University of Denver, Colorado. Before joining the University of Ghana as a lecturer, she worked with the Department of Social Welfare in Ghana as a social development officer responsible for family and juvenile court cases. She also worked as a social work consultant for the United Nations High Commissioner for Refugees, Ghana Office, and for the International Organization for Migration in Ghana. Her research interests are in social policy, child welfare, and gender issues.

Graciela Haydée Tonon, Licenciada en Trabajo Social (Licensed Social Worker), has worked for the past 16 years as a school social worker in public and private schools at kindergarten, primary, and high school levels in Greater Buenos Aires, Argentina. She is also a professor at the Universidad Nacional de la Matanza and at the Universidad Nacional de Lomas de Zamora. Professor Tonon also worked for the Provincial Court, is director of a research project titled "The Quality of Children's Lives," and is the author of several articles about social work and children at risk.

Erja Väisänen, BA, DSW, is a school social worker in Vantaa, Finland, and has worked as a school social worker for 15 years. She has been a member of Koulukuraattorit-Skolkuratorer Ry (The School Social Work Association of Finland) since 1987. She was secretary of the association between 1991 and 1994 and chairman between 1995 and 1998.

Aila Wallin, BSW, has worked for 15 years as a school social worker, and for five years as a consultant in her own company, AikaIHMINEN Consulting, Riihimäki, Finland. She has undertaken research on substance abuse among children and young people in Finland and is leading the postgraduate training programs in school social work in Finland. For 18 years she has been active in Koulukuraattorit-Skolkuratorer Ry (The School Social Work Association of Finland), including several years as a member of the association's board and seven years as its membership secretary

John Wilhelm, MSW, is a school social worker in the Toronto Catholic District School Board, Ontario, Canada. He has worked for 11 years as a school social worker as well as exercising major responsibilities in social work professional associations. He is past chair of the School Social Work Committee of the Ontario Association of Social Work and a recent member of the Minister of Education's Advisory Council for Special Education.

Victor Wong, PhD, is Assistant Professor at the Department of Social Work, Hong Kong Baptist University and has been employed as a university social work teacher since 1991. Prior to this he had been a community-based youth worker for six years. His research interest and teaching subjects are in the areas of youth, health, and public administration. Among his books are *Youth and Empowerment: Theory and Practice* (Hong Kong Policy Viewers), co-edited with Sammy Chiu, and *The Political Economy of Health Care Development and Reforms in Hong Kong* (Ashgate).

Wilfried Wulfers, PhD, has many years of experience as both a school teacher in a comprehensive school and as a school social worker in Hessen, Germany. He also has responsibility for school social work issues for the labor union in Hessen, Gewerkschaft Erziehung und Wissenschaft, and provides further education training events for both teachers and school social workers at the Hessische Institut für Pädagogik. He has published widely within Germany in the area of school social work.

Eizaburo Yamashita, MSW, is an instructor at the Japan School of Social Work, Tokyo, Japan. Previously, he spent 11 years as a school social worker. He is the author of numerous articles and several books on school social work and education and is President of the School Social Work Association of Japan.

INTRODUCTION

Marion Huxtable and Eric Blyth

Children growing up in the 21st century live in a world closely linked by international trade, travel, and electronic media, particularly the Internet. Globalization is the term that has been coined for this accelerated process of interdependence and contact between countries. Children all over the world are increasingly affected by many common influences, such as television, and face similar problems including changes in the family, changing values, social injustice, poverty, and violence. This book examines how the profession of school social work is helping children around the world reach their potential through education.

In recent years there have been several texts discussing international issues in social work and the impact of global interdependence on social work policy and practice (see, for example, Healy, 2001; Hokenstad & Midgley, 1997; Lesnik, 1999; Lyons, 1999; Mayadas, Watts, & Elliot, 1997; Midgley, 1997a). These works identify a number of interrelated global issues that affect social work and issues with which social work should be concerned, including poverty, social justice and human rights, population growth, migration, disasters, conflict, displacement, social development, sustainable growth, and the environment. These issues are especially relevant for today's children in two major ways. First, as the most powerless members of world society, children bear the brunt of these global social problems. Holt (1997), for example, draws the attention of social workers to "the threats to future generations of children that are posed by the pervasive degradation of the natural environment" (p. 41). We briefly discuss some of these threats below. The second aspect is potentially more optimistic while at the same time posing challenges for today's adults, whether they are parents, teachers, social workers, or politicians. If we care sufficiently about the future of the world and its peoples, then today's children are the force through which such care can be nurtured and allowed to flourish. If we fail to tackle these issues now, another generation will have passed by. Education is the key to solving these problems. We frequently speak in terms of education from the perspective of individual growth and personal advancement, but Midgley (1997b) reminds us of the role of education in promoting social development more widely, noting that investment in primary education and improving the education of women in developing nations show a particularly high rate of return.

School Social Work Worldwide highlights one of the key threads of contemporary international social work: the need to learn from each other. The editors, as citizens of two of the world's wealthiest nations, are conscious of Midgley's (1977b) warning against "professional imperialism". Several chapters in this book make reference to the legacy of European (particularly British) imperialism from the 16th century onward and the imposition of alien cultural norms and practices. We hope that we have avoided the trap of perpetuating such imperialism and believe that we can all profitably learn from one another.

EDUCATING THE WORLD'S CHILDREN

School Social Work Worldwide is about the role of social work in educating the world's children. It describes how school social workers are working to include all children in schools that meet their needs and prepare them to fulfill their potential.

On October 12, 1999, approximately 214,000 children were born around the world, bringing the population on planet Earth to six billion. The proportion of children under the age of 15 in the world's nations varies from 14 percent to over 50 percent. In European countries, between 14 and 20 percent of the population is under 15 years of age, while in many countries in Africa and Asia, the percentage of children ranges from 30 percent to over 50 percent (Statistics Division of the United Nations, 1999).

Universal education was a creation of the 20th century. By 1997, there were 668 million children enrolled in primary schools, 398 million in secondary schools, and 88 million young adults in tertiary education (United Nations Educational, Scientific and Cultural Organization, 2000). However, 130 million children (12 percent of the total) are still not in school (United Nations Children's Fund, 2000). Illiteracy in most developed countries has been reduced to a negligible level following several decades of universal education. However, in many less-developed countries, literacy rates remain as low as 50 percent because of low school enrollment levels. The United Nations Educational, Scientific and Cultural Organization [UNESCO] (United Nations Educational, Scientific and Cultural Organization, 2000) lists illiteracy rates for 163 countries. Of these, 54 countries report more than 20 percent of males over 15 years of age are illiterate. Seventy-four countries report that more than 20 percent of females over 15 years of age are illiterate, reflecting the under-enrollment of girls in school.

The continued existence of child labor contributes to underenrollment in school. The latest study by the International Labour Organization (Ashagrie, 1998) produced estimates that there are 250 million children aged five to 14 working, 110 million (44 percent) of whom are girls. Of the 250 million child workers, 120 million work full-time, a number which is 10 million fewer than the number of children not enrolled in school. Many of these 10 million are girls who were not counted in the ILO survey because they work in the home, doing housework, and caring for younger children or sick family members. UNESCO figures show fewer girls than boys enrolled in schools worldwide. In primary schools around the world, 46 percent of the children enrolled are female, in secondary schools 44 percent are female, and in institutions of higher education 46 percent are female (United Nations Educational, Scientific and Cultural Organization, 1999). The underenrollment of girls is of concern, both for their own future well-being and that of their children.

Patterns of child labor reflect a gap between rich and poor countries. In Africa, 41 percent of children are working; in Asia (exclusive of Japan), 21 percent; in Latin America, 17 percent; and in Oceania, 10 percent (Ashagrie, 1998). These working children are exposed to hazardous conditions and injuries in many types of work. Girls are also employed as prostitutes, exposing them to AIDS and other sexually transmitted diseases. For example, in the United States, 300,000 juveniles, mostly female, are engaged in prostitution, and the number is 100,000 in Thailand (United Nations Children's Fund, 1994). Boys, on the other hand, are easily recruited, using intimidation, as child soldiers, with about 300,000 around the world in 25 countries (United Nations Children's Fund, 1996). The United Nations Children's Fund organized a successful campaign that led to passage of a United Nations Security Council Resolution on child soldiers in August 1999. This resolution was another step toward raising the minimum age for recruitment into armed service to 18 as proposed for the Optional Protocol to the Convention on the Rights of the Child (United Nations Children's Fund, 2000).

Not only are these working children exposed to physical harm, but they are also denied the fulfillment of potential that they can only realize through education. Most of them will continue in unskilled work or bonded labor, with low pay, for the rest of their lives.

THE RIGHT OF EVERY CHILD TO EDUCATION

The primary mission of school social work during the 20th century has been to help every child enroll and complete school successfully. A summary of international milestones in reaching this goal shows that the world is making progress toward recognizing and supporting this mission. The right to education is one of the rights of children encoded in the United Nations Convention on the Rights of the Child, an agreement between nations that is recognized by all countries except the United States and Somalia (United Nations Children's Fund, 2000). In 1959, the United Nations General Assembly first declared that education was the right of every child. Four world conferences were held in the early 1960s to help establish regional goals to provide primary education to all children, and, by 1980, primary enrollment had doubled in Latin America and Asia and tripled in Africa. However, one-third of all six to 11 year olds in developing countries and about one-twelfth in industrialized countries were not in school. The debt crisis in the 1980s resulted in the suspension of many loans to developing countries, which led to slower growth in public sector services including education. In 1990, the Convention on the Rights of the Child codified the right to education for all children into international law. One hundred and fifty-nine countries at the World Summit for Children agreed on goals for education, including universal access to basic education and completion of primary school by at least 80 percent of primary school children by the year 2000 (United Nations Children's Fund, 1999). UNESCO figures indicate that this goal has been exceeded (United Nations Educational, Scientific and Cultural Organization, 2000).

As progress is made toward universal basic education, special efforts must be made to include disadvantaged groups, such as children with disabilities and working children. In 1993, the United Nations Standard Rules on the Equalization of Opportunities for Persons with Disabilities were adopted by the United Nations General Assembly, recognizing the principle of equal educational opportunities for children with disabilities. In 1997, the participating governments at the International Conference on Child Labor in Oslo declared all work that interferes with the child's education unacceptable, and agreed on goals for universal and compulsory basic education, with a particular emphasis on the education of girls (United Nations Children's Fund, 1999). Educating girls brings them into the workforce and reduces the number of children they have, helping to reduce poverty, overpopulation, and emigration from poorer countries to richer ones. The World Bank promotes education for girls in developing countries as a way of strengthening economic development (The World Bank, 1994).

SUCCESS IN SCHOOL AND THE MISSION OF SCHOOL SOCIAL WORK

After universal education has been established, the mission of school social work moves toward ensuring that children complete school successfully. Most school social workers are practicing in industrialized countries where universal compulsory education has been established for decades. Supporting regular school attendance with social work skills continues to be an important part of their contribution to children's achievement in school in many countries, and reducing the social problems that interfere with school attendance is always a part of attendance work. However, many other activities have been added to school social work involving working with school children, families, schools, and communities. Even when access to school is guaranteed, children face a variety of obstacles in their personal and family life or within the school system. The school social work mission is to help school children, families, schools, and communities to remove these obstacles, and to advocate a school setting that promotes success for all children.

Children face personal obstacles such as disabilities, physical and mental health problems, drug use, adolescent pregnancy, and learning problems. Family problems include domestic violence, divorce, child abuse, homelessness, and family illnesses. In school many children face poor facilities, ineffective teaching, bullying, and abuse by staff. Classroom management is becoming more difficult even in countries with a tradition of obedient students and respected teachers. In Japan the term "collapsed classroom" has been coined to describe classrooms of unruly, demanding students (Jordan and Sullivan, 1999). Community-wide problems that make school difficult for many children are violence, crime, decaying neighborhoods, lack of community services, racism, and poverty. All children perceived as minorities in their communities because of their religion, language, ethnic group, or immigrant status are also at risk for difficulties in school. These wide-ranging obstacles to success in school are the focus of school social work today. The range of problems includes everything in a child's life that interferes with the child's education.

THE OBSTACLES TO SUCCESS IN SCHOOL

The problems outlined above affect children in all countries, rich and poor. The social ills of childhood are remarkably similar in every country and community. Poverty is often the greatest hindrance to children's education because poor children are pushed too soon into work, poor families cannot afford the resources to keep children in school, and poor school systems have inadequate facilities and equipment. The greatest problem is the wide gap between the wealth of industrialized nations and the poverty of developing countries. However, poverty affects children in rich countries as well as poor ones, with an increasing disparity in the quality of life between rich and poor families in several countries. In the United States, which is sometimes seen as the prototypical wealthy industrialized nation, one in six children lived below the poverty level in 1999 (Children's Defense Fund, 2000). The economic boom of the 1990s produced great wealth for large numbers of people in the United States, without any increase in quality of life for the poorest. School social workers continue to play their historical role in helping these children achieve a good education, which is usually the most effective way out of a life of poverty.

Today's children are affected deeply by violence, whether through war; violence in communities, in school, at home; or simply through the steady bombardment of violence on television and in video games. In 1997, a 14-year-old boy was arrested in Japan for the murder and mutilation of an 11-year-old playmate. The killer left a note in the mouth of the victim saying the murder was committed as revenge against the school system. Experts blamed the breakdown of family values, a repressive school system, and the influence of violent movies and video games (Moosa, 1997). In 1999, 16 people in the United States and one in Canada were killed in school shootings, and 4 were wounded in a shooting at a school in the Netherlands (Ribbon of Promise, 1999). These tragic events, while rare, command public attention and have an impact on school safety protocols, which range from installing metal detectors in schools to developing better procedures for helping troubled students. Many children are affected by corporal punishment in schools, playground bullying, suicides, and sexual harassment. Corporal punishment in schools has been banned in most European schools, but is still practiced widely in several of the countries featured in this book (for example, in Ghana and Korea). Meanwhile, the United States is the only country in the world that still inflicts the death penalty on youths (Richey, 2000), a reflection of its continued refusal to ratify the UN Convention on the Rights of the Child. School social workers around the world are involved in researching, developing, and implementing programs to help both aggressors and victims. Social work expertise in family issues, such as child abuse and domestic violence, and in mental health make school social workers well-suited for helping schools develop antiviolence programs that reduce the likelihood of violence in schools while helping troubled children who sometimes become the perpetrators of violent crimes.

While children in most parts of the world are healthier overall because of better public health measures and immunization, chronic illness, preventable accidents, mental illness, teenage pregnancy, suicide and drug problems are still common problems for school children. A survey by the European Monitoring Centre for Drugs found that 35 percent of British teens and 21 percent of German teens have used cannabis. In Finland, where drug abuse was until recently of minor significance, there has been an increase in concern about teen deaths from overdose (Helsingen Sanomat, 1999). Recent figures from the Centre for Addiction and Mental Health in Canada found that 67 percent of Ontario teens used alcohol and 29 percent used cannabis in 1999 (Centre for Addiction and Mental Health, 1999). A team of school personnel, including teachers, school nurses, and school social workers, is well-placed for observing children's health, providing instruction on staying healthy and helping children obtain treatment. Much preventive help and early intervention takes place in schools around the world, and school social workers play a major role in such teamwork by counseling children and their families, as well as in promoting healthy life styles. School social workers increasingly use research on resiliency to help children learn to cope with stress, rather than relying on the medical model of looking for symptoms and recommending treatment (The Search Institute, 1996; Werner & Smith, 1989).

Family issues, such as the increase in divorce, single parenting, and domestic violence, are brought to class every day in every country. In Russia, Sweden, Finland, Norway, the United Kingdom, the United States, Canada, and Hungary (several of the countries featured in this book) the divorce rate in 1996 was at least 40 percent of the marriage rate, indicating that large numbers of children do not live with both parents, exposing them to increased poverty and stress (Lycos Network, 1996). In Canada, for example, 76 percent of children aged 0 to 11 live with both parents and 16 percent live with a single parent according to the 1996 census (Statistics Canada, 1996). In the United States, 32 percent of all births are to unmarried women, providing a lower level of security to these children from the outset (Children's Defense Fund, 1998). School social workers work disproportionately with children from homes having only one parent, to help obtain resources and to provide additional support for their education. In countries where divorce is common and has little stigma, such as the United States, school social workers find little resistance to providing special assistance for such children. In countries where divorce is less common and still stigmatized, such as Japan, children of divorced parents often suffer much more from feelings of being different and feelings of isolation from their peers. In Japan, in spite of the low rate of divorce, many fathers play little active roles in the lives of their children, and some experts blame the increase in delinquency, school violence, and child abuse on the excessive stress this places on mothers. A campaign by the Child and Family Bureau at the Health and Welfare Ministry is attempting to encourage more involvement by fathers (Matsushita, 1999).

As populations have become more mobile in the second half of the 20th century, communities have become diverse. People are moving from the developing countries where there are high birth rates to the industrialized countries that have low birth rates. When children move to new communities, they often face prejudice because of minority status. Much of the mobility has been due to the great increase in refugees, of whom 21.5 million were considered as being of concern to the United Nations High Commissioner for Refugees in 1999 (United Nations High Commissioner for Refugees, 1999). One out of every 280 people on earth is counted by UNHCR as displaced from their homes. Economic problems are also driving large-scale migrations. The United States adds about three quarters of a million immigrants a year to its population of 270 million (The Federation for American Immigration Reform, 1996). The United States has historically been a country of immigrants, but now European countries, previously with relatively homogeneous populations, are also receiving influxes from the south and east. Immigrant children face anti-immigrant, even xenophobic, reactions, occasionally supported by right-wing political parties. To deal with these massive population shifts, school systems in every country must provide for children who speak different languages, have different customs, and need extra help to succeed in school. Schools are also in the forefront of teaching tolerance, dealing with inter-group conflicts, and helping immigrant children adapt while retaining their heritage.

Schools have traditionally been second only to the family in socializing children, yet their role is now even greater as both nuclear and extended families are shrinking. Schools not only teach reading, writing, and mathematics, but are assuming a primary role in helping children cope with the problems described above, which previously were handled by families alone. School social workers work with members of other disciplines to create an environment in which children not only are actively involved in their own learning, but also flourish and become resilient.

How School Social Work Developed around the World

The earliest development of school social work is closely related to the introduction of compulsory attendance. Laws requiring compulsory and universal school attendance are the norm worldwide for increasing literacy and improving the educational level of the population. The eradication of illiteracy follows the implementation of such laws. For example, compulsory education began in England at the end of the 19th century, in Canada in the 1870s, and every state in the United States had passed compulsory attendance laws by 1918 (Allen-Meares, Washington & Welsh, 2000). Illiteracy is minimal in developed countries with compulsory attendance laws. The trend is to introduce a compulsory system of education for at least basic education, and to add additional years to the requirement as demand increases for a more sophisticated workforce. While many countries have achieved the basic goal of a fully literate society through universal school attendance, others are still working toward that goal. In Ghana, for example, 22.5 percent of men and 41.6 percent of women were illiterate in 1997 (United Nations Educational, Scientific and Cultural Organization Statistical Yearbook, 1999). Ghana aims to provide basic education for every child by 2005 through the introduction of FCUBE: Free, Compulsory, Universal, Basic Education (Ghana Education Service, 1996).

Following the introduction of universal education, many children throughout the world were unable to take advantage of their new right to attend school. The need for children to work to supplement family income, the family's lack of understanding of the benefits of education, and many physical and social problems interfered with children attending school. Schools needed officials to enforce attendance and families needed help to make it possible to send their children to school.

In England, the role of *school attendance officer* was born, and over a century later, has evolved into the position of *education welfare officer* or *education social worker*. In the United States, private agencies in three East Coast cities placed *visiting teachers* in the schools to provide contact between home and school and promote school attendance. The role of the visiting teacher developed a true social work approach early on, incorporating much from the mental hygiene movement, and has evolved steadily to include a variety of roles and services over the past 90 years. The title *school social worker* was adopted in the 1930s (Costin, 1969).

The Nordic countries introduced school social work between the 1940s and 1970s. The role includes both social work and guidance/counseling with a strong emphasis on prevention. The professional title of *school curator* ("one who cares") reveals the underlying principle. Canadian school social work also started in the 1940s. Its roots were both in the work of attendance officers from the earlier part of the 20th century, which in turn developed out of truancy work in the last quarter of the 20th century, and in the mental hygiene movement. The Netherlands also introduced school social work in the 1940s.

Social welfare personnel in Ghana were assigned to work with schools in the 1950s, and in the 1960s the Ghana Education Service started its own school welfare service to ensure that children attend school and that their needs are met so that they can benefit from their education. Part of the current role of school social workers in Ghana is to provide services, such as food services in schools, that help to increase enrollment. In the 1960s Argentina started to provide school social work service, followed by Australia, Germany, Poland, and Hong Kong in the 1970s, and Korea in the 1980s.

School social work is a new development in Austria, New Zealand, Switzerland, Saudi Arabia, Sri Lanka, Macedonia, and several Eastern European countries, including Russia, Latvia, Hungary, and Estonia, and has been demonstrated only as a small pilot program in Japan. School social workers in programs that started within the last 30 years are typically still defining the role and interpreting it to the consuming public and to fellow professionals.

School social workers have the skills and knowledge to help solve problems of underachievement, school violence, and poor attendance. Without social work intervention, children are often excluded, punished, or drop out of school. School is also the logical location for providing social work services to children who need help for a wide variety of problems. Fortunately school social work is growing. Several countries have recently started school social work services, and in countries such as the United States and the Netherlands it is becoming stronger. Over 21,000 school social workers are known to be active around the world, but most of the world's children do not have the advocacy of a school social worker. In the United States, there are over 14,000 school social workers, yet many schools have no access to a school social worker. In Sweden there are about 2,000 school social workers, yet school social work is not seen as a priority. Other countries, such as Australia, have school social workers, but in such small numbers that the service is restricted to a few basic functions such as crisis intervention. Many countries, including Japan, do not have social work in schools. Education is extremely important in Japanese culture, and Japanese students achieve at a high level. In recent years, however, there have been signs of tension in the system and stress among students, yet the school system has been slow to change to meet students' needs and to provide support programs such as school social work.

Little is known about social work services to children in many parts of the world because of a lack of international comparative studies in the field of social work. For example, there is a lack of information about social work in schools in some parts of Europe, especially the Mediterranean countries, much of Africa, Asia, and Central and South America.

THE ROLE OF SCHOOL SOCIAL WORK

The origins of the earliest school social work programs (in the United Kingdom and the United States) were in attendance work following the intro-duction of universal compulsory attendance. However, there has been a steady trend toward a broader definition of the role. In countries that introduced school social work after child labor was no longer a routine hindrance to school attendance, school social work was brought in to attend to a range of social and emotional needs of the students. Often, these social or emotional needs result in poor attendance and interfere with the student's success in school. As a result, attendance work, with its complex underlying problems, continues to be a staple of school social work service, although in many places it is no longer the main activity.

In tracing the origins and development of school social work in various parts of the world it is clear that the role has changed over time and varies from country to country. For example, in the United States, the visiting teacher of 1906 who visited homes to support compulsory attendance laws, improve home/school communication, and attend to child welfare, has become the school social worker of the 21st century with wide-ranging responsibilities in special education, mental health, advocacy, program development, and home/school/community liaison. The role is never static but changes as the needs of the students and schools change. Similarly, each country has placed its own stamp on the work while drawing on some of the training and research available from those countries where school social work is well-developed.

Content of This Book

Each chapter of *School Social Work Worldwide* reports the history and current status of school social work in a different country or region. Demographic, social welfare, and political information is included at the start of each chapter to show the influences that affect children and their education in that country. Data on social indicators related to children and youth are provided in sidebars for easy reference. Authors describe the education system in their country and the major current issues in education, including educating disabled children, preventing violence in schools, and raising educational standards. Following this background information, each chapter shows how, when, and why school social work was developed, describes the role and activities of school social workers, outlines the training and certification required, and discusses current concerns. The chapters conclude with a summary of policy and practice issues for the future direction of the profession.

The editors have arranged the chapters in the approximate order in which school social work appeared, so that if the chapters are read in this sequence, the reader will follow its expansion around the world, and notice stages of development as well as differing models of practice. Early models of school social work in the United Kingdom and the United States were designed to increase enrollment and improve attendance. These early programs and those that developed later in the other countries in the book evolved to include much more than attendance work. The concluding chapter is about efforts to introduce school social work into Japan.

The book exemplifies the value of practitioners collaborating with researchers and educators in developing the literature of the profession. Most of the authors in this book are either school social workers or professors of social work who have both practiced school social work and carried out research. They understand not only the development of school social work, but also have first-hand knowledge of the problems of today's children and youth. Since most of the countries in the book have only a modest school social work literature, the authors have searched records of professional associations and made personal contacts, in addition to reviewing social work texts, in order to present a complete description of the field. The book itself is one illustration of how society can benefit from the accelerated pace of international contact in the 21st century.

The conclusion summarizes the common issues that affect school children at the beginning of the 21st century and the common themes in school social work practice around the world. In addition to indicating the commonalities, the editors also describe differences in school social work practice around the world, and show how these differences emerged both from national traditions in the helping professions and from political influences. The conclusion helps school social workers, social work educators, and policy makers see how the tradition of school social work in their own country matches the trends around the world. In today's global environment, professionals may learn as much from peers in other countries as from the social worker next door. The conclusion also raises issues for social work educators about how social work students are prepared to work in schools, and about the inclusion of international themes in social work education. The editors draw conclusions about the direction of school social work and how this profession can become a more effective agent in ensuring an appropriate education for all of the world's children.

REFERENCES

Allen-Meares, P., Washington, R. & Welsh, B. (2000). *Social Work Services in Schools* (pp.31–32). Needham Heights, MA: Allyn and Bacon.

Ashagrie, K. (1998). *Statistics on working children and hazardous child labor in brief.* Geneva: International Labour Organization.

Centre for Addiction and Mental Health. (1999). *Ontario student drug use survey* [Online]. Available: http://www.camh.net/addiction/ont_study_drug_use.html

Children's Defense Fund. (2000). *Every child deserves a fair start* [Online]. Available: http://childrensdefense.org/fairstart-faqs.htm

Costin, L. (1969). A historical review of school social work. *Social Casework, 50,* 439–453.

Ghana Education Service. (1996). *Free Compulsory Universal Basic Education.* Accra, Ghana: Ministry of Education.

Healy, L. (2001). *International social work: Professional action in an interdependent world.* Oxford: Oxford University Press.

Helsingin Sanomat. International edition. *Police to crack down on drug trade in Greater Helsinki.* (First published in print 10.11.1999) [Online]. Available: http://www.helsinki-hs.net/today/101199-03.html

Hokenstad, M.C. & Midgley, J. (Eds.). (1997). *Issues in international social work: Global challenges for a new century.* Washington, DC: NASW Press.

Holt, M. D. (1997) Social work, the environment and sustainable growth. In M. C. Hokenstad & J. Midgley (Eds.). *Issues in international social work: Global challenges for a new century.* (pp. 27–44). Washington, DC: NASW Press.

Jordan, M. & Sullivan, K. (1999, January 24). Japanese schools' authority in recess. *Washington Post,* p.A01.

Lesnik, B. (Ed.). (1999). *International perspectives in social work: Social work and the state.* London: Pavilion.

Lycos Network. (1996). *World Statistics: Percentage of divorces in selected countries.* [Online]. Available: http://infoplease.lycos.com/ipa/A0200806.html

Lyons, K. (1999). *International social work: Themes and perspectives.* Aldershot: Ashgate.

Matsushita, Y. (1999, June 16). Japanese children ask, "Where's otosan?" *Christian Science Monitor,* p.13.

Mayadas, N.S., Watts, T.D. & Elliot, D. (Eds). (1997). *International handbook on social work theory and practice.* London: Greenwood Press.

Midgley, J. (1997a). *Social welfare in global context.* Thousand Oaks, CA: Sage.

Midgley, J. (1997b). Social work and international social development. In M. C. Hokenstad & J. Midgley (Eds.). *Issues in international social work: Global challenges for a new century.* (pp. 11–26). Washington, DC: NASW Press.

Moosa, E. (1997, July 3). Law to blame for kid crime? *The Japan Times,* p.3.

Ribbon of Promise. (1999). *Statistics on school shootings.* http://www.ribbonofpromise.org/about.html

Richey, W. (2000, February 1). In executing youths, U.S. stands alone. *The Christian Science Monitor*, p.1.

Statistics Canada. (1996). *Canadian statistics: Marriage and divorce.* [Online]. Available: http://www.statcan.ca/start.html

Statistics Division of the United Nations (1999). *Indicators on population*, United Nations Statistical Yearbook, Series S, No 19. [Online]. Available: http://www.un.org/Depts/unsd/statdiv.htm

The Federation for American Immigration Reform. (1996). *Immigration overview.* [Online]. Available: http://www.fairus.org/html/research.html

The Search Institute. (1996). Healthy communities, healthy youth. A national initiative of Search Institute to unite communities for children and adolescents.

The World Bank. (1994). Enhancing women's participation in economic development. Policy Papers: Stock No. 12963. World Bank Publications. [Online]. Available: http://www.worldbank.org/html/extpb/abshtml/12963.htm

United Nations Children's Fund. (1994). *Breaking the walls of silence (A UNICEF background paper on the sexual exploitation of children).* [Online]. Available: http://www.unicef.org/pon95/chil0015.html

United Nations Children's Fund. (1996). *Impact of armed conflict on children.* Report of the expert of the Secretary General, Grac'a Machel.

United Nations Children's Fund. (1999). *The state of the world's children.* [Online]. Available: http://www.unicef.org/sowc99/

United Nations Children's Fund. (2000). *The state of the world's children.* [Online]. Available: http://www.unicef.org/sowc00/

United Nations Education, Science and Cultural Organization Institute for Statistics. (2000). *Education and Literacy.* [Online]. Available: http://unescostat.unesco.org/en/stats/stats0.htm

United Nations Educational Scientific and Cultural Organization. (1999). *Statistical yearbook.* [Online]. Available: http://www.unesco.org/education/information/wer/WEBtables/Ind2web.xls

United Nations High Commissioner for Refugees. (1999). *UNHCR and Refugees.* [Online]. Available: http://www.unhcr.ch/un&ref/numbers/table1.htm

Werner, E. & Smith, R. (1989). *Vulnerable but invincible.* New York: Adams, Bannister, Cox.

1 SCHOOL SOCIAL WORK IN THE UNITED KINGDOM: A KEY ROLE IN SOCIAL INCLUSION

Eric Blyth and Helen Cooper

Social Indicators* — United Kingdom	
Population	59,541,000
Percentage under age 15 years	19
Percentage urban (2000)	90
Life expectancy at birth	75.7 men, 80.7 women
Fertility rate	1.61 children per woman
Percentage of illiterate adults	Not available
Per capita GDP in $U.S. (1999)	24,323
Percentage unemployed (November 1999)	6.0

*Social Indicators. From the Statistics Division of the United Nations. Refer to notes on page 249.
Reference: http://www.un.org/Depts/unsd/indicators/indic2a.htm

NATIONAL CONTEXT

The United Kingdom (UK) has a population of just less than 60 million, of whom 83 percent live in England, 9 percent in Scotland, 5 percent in Wales, and 3 percent in Northern Ireland (Stationery Office, 1998). Minority ethnic groups account for approximately 5 percent of the total population, with the largest groupings (Indians, African-Caribbeans, Pakistanis, Africans, Bangladeshis, and Chinese) representing the UK's imperial heritage (Stationery Office, 1991). For the most part, minority ethnic populations are located in urban areas, many of which have experienced recent economic decline resulting from the demise of traditional manufacturing industry that underpinned local economies.

In the aftermath of Word War II, the UK developed a comprehensive welfare program, funded through taxation and social insurance contributions. This welfare program included a national health service, a national education system, and social security to provide subsistence incomes for those unable to provide for themselves because of sickness, disability, old age, or unemployment. Significant aspects of this provision remain in place more than half a century later, having survived many reforms.

There is evidence that an overall increase in prosperity in the UK has not been uniformly experienced throughout the population. There has, in fact, been a significant growth in childhood poverty and widening of socioeconomic divisions. The government's Department of Social Security (1999) concluded that a third of all children in the UK lived in poverty (defined as household income of less than half the national average income) and that the number of children living in poverty had tripled since 1979. In 1994 a national child care agency, NCH: Action for Children (1994) claimed that "the gap between rich and poor is as wide today as it was in Victorian times, and charities are increasingly being forced to 'carry the can' for crisis situations in the lives of children, young people and families in need." It provided a graphic illustration of life on the poverty line in 1990s Britain, claiming that a family on Income Support (a state benefit payable to low-income families to supplement family income) "could not afford the diet fed to a similar child living in a Bethnal Green [East London] Workhouse[1] in 1876."

A number of groups have been identified as being at particular risk of educational disadvantage, through low achievement, poor attendance, or exclusion from school (see Social Exclusion Unit [1998] for an overview of research evidence). These include:

- students with "special education needs"
- young people in public care
- minority ethnic children
- children from "traveler" families (families with an itinerant lifestyle)
- young people who care for a sick or disabled family member ("young carers")
- children living in families "under stress"
- pregnant schoolgirls and teenage mothers, with the UK having one of the highest rates in the developed world (Department for Education and Employment, 1999a).

Concerns for specific disadvantaged groups in the population have recently crystallized into broader concepts such as the "underclass" (Murray, 1990) and "social exclusion" (Social Exclusion Unit, 1998). We discuss these further in the section titled "Issues for Future Directions."

---

[1]The 'workhouse' was an institution that provided subsistence and accommodation in virtually custodial conditions for destitute individuals and families. On entry to a workhouse, families were invariably separated into segregated male and female quarters.

Education in the UK

The distinct traditional and cultural differences between different parts of the UK are reflected in a different legal system in operation in England and Wales compared to the systems in Northern Ireland and in Scotland. Overall responsibility for the formulation of national policy for education and for the maintenance of education standards lies with national governments. In England this responsibility is exercised by the Department for Education and Employment; whereas in Scotland, Northern Ireland and Wales, the Scottish Parliament and Northern Ireland and Welsh Assemblies, respectively, discharge these functions.

Legislation in the constituent countries of the UK requires that each child aged between five (four in Northern Ireland) and 16 must receive "efficient, full-time education suitable to [his/her] age, ability, aptitude and to any special educational needs [he/she] may have." Although most children are educated through attendance at a public-sector school, the law allows for children to be educated other than by attendance at school, so long as their parents can provide evidence of the suitability of the education being provided. In 1997–1998, a total of 9,972,800 children were registered at public-sector and private schools. Of these, approximately 5.5 million were attending nursery and primary schools (for children up to the age of 11 years) and approximately 3.75 million were attending secondary schools (for students aged between 11 and 18 years). Approximately 3 percent of the total student population (282,000 students) had statements of special educational need, of whom just over 100,000 attended a segregated school catering for students with particular disabilities or learning difficulties (Department for Education and Employment, 1998a).

Statistics concerning unauthorized absence from school (that is, absence which has not been authorized by the school's head teacher) and exclusion (expulsion or suspension) have been systematically analyzed only since the early 1990s (Social Exclusion Unit, 1998). These reveal that at primary schools, 0.5 percent of school time is lost to unauthorized absence, approximately half the time that is lost to unauthorized absence at secondary schools.

These figures have been relatively stable during this period, although anonymous surveys of students themselves indicate significantly higher levels of unauthorized absence than indicated by official attendance registers (O'Keeffe, 1994). There have been suggestions that, because schools have had to record unauthorized absence statistics in their published performance data, some have underreported the level of unauthorized absence because of its potential implications for the school's image.

Statistics for exclusion from school reveal a somewhat different picture. Whereas the number of students excluded is small in relation to the total school population, the rate of permanent exclusion (expulsion) recently has increased rapidly, from 3,000 in the 1990–1991 school year to 13,500 in the

1996–1997 school year. However, the Audit Commission (1999), a government body that audits financial accountability in public bodies, has subsequently indicated that the annual number of permanent exclusions had declined to 12,800. As with attendance, sources other than official records indicate that the official rate of exclusion has hidden a much higher incidence of unofficial and illegal exclusion. Data concerning fixed-term exclusions (suspension) are less readily available because schools were not required to notify the local education authority (see below) of a student's temporary exclusion before September 1999. However, the Audit Commission (1999) estimated that approximately 150,000 students are excluded annually for a fixed period. Government concern with the limited education for children excluded from school, thus increasing their risk of marginalization both from education and from membership in society itself, has resulted in new measures intended not only to halt but also to reverse these trends and to provide alternative education provision for excluded students.

Day-to-day responsibility for the provision of education for children is largely decentralized to local education bodies (referred to as local education authorities [LEAs] in England and Wales, education authorities in Scotland, and education and library boards in Northern Ireland). These comprise part of the machinery of democratically elected local governments that have limited revenue-raising powers, principally by means of local residential and business property taxes. However, the main source of income of local education bodies is provided by national government, enabling national government to exercise extensive power over local expenditure and service provision.

National government also exerts control over education provision in public-sector schools through: the National Curriculum in England and Wales (different provisions apply in Scotland and Northern Ireland), national tests undertaken by all students at ages seven, 11, and 14, in addition to public examinations undertaken at the end of the period of compulsory education; through the annual publication of schools' performance (including details of attendance and exclusion levels and students' academic achievement); and through the inspection of individual schools and education authorities. A further example of the role of central government, and one affecting education social work in particular, was the establishment of a program in 1990 designed to improve student behavior and attendance. Under this program, currently designated as the Social Inclusion: Pupil Support program, which is jointly funded by national and local government, local authorities are required to submit proposals for project funding to central government, such specific targeting providing for greater central government control of resource deployment. We provide examples of such projects below. Additionally, in 1998, the prime minister established a ministerial task force representing various government departments to monitor the progress of schools and local education authorities in tackling unauthorized absence (Social Exclusion Unit, 1998).

Statutory bodies are also required to take account of the European Convention on Human Rights and Fundamental Freedoms, which was incorporated into domestic legislation in different parts of the UK during 1999 and 2000. The main impact of the European Convention on UK education to date has been the abolition of corporal punishment in schools. The UK is a signatory to the United Nations Convention on the Rights of the Child. However, the UN Convention does not have the force of law and it is questionable how far it has affected education, except to flag the failure of children's rights to influence UK education legislation and provision (Lansdown, 1996).

Provision for the education of students with special educational needs, a categorization that includes children who have a physical or sensory disability, learning difficulties or behavioral, emotional or relationship difficulties, is based on the report of a government-appointed Committee of Enquiry (HMSO, 1978) and upon which subsequent special education legislation is based. According to the Committee, approximately one in six children at any one time and up to one in five at any time during their school careers would require some form of special educational provision. This is primarily school-based but supplemented when necessary with external support (Department for Education and Employment, 1994a), and a smaller group of students with significant disabilities (approximately 2 percent of the total school population) should be formally assessed and issued with a statement of special educational need, prescribing legal entitlements to specified educational provision subject to periodic statutory review. As official statistics show, the proportion of the school population provided with a statement of special educational need is somewhat higher than the Committee envisaged—approximately 3 percent. Under provisions of the 1996 Education Act, there is a general duty to provide appropriate education within a mainstream school, whenever possible, for students with a statement of special educational need. However, the basic principle of integration is qualified by the requirements to take account of the wishes of the child's parents, to ensure the efficient use of resources and to ensure the efficient education of other children. As a consequence, about half of all students with a statement of special educational need are educated separately from their peers in a special school or other type of educational unit, a proportion that has changed little over the years (Department for Education and Employment, 1998a). The special education system in the UK has received considerable criticism. For example, Barnes, a university teacher who has a visual impairment, finds little evidence of the beneficial effect of special schools, which he describes as "a fundamental part of the discriminatory process, not simply because they create and perpetuate artificial barriers between disabled children and their nondisabled peers, but also because they reinforce traditional individualistic medical perceptions of disability, and generally, fail to provide their pupils with either an adequate education or the skills necessary for adulthood" (Barnes, 1994, p. 42).

A more radical approach to the education of disabled children, and one that has wider applicability in the light of recent attention given to the concept of social exclusion and its remediation, is the idea of inclusion. Inclusion is defined as "a philosophy which views diversity of strengths, abilities, and needs as natural and desirable, bringing to any community the opportunity to respond in ways which lead to learning and growth for the whole school community and giving each and every member a valued role. Inclusion requires striving for the optimal growth of all pupils in the most enabling environment by recognizing individual strengths and needs" (The Council for Disabled Children [1994] cited in Russell, 1995, p. 20).

HISTORY OF SCHOOL SOCIAL WORK IN THE UK

In the UK, "school social work" is not a term that enjoys widespread usage. Although the title "education social work" (ESW) is used in some parts of the country, the terms "education welfare service" (EWS) and "education welfare officer" (EWO)—the designation 'officer' emphasizing the EWO's status as a local government official—are more commonly used both by LEAs and by government.

The EWS has its origins in the late 19th century as a school attendance enforcement service, a function that to a large extent continues to define its role. The officers of this service, school attendance officers, were originally employed by education boards, which had the responsibility for providing public schooling in specific local communities. Despite the focus on attendance enforcement, from the earliest days school attendance officers were aware of the impact of personal problems and social and economic disadvantage, what would today be perceived as social exclusion, on the children's ability to take advantage of educational opportunities. In 1897, Robert Aitken, the president of the attendance officers' national association stated, "Those with whom we are in contact require our sympathy and all our counsel. Children brought up too often in poverty and squalor and huddled in wretched homes, what thought have they for good education? School life can never succeed, or the influence of school, while home life is cramped and crushed by insanitary and often immoral surroundings" (cited in Coombes & Beer, 1984, p. 6).

More than a century later, the professional descendants of the school attendance officers, EWOs or ESWs, remain employed by the administrative descendants of the school boards. EWOs, therefore, are not employed directly by schools, so they have always retained a measure of independence from school managers and administrators. Education welfare services have also developed independently of statutory social work services for children and families provided by local authority social services departments, which have tended to focus on child protection and are typically associated by the public with the forcible removal of children from their homes. Because of the potentially stigmatizing aspects of child protection work, many EWOs have resisted describing themselves as social workers.

Although local education bodies have statutory responsibilities regarding the enforcement of compulsory education, the regulation of the employment of children of compulsory schoolage and overseeing children of compulsory schoolage employed in paid entertainment, they have no legal obligation to provide an EWS, nor to employ EWOs. Consequently, the service itself has no inherent statutory mandate.

The lack of both a statutory basis and of any national standards is seen as a major reason for the wide variation to be found among different education welfare services throughout the country. The functions of these education welfare services depend to a significant extent on the policies and resources of individual employer agencies.

Crucially, these differences affect both funding and staffing levels. For example, in a national survey of English education welfare services conducted between September 1991 and January 1992, Halford (1994) showed that staffing to student ratios in different LEAs ranged from 1:719 to 1:10,035. Later figures from one of the country's two professional education associations, the National Association for Social Workers in Education, showed EWO to student ratios ranging from 1:1,350 to 1:6,500 (NASWE, 1996). A survey undertaken by the Audit Commission showed that allocation of EWS resources across different English and Welsh LEAs varied by a factor of four, although its estimate of local need as measured by attendance levels suggested that "the variation of staffing across services is not huge" (Audit Commission, 1999, p. 39). For the whole of the UK there are approximately 5,500 EWOs or ESWs, although this represents a "best guess" because no national statistics are maintained.

Education welfare has experienced mixed fortunes regarding funding in recent years. Education support services, such as the EWS, suffered funding restrictions, as did other public services, as a consequence of Conservative administrations' reductions in public expenditure that were begun in the 1980s. Conversely, funding has been directed toward education welfare since 1990, as well as into schools and other support services, through targeted Social Inclusion: Pupil Support initiatives aimed at improving student behavior and attendance. Many current projects involve the development of more accurate and reliable systems of attendance recording and monitoring through the use of information technology, establishing cooperative interdisciplinary teams and employing whole school approaches. Given that national government has contributed the main element of funding to these projects, it has been able to influence the nature of the work that will be supported, for example through the use of Truancy Watch programs (designating areas, usually shopping centers, as "zero tolerance" areas for nonattendance and staffed by multidisciplinary teams such as the police and EWOs).

There are two separate national education welfare associations—the National Association of Social Workers in Education (NASWE) and the Association for Education Welfare Management (AEWM). The association that subsequently became NASWE was formed in 1884, and the association that is now AEWM was established in the early part of the 20th century. Each association produces a newsletter, the "Education Social Worker" published by NASWE and the "Education Welfare Manager" published by AEWM. The two associations provide a wide range of membership services, including information exchange and training. They also undertake public relations, advise national and local government, and lobby on behalf of the profession to maintain and improve standards. For example, NASWE was represented on the advisory group for a study on the management of school attendance and exclusion undertaken by the Audit Commission (1999). The two associations are also members of an umbrella organization, the Training Advisory Group, which also involves the Department for Education and Employment, OFSTED (the Office for Standards in Education, the statutory inspection body for schools), and educational institutions. The Training Advisory Group was set up in 1983 to coordinate national training for the EWS.

SCHOOL SOCIAL WORK ROLE

There is general consensus that a central responsibility of the education welfare service is to deal with school attendance (Atkinson *et al.*, 2000a, 2000b; Department of Education and Science, 1984, 1989a, 1989b; Halford, 1994; OFSTED, 1995a). Quantification by the Audit Commission (1999) of typical national referral patterns to the EWS revealed that 73 percent of referrals were for nonattendance. Atkinson *et al.* (2000a) report that 99 percent of respondents cited school attendance as a main area of activity.

In most areas, the education welfare service also monitors and regulates the employment of children of compulsory school age, including children engaged in paid entertainment. Many individual services have developed additional functions and broadened their role to ensure that "children are able to benefit to the full from whatever educational opportunities are offered them" (Department of Education and Science, 1984).

In practice, this means that EWOs are involved in a wide range of work, primarily direct work, with children and young people and their families.

This work includes:

- pre-school age children (for example, helping parents obtain nursery and other day care placements)
- child employment and licensing child entertainment
- inter-agency liaison, in particular regarding child protection and youth justice
- securing alternative education provision for students who are persistent nonattenders and students excluded from school
- young carers
- pregnant students and school-age mothers
- children from traveler families
- children in public care
- students with special educational needs
- survivors of abuse
- students experiencing attendance difficulties
- students exhibiting behavior or relationship difficulties (for example, problems with offending, bullying, alcohol, and drug use)
- parents of any child in the preceding categories
- preparing reports for courts, when a young person is involved in the youth justice system, when legal proceedings have been instigated to protect a child from abuse or neglect or in connection with nonattendance at school, or when a parent is prosecuted for failing to ensure his or her child's attendance at school
- providing advice concerning welfare benefits, such as free school lunches and free school clothing, and administering these benefits
- contributing to in-service training programs for teachers.

Typically, an EWO will be responsible for a "pyramid" of schools, that is, one high school and its "feeder" primary schools. More than one EWO may work with an individual school or pyramid where there are particularly high levels of social difficulties.

TRAINING FOR SCHOOL SOCIAL WORKERS

In the UK, the recognized national qualification for social work is the Diploma in Social Work awarded by the national validating body, the Central Council for Education and Training in Social Work (CCETSW), following completion of a prescribed course of study at a university or college. Currently, there are various modes of part-time, full-time, employment-based, and distance learning leading to the Diploma in Social Work that may be studied at nongraduate, undergraduate and post-graduate levels and which can be completed in as little as two years' full-time study, although the government has recently indicated that future professional social work qualification will be standardized at first degree level.

The Diploma in Social Work is a generic qualification and, since the early 1970s, there have been no specialist social work qualifications, although in 1998 the government introduced a specialized Diploma in Probation Studies qualification for Probation Officers. Whether this will herald a return to dedicated professional qualifications for different specialties, as existed before the 1970s, remains to be seen. Dedicated post-qualifying training is available in many specialties, although not in education welfare, and most such training is optional, given that there is no tradition of formal continuing professional development in social work in the UK. Continuing professional development is currently mandatory only for social workers carrying out statutory duties under mental health legislation and, in 2000, the government introduced specialist post-qualification training for social workers involved in child care, although this will not extend to education welfare.

No formal certification at either national or local level, other than that provided through acquisition of the Diploma in Social Work, is required for any social workers in the UK, although the planned introduction of a General Social Care Council in England and Wales (and parallel bodies in Northern Ireland and Scotland) will incorporate arrangements for ensuring maintenance of standards through a statutory registration system for social workers and other workers in social care. At the present time, it has not been established whether the mandate of any of these Councils will extend to education welfare. Any failure to include education welfare in the new regulatory system would be a missed opportunity to promote and ensure high standards in the service.

Very few Diploma in Social Work programs address the particular needs of prospective EWOs. The only dedicated program known to us was inaugurated at the University of Salford in 1999, although a number of universities that offer modular programs, such as the University of Huddersfield, permit students to choose academic modules and assessed practice placements that provide suitable teaching and learning for a career in education welfare. Although CCETSW has commissioned some curriculum development work for Diploma in Social Work programs (CCETSW, 1992, 1995a, 1995b), this effort needs to be seen in the wider context of the government giving no clear indication whether education welfare officers should possess any formal qualification at all. Rather, the government has merely confirmed that individual employing agencies have responsibility to determine what "qualifications, skills and experience EWOs need" (Department for Education and Employment, 1999b, p. 4).

In practice, few employers demand formal qualifications as a condition of employment as an EWO and, although there are no recent national data, Halford (1994) found that one-fifth of LEAs employed no social work qualified staff at all. The same study revealed that only about one-fifth of education welfare staff held a recognized professional social work qualification, although this in itself represented a thirty-fold increase compared with qualification levels previously recorded by MacMillan (1977). There is no evidence to suggest that professional qualification levels have changed markedly during the past decade, in our view placing EWOs at considerable disadvantage when dealing with other professional groups, especially teachers, other educational professionals (such as psychologists), and other social workers.

Generally, opportunities for continuing education, such as specialized school social work conferences, post-qualifying or post-graduate qualifications, are limited. Each of the two professional associations organizes an annual conference for its members, and other educational and childcare organizations hold conferences and training events on relevant topics, such as youth crime, exclusion from school, school attendance, and special educational needs. The Training Advisory Group, to which we have already referred, also arranges short national and local training programs, usually focusing on specific themes. Additionally, there have been a number of national events sponsored by the Department for Education and Employment to disseminate ideas about "good practice" resulting from projects funded under the Social Inclusion: Pupil Support program and its precursors.

ISSUES FOR FUTURE DIRECTION

There are three key areas for education welfare: clarifying its role; evaluating the outcomes of intervention, and evaluating its relationship with other agencies. As we have indicated, the origins of education welfare lie in the enforcement of compulsory school attendance. Attendance work accounts for approximately 75 percent of referrals to the EWS, and the government has made it clear that the central role of education welfare should remain concentrated on improving school attendance (Audit Commission, 1999; Department for Education and Employment, 1999c). The Audit Commission (1999) has highlighted government ambivalence about EWS involvement in work that is unrelated to attendance, which it seems to regard as a default function and which is likely to be encouraged when EWO's hold a professional social work qualification: "There is a natural tendency in EWS's to meet demands not met by local authority social services [departments]. Where local factors mean that such demands cannot be reduced by LEA policy, their impact on an EWS's workload needs to be acknowledged; elsewhere, LEAs may wish to consider staff specialisation *or refocusing of the service on attendance work*" [italics added] (p. 40).

Improving school attendance is seen as a key feature of the government's strategy for tackling underachievement and disaffection among school children in the UK and for promoting social inclusion (Social Exclusion Unit, 1998). To this end, the government has developed a range of approaches. First, it has established targets requiring schools and LEAs to reduce levels of both unauthorized absence and exclusion by one-third by 2002, under provisions of the School Standards and Framework Act of 1998. Second, it has encouraged and extended the use of legal sanctions to enforce school attendance, introducing new powers under the Crime and Disorder Act, 1998, to bring greater pressure to bear on parents, although doubt about the likely effectiveness of these measures has been raised by leading child care organizations (Scanlan, 1998). More recently, the government has significantly increased the maximum fine levels for parents convicted of school attendance offenses. However, the empirical evidence that exists casts serious doubt on the impact of much parental prosecution on school attendance (Blacktop & Blyth, 1999). Indeed, it may well be argued that too much effort is being deployed on older students with attendance problems, whose attendance is unlikely to show much improvement, at the cost of preventive action with younger students showing initial signs of disaffection. NASWE, in conjunction with the UK's largest public-sector trade union, has described attendance enforcement as "a simplistic solution to a complex problem that requires a more strategic approach, more resources and a commitment to early intervention, proper follow-up and support" (UNISON & NASWE, 1998).

A second, and in our view more positive, strand of intervention has been the funding of innovative work introduced as part of what is now known as the Social Inclusion: Pupil Support program. Below we outline some examples of the type of projects that have been introduced involving education welfare staff (Department for Education and Employment, 1999c).

At Stewards School, Essex, a program of "first-day contact" was introduced, with the aim of contacting all parents of students within targeted year groups who were absent from school without permission. Following morning registration, details of students who were absent without permission were passed to the contact team. After further checking to ensure that the student had not subsequently arrived to school late, a telephone call was made to the child's home. When it was not possible to establish telephone contact, a home visit was made by an EWO. When the EWO home visiting service was withdrawn, the school's administrative team and teachers continued with the telephone system. The levels of unauthorized absence were cut by half during the exercise. Another project using telecommunications was developed by the Liverpool LEA, which issued parents of identified "habitual truants" in a small number of project schools with pagers so that they could be contacted when their child was out of school. The scheme was so successful that it was extended across the LEA at the end of the pilot phase. Pagers were also used to convey positive messages to parents about their children's schoolwork.

In Kirklees Education Social Work Service (where one of the authors was employed as an education social worker), an attendance support team has been set up to work with students experiencing a range of difficulties. One of the projects initiated by the team is to work with students transferring from primary school to high school (at age 11), because there is evidence of a significant decrease in attendance at high school compared to attendance levels at the feeder primary schools. Kirklees Education Social Work Service also employs a number of specialist workers such as an employment officer, whose role is to ensure that children of school age are not being employed illegally because employment can have adverse implications for childrens' health and education.

Kirklees also employs a "looked after" children officer who works closely with the local authority social services department to try to raise the attendance and achievement levels of children accommodated by the local authority.

Traditionally, EWOs have tended to work with individual students— or groups of students—and their families. However (given the lack of evaluation of intervention), the Audit Commission (1999) has questioned whether individual casework can exert more than a peripheral effect and whether a greater impact may be achieved by promoting improvements in schools' management of absence and behavior. The Department for Education and Employment (1999c) suggests that this is likely to lead to a greater emphasis within the EWS on providing "strategic advice and guidelines to schools on attendance, including policy development and good practice, monitoring school performance and, where necessary, challenging underperformance" (p. 16).

Uncertainty about the role of education welfare clearly affects decisions concerning its training needs. Given the government's preference for education welfare to be primarily focused on attendance, it might be argued that a professional social work qualification is unnecessary and, indeed, few social work qualifying programs would be equipped to provide the necessary specialist academic and practice curriculum. This is reflected in two quite different programs dedicated to education welfare staff, the new Diploma in Social Work program at the University of Salford and the Diploma in Education Welfare Studies at the University of the West of England, although the latter does not meet curriculum requirements for recognition as a professional social work qualification. Given the cost of professional training and the limited resources available to LEAs, without clearer direction from government, we do not foresee significant changes in qualification levels within the service.

Little evaluation of mainstream EWO work appears to take place (Audit Commission, 1999), the work of Kazi (1998) and Kazi & Wilson (1996) providing rare exceptions. However, given that one of the criteria for project funding under the Social Inclusion: Pupil Support program is that evaluation is undertaken, we can expect that, in time, evidence about the outcomes of innovative programs will provide useful information about new directions for effective services for school children.

As we have indicated, the EWS has always been independent from schools, an independence that has been fiercely protected by the service. However, for a number of years, national government has questioned whether managerial responsibility for the service should be transferred to schools directly, considering that such an arrangement "would help schools respond quickly to problems of nonattendance" (Department for Education and Employment, 1999c, p. 16). In September 2000 the government initiated a one-year pilot program in 15 LEAs to transfer managerial responsibility for secondary school level EWS provision directly to schools. At the launch of the program, the Minister for Schools said:

'The aim of these pilots is to see whether giving headteachers more day-to-day control over the attendance functions of Education Welfare Services has an impact on truancy and levels of school attendance....The pilots will help us identify the best ways to enable heads to act quickly to tackle truancy, to support home-school liaison and ensure education and social services work together effectively' (Department for Education and Employment, 2000a).

However, dealing effectively with attendance problems may bring EWOs into conflict with schools—when, for example, students have been de-registered or excluded illicitly and risk becoming lost in the education system (OFSTED, 1998; Stirling, 1992)—indicating to us the value of their continuing independence from school management.

In the light of increasing evidence about the interplay of educational difficulties and wider social, cultural or health issues, the need for close cooperation between education, health, and social services is inarguable, although in practice, competing demands have meant that such cooperation has been all too rare (e.g. OFSTED, 1995b). Indeed, Webb (1994) highlights the lack of adequate support to children and families experiencing difficulties: "Schools often provide the most readily available and accessible source of counselling and information. Consequently many schools appear to have become an unfunded branch of the social services" (p. 71).

More recently, there has been increasing awareness of the importance of educational achievement for improved life chances and of the role of schools in the welfare network, and in providing a focus for community support and service delivery (Vernon and Sinclair, 1998). The government has proposed cross-welfare links to tackle disadvantage and underachievement, for example, the creation of multi-disciplinary 'youth offending teams' involving police, education, social services, probation and health services. Another example is a new service, Connexions, aimed at 13–19-year-olds to improve the coherence of what is currently provided through the careers service, schools, social services, youth and education welfare services to encourage more young people to remain in education (Department for Education and Employment, 1999c, 2000b). In the context of increased fragmentization of the EWS via devolution of service management to schools, the significance of EWS involvement in the Connexions program for its survival has been highlighted by the outgoing President of NASWE:"If we are not in Connexions we will be isolated and dismembered to work under individual schools agenda's" [*sic*] (Sunderland, 2000).

CONCLUSION

As we have indicated in this chapter, education welfare in the UK has experienced, and continues to experience, its own problems of exclusion and marginalization. Future prognosis is made difficult by major new initiatives whose outcome is yet to be evaluated, such as the introduction of the Connexions program, experimentation with new managerial arrangements and, not least, by the prospect of a general election during 2001 (although current indications suggest this will not see the return of a Conservative administration).

Given the pledge of Prime Minister Tony Blair before the 1997 general election that his party's three top priorities were "education, education and education," educational issues have featured high on the agenda of the present government. Concern with the problems of social exclusion led to the establishment of the Social Exclusion Unit (1998), whose first task was to investigate nonattendance and exclusion from school. The work of the unit, defined as promoting social inclusion, has dovetailed with other initiatives to improve standards of literacy and to raise academic achievement (Department for Education and Employment, 1997, 1998b; Department of Health, 1998; OFSTED, 1999).

The government has also recognized that multifaceted barriers to the promotion of social inclusion are beyond the capacity of any single organization or professional group to resolve unaided, coining the idea of "joined up solutions to joined up problems" (Social Exclusion Unit, 1998) to demonstrate the need for multi-agency and multi-disciplinary responses to such problems (Department for Education and Employment, 2000b). In our view the future of education welfare will depend on its success in responding to concerns on the political agenda and forming alliances through participation in the collaborative effort to promote social inclusion.

REFERENCES

Atkinson, M., Halsey, K., Wilkin, A. & Kinder, K. (2000a). *Raising attendance 1: Working practices and current initiatives within the education welfare service.* Slough: National Foundation for Educational Research.

Atkinson, M., Halsey, K., Wilkin, A. & Kinder, K. (2000b). *Raising attendance 2: A detailed study of education welfare service working practices.* Slough: National Foundation for Educational Research.

Audit Commission (1999). *Missing out: LEA management of school attendance and exclusion.* London: Audit Commission.

Barnes, C. (1994). *Disabled people in Britain and discrimination: A case for anti-discrimination legislation.* London: Hurst & Co.

Blacktop, J. & Blyth, E. (1999). School attendance and the role of law in England and Wales. In Blyth, E. & Milner, J. (Eds.), *Improving school attendance* (pp. 36-54). London: Routledge.

Central Council for Education and Training in Social Work (1992). *Preparing for work in the Education Welfare Service* (Improving Social Work Education and Training No. 13). London: CCETSW.

Central Council for Education and Training in Social Work (1995a). *Education, social work and the law: Preparing for professional practice* (Improving Social Work Education and Training No. 17). London: CCETSW.

Central Council for Education and Training in Social Work (1995b). *Preventing behavior problems: Practice issues in education social work* (Improving Social Education and Training no. 19). London: CCETSW.

Coombes, F. & Beer, D. (1984). *The long walk from the dark.* Birmingham: National Association of Social Workers in Education.

Department for Education (1994a). *Code of practice on the identification and assessment of special educational needs.* London: Department for Education.

Department for Education (1994b). *Exclusions from school* (Circular No. 10/94). London: Department for Education.

Department for Education (1994c). *Pupil behavior and discipline* (Circular No. 8/94). London: Department for Education.

Department for Education (1994d). *The education by LEAs of children otherwise than at school* (Circular No. 11/94). London: Department for Education.

Department for Education & Department of Health (1994). *The education of children with emotional and behavioural difficulties* (Circular No. 9/94. DH LAC (94) 9). London: Department for Education & Department of Health.

Department for Education and Employment (1997). *The implementation of the national literacy strategy.* London: Department for Education and Employment.

Department for Education and Employment (1998a). *Education and training statistics for the United Kingdom 1998.* London: Department for Education and Employment.

Department for Education and Employment (1998b). *Extending opportunity: A national framework for study support*. London: Department for Education and Employment.

Department for Education and Employment (1999a). *Social inclusion: Pupil support* (Circular 10/99). London: Department for Education and Employment.

Department for Education and Employment (1999b). *Social inclusion: The LEA role in pupil support* (Circular 11/99). London: Department for Education and Employment.

Department for Education and Employment (1999c). *Tackling truancy together: A strategy document*. London: Department for Education and Employment.

Department for Education and Employment (2000a). *Jacqui Smith announces pilot areas for devolving education welfare services to secondary schools*, Press Notice 321/00, 14 July. London: Department for Education and Employment.

Department for Education and Employment (2000b). *Connexions: The Best Start in Life for Every Young Person*. London: Department for Education and Employment.

Department of Education and Science (1984). *The education welfare service*. London: HMSO.

Department of Education and Science (1989a). *Discipline in school* (Report of the Committee of Inquiry Chaired by Lord Elton). London: HMSO.

Department of Education and Science (1989b). *Attendance at school* (Education Observed, 13). London: HMSO.

Department of Health (1998). *Quality protects programme - transforming children's services* (Circular LAC [98] 28). London: Department of Health.

Department of Social Security (1999). *Opportunity for all: Tackling poverty and social exclusion*. London: Department of Social Security.

Halford, P. (1994). *The Education welfare/education social work service in England and Wales: A critique of its organisation and role*. Unpublished Mphil dissertation, University of Southampton, Southampton, England.

Her Majesty's Stationery Office (1978). *Special educational needs* (Report of the Committee of Enquiry Into the Education of Handicapped Children and Young People. Cmnd. 7212). London: HMSO.

Kazi, M. (1998). Examples of research in education social work. In Kazi, M. (Ed.). *Single case evaluation by social workers*. Aldershot: Ashgate.

Kazi, M. & Wilson, J. (1996). Applying single-case evaluation in social work. *British Journal of Social Work, 26*, 5, 699–717.

Lansdown, G. (1996). Implementation of the UN Convention on the Rights of the Child in the UK. In John, M. (Ed.). *Children in our charge - the child's right to resources*. London: Jessica Kingsley Publishers.

Learmonth, J. (1995). *More willingly to school? An independent evaluation of the truancy and disaffected pupils GEST programme*. London: Department for Education and Employment.

MacMillan, K. (1977). *Education welfare: Strategy and structure.* London: Longman.

Murray, C. (1990). *The emerging British underclass.* London: Institute of Economic Affairs.

National Association of Social Workers in Education (1996). *NASWE data book.* London: NASWE.

NCH: Action for Children (1994). *The workhouse diet and the cost of feeding a child today.* (Press release February 1). London: NCH: Action for Children.

OFSTED (1995a). *The challenge for education welfare.* (A report from the Office of Her Majesty's Chief Inspector of Schools. Ref 17/95/NS). London: OFSTED.

OFSTED (1995b). *Access, achievement and attendance in secondary schools.* London: OFSTED.

OFSTED in conjunction with the Audit Commission (1998). *Inspection of Manchester Local Education Authority.* London: OFSTED.

OFSTED (1999). *Raising the attainment of minority ethnic pupils: School and LEA responses.* London: OFSTED.

O'Keeffe, D. (1994). *Truancy in English secondary schools.* London: HMSO.

Russell, P. (1995). Policy and diversity: addressing values and principles when developing a school policy for children with special education needs. In National Children's Bureau, *Schools special educational needs policies pack: Discussion papers I.* (p. 20). London: National Children's Bureau.

Scanlan, D. (1998). *The Crime and Disorder Act of 1998: A guide for practitioners.* London: Callow Publishing.

Social Exclusion Unit (1998). *Truancy and school exclusion.* (Report by the Social Exclusion Unit). London: The Cabinet Office.

The Stationery Office (1991). *Population trends 72.* London: The Stationery Office.

The Stationery Office (1998). *Annual abstract of statistics.* London: The Stationery Office.

Stirling, M. (1992). How many pupils are being excluded? *British Journal of Special Education, 19,* 4, 128–130.

Sunderland, M. (2000). Presidential parting piece. *The Education Social Worker, 244,* p. 25.

UNISON & National Association of Social Workers in Education (1998). *Truancy and social exclusions: An interim report.* London: UNISON.

Vernon, J. and Sinclair, R. (1998). *Maintaining children in school: The contribution of social services departments.* London: National Children's Bureau.

Webb, R. (1994). *After the deluge: Changing roles and responsibilities in the primary school* (Final Report of Research Commissioned by the Association of Teachers and Lecturers). London: Association of Teachers and Lecturers.

2 SCHOOL SOCIAL WORK IN THE UNITED STATES: A HOLISTIC APPROACH

Debra M. Hernandez Jozefowicz, Paula Allen-Meares,

Mariann A. Piro-Lupinacci, and Randy Fisher

Social Indicators* — United States	
Population	285,926,000
Percentage under age 15 years	22
Percentage urban (2000)	77
Life expectancy at birth	74.6 men, 80.4 women
Fertility rate	1.93 children per woman
Percentage of illiterate adults	Not available
Per capita GDP in $U.S. (1999)	32,778
Percentage unemployed (1999)	4.2

*Social Indicators. From the Statistics Division of the United Nations. Refer to notes on page 249.
Reference: http://www.un.org/Depts/unsd/indicators/indic2a.htm

NATIONAL CONTEXT

Social conditions across the nation contribute to the state of students entering school. Below are demographic, political, and social trends that influence contemporary American education and social work services in the schools.

There are 70 million children under the age of 18 years in the United States (Children's Defense Fund, 1998a). Thirty-six million are enrolled in the kindergarten to eighth grades (age five years to 13 years), and 14 million are enrolled in the ninth to twelfth grades (age 14 to 17 years). Since 1970, nearly 100 percent of all five to seventeen-year-olds have enrolled in schools. During this time, there have been considerable shifts in enrollment rates at the pre-primary and post-secondary levels. In 1970, 20 percent of all three- to four-year-olds were enrolled in preschool programs, compared to 50 percent of all three- to four-year-olds in 1994. In 1994, 12 million students were enrolled at baccalaureate level or below, and two million were in graduate programs, a 10 percent increase from 1970 (Digest of Education Statistics, 1995). Thus, in addition to a continued focus on elementary and secondary students, school social workers need to attend to the growing numbers of pre-primary and post-secondary students.

The United States is one of the most culturally diverse nations of the world. Currently, 72 percent of Americans are of European descent, 12 percent of African descent, 11 percent of Hispanic, 4 percent of Asian or Pacific Islander, and 1 percent is Native American, Eskimo or Aleut (U.S. Bureau of the Census, 1998). As a result of increased birthrates among indigenous ethnic minority groups such as Latinos and African Americans, as well as increased immigration from outside countries, the United States is becoming more diverse. It is estimated that by the middle of the 21st century, students of color will be the majority population across the nation. As a result, schools will need to be responsive to increased cultural diversity.

Divorce rates have been steadily declining over the past decade. Presently, 19.4 million (10 percent) of adults report being currently divorced (U.S. Bureau of the Census, 1999). Single parenthood is on the rise, with 32 percent of all births occurring for unmarried women (Children's Defense Fund, 1998a). There are approximately 480,000 children in the United States foster care system, with an increasing number being placed with extended family members (Children's Defense Fund, 1998a). A significant number of U.S. families are adopting children from other countries. Finally, there are increasing numbers of children in American schools whose parents are openly gay and lesbian.

The median family income for a family of four in the United States is $49,687. Approximately 15 percent of all families, including one out of every four children, live at or below the poverty threshold ($16,000 for a family of four) (Children's Defense Fund, 1998a). Although 68.6 percent of the population living in poverty is European American, a disproportionate number of African American (25.6 percent) and Hispanic (46.6 percent) families fall below the poverty line (U.S. Bureau of the Census, 1997). Living in poverty is associated with a host of challenging life circumstances, including homelessness; high mobility; lack of food, clothing, and health insurance; increased exposure to drugs, violence and neglect; and little social or political power. In the United States, education has also been viewed as a vehicle out of poverty. School social workers view their role as one of promoting equal opportunity and social equality.

Researchers and policy makers in the United States have been concerned about the increasing gap between the rich and poor (Danziger et al., 1994). While poor and working class families can afford less and less in today's economy, some upper-middle-class families can afford more and more. Schools and school social workers may be called on to confront increasingly distanced and disaffected groups of students, and they are likely to be challenged to work across districts and communities in new and creative ways.

In the past decade the nation has experienced considerable economic growth. However, many men and women are finding it increasingly necessary to work more hours to make ends meet. In addition, changing attitudes about women's work, and the impact of welfare-to-work programs have meant that more parents are in the workforce than ever. As a result, it is estimated that five million children are left at home unattended by their parents (Children's Defense Fund, 1998b). In response to these trends, schools have needed to be more flexible and creative in how to involve parents in the education of their children, ensuring the safety of students to and from school, transporting students, and providing before- and after school-care. For instance, in 1993–1994, only 19 percent of American public schools offered extended day care programs (Children's Defense Fund, 1998a). Recently, the National Department of Education provided $40 million to schools to fund extended day care programs. (Children's Defense Fund, 1998b). Parents from disadvantaged backgrounds also benefit from on-site childcare while attending secondary or post-secondary schools (e.g., Gonchar, 1995).

While the nation has been economically healthy, the federal government has decreased its fiscal commitment to many welfare programs. The Welfare Reform Act of 1988 and the Work and Responsibility Act of 1994 were designed to increase families' abilities to provide for themselves financially, as well as decrease the number of welfare recipients. The Acts called for child support enforcement, creation of employment programs that included benefits such as child and health care, and increased flexibility in allowing states to deny benefits (Allen-Meares, 1996). As a result, there has been a 30 percent decrease in the number of welfare recipients between 1993 and 1997 (Children's Defense Fund, 1998a). In 1996, President Clinton signed the Personal Responsibility and Work Opportunity Reconciliation Act (P.L. 104-193). As a result, it is estimated that millions of American children and families will remain in or move into poverty in the coming decades (Children's Defense Fund, 1996).

PROBLEMS FACED BY CHILDREN AND YOUTH IN THE UNITED STATES

The Goals 2000: Educate America Act calls for early school readiness; school completion; increased student achievement; national performance standards; quality vocational training; adult literacy; safe, disciplined, drug-free school environments; increased parental participation; skills and professional development for teachers; and increased fiscal flexibility allowing for local school reform (Allen-Meares *et al.*, 1996). Further, in his 1997 State of the Union address, President Clinton identified education as his number-one priority, and added the following objectives to the national agenda: expanding the options of parents to select from a variety of educational options, increased school and teacher accountability, modernization of buildings, universal access to post-secondary education, improvement of adult education, and connection of every classroom to the Internet to encourage technical literacy (President Clinton's Call to Action, 1997). Many of these goals support the presence and relevance of school social work practice and offer new opportunities.

Americans have been consistently concerned about social problems affecting children and youth, including substance use, teen pregnancy, HIV infection, violence, suicide, abuse and neglect, and family violence. Below is a brief overview of the issues children and youth in America face.

In the last decade, cigarette smoking among children and adolescents has increased, particularly among 13- and 14-year-olds. Approximately 20 percent of 12- through 17-year-olds use alcohol, a decrease of 30 percent from 1979. Forty-six percent of 18- through 25-year-olds reported binge drinking, a trend that has raised concerns across American's college campuses. The highest rates of illicit drug use are found among 16- through 17-year-olds (19.2 percent) and 18- to 20-year-olds (17.3 percent) (National Center for Health Statistics, 1999). Every day in America 311 children are arrested for alcohol offenses, and 403 are arrested for drug offenses. The increased death rate for 15- through 24-year-olds is attributed to accidents that are the result of driving under the influence of alcohol or other drugs (Campaign for our Children, 1998).

Although adolescence is a time when sexual identity formation and relationships are heightened, 27 percent of women and 16 percent of men reported being sexually victimized at the median age of 9.9 and 9.6 respectively (Faulkner, 1999). In addition, 50 percent of rape victims are under the age of 18, and one out of six are under the age of 12. Those in families with low incomes are twice as likely to be victims of sexual assault (Abuse and Incest National Network, 1994). Increasingly, date rape and relationship violence during adolescence and young adulthood are topics being addressed in the literature.

For heterosexual youth, early sexual activity places adolescents at risk of sexually transmitted diseases and early, unwanted pregnancies. In general, the prevalence of sexually transmitted diseases, including HIV infection, is on the rise among the nation's youth (Center for Disease Control, 1999). Every minute a baby is born to a teen mother (Children's Defense Fund, 1998c), resulting in one million young mothers in the United States each year. Teenage mothers are less likely to complete school, and are more likely to have another baby. Children born to teen mothers are more likely to be poor, have health problems, drop out of school, and become teen parents themselves (McWhirter et al., 1998).

In addition to issues faced by heterosexual children and youth, gay, lesbian, and bisexual students face considerable mental health and relationship issues that schools need to address. For instance, fear of losing significant others, as well as actual rejection by family and friends, contribute to high levels of suicidal ideation and suicide in gay and lesbian youth (Hunter & Schaecher,

1987). In addition, homosexual and bisexual youth are increasingly becoming targets of harassment and outright violence. School social workers are critical in supporting these students, encouraging an atmosphere of acceptance among students, and promoting the creation of alternative environments free of harassment and violence (Hunter & Schaecher, 1987).

Depression, low self-esteem, and acting out behaviors are mental health issues schools consistently confront. Approximately 20 percent of children and adolescents are significantly depressed, while many more have low feelings of self-worth. Those who feel depressed, overwhelmed, and hopeless about the future often consider suicide. Suicide is the third leading cause of death among adolescents and young adults in the United States, and continues to be on the rise (McWhirter *et al.*, 1998).

On a daily basis, many children are living with violence in their homes, schools, and communities, challenging their fundamental needs for safety and leading to fears and anxieties that are counterproductive to learning (Steele & Couillard, 1994). For some children, school is a respite from violence. For others, school is a source of harassment and stress (McWhirter *et al.*, 1998).

EDUCATION IN THE UNITED STATES

Most students attend public schools, which provide a free education for students from ages five to 18. Elementary or primary schools typically house kindergarten to fifth or sixth graders (ages five to 11), although some primary schools house kindergarten to eighth graders. Secondary schools include middle schools (grades six to eight), junior high schools (grades seven to nine), and high schools (grades nine to 12). Increasingly, children are being socialized into pre-primary school settings as early as age two, and with the advent of the Individuals with Disabilities Education Act (IDEA) and P.L. 100-297, the Elementary and Secondary School Improvement Amendments of 1988, public schools must provide services to special needs and at-risk infants and preschoolers. Post-secondary education includes proprietary schools, community colleges, and public and private universities.

A significant number of American students attend private schools. Thirty-two percent of private schools are Roman Catholic, 47 percent are Christian non-denominational, and 21 percent are non-sectarian, special-needs schools (Office of Non-Public Education, 1999). There has been an increase in the presence of alternative public and private educational experiences, such as home schooling, Internet schooling, and new, innovative charter schools. Such trends have received little attention by the general public in terms of their implications for students and the nation, but have drawn attention to the use of public tax money to support home schooling and other schooling opportunities under the auspices of the private sector.

There have been increased concerns about the quality of education in America, both in terms of the ability of schools to instill basic level competencies, as well as produce high achievers, particularly in math and science. At the same time, educators have recognized the inherent biases in assessment tools, such as standardized achievement tests and psychometric evaluations that result in pupils being classified along racial, gender, and economic characteristics.

One form of student disengagement/disaffection is student absenteeism. Absences from school are one of the biggest predictors of school achievement and dropout rates. School social work practice began as a result of compulsory attendance laws, and school social workers in the early 1900s often served as attendance officers.

Ultimately, 25 percent of any given school cohort will leave school early. Everyday, 2,489 White students, 606 African American students, and 967 Hispanic students do not complete their schooling (Children's Defense Fund, 1997). Adolescents in families with low incomes are five times more likely to drop out of school than adolescents in families with above-average incomes (National Center for Education Statistics, 1996). Given that there are significant personal and societal costs to school dropout, school social workers have an opportunity to develop dropout prevention programs (see, for example, Jozefowicz, 1996).

Normative school transitions such as movement into high schools, and non-normative transitions such as those following a move of the family home, significantly affect students and schools. For instance, it has been found that some students making the transition to junior high school suffer academic and affective declines that contribute to later academic performance, early school leaving, and overall adjustment (Eccles *et al.*, 1997; Simmon & Blyth, 1987).

Since the mid-1880s, our nation has provided an education for children with disabilities. However, it was not until 1975, when P.L. 94-142, the Education for All Handicapped Children Act, was created, that students with disabilities were entitled to a free, appropriate, public education (FAPE). Children with disabilities had the right to education in the least restrictive environment (LRE), which included special services to disabled students in age-appropriate classrooms with a special education teacher, as well as "mainstreaming" into regular education classrooms with support services.

In 1990, P.L. 101-476, the Individuals with Disabilities Education Act (IDEA), was implemented. This Act was designed to ensure that states and local communities provided early intervention services and education to all infants and toddlers with disabilities and assistance to their families.

Students qualify for special education services when they are identified as having learning disabilities, speech and language delays, developmental disorders such as autism, severe cognitive impairments such as mental retardation, physical handicaps, or serious emotional disturbances. In the United

States, 5.6 million individuals under the age of 22 were enrolled in special education programs in 1995–1996 under the Individuals with Disabilities Education Program (Children's Defense Fund, 1998a). Between 1995 and 1997, the rate of children in special education programs increased 47 percent, a rate greater than the total increase in overall public school enrollment (National Center for Education Statistics, 1997).

P.L. 94-142 and P.L. 101-476 have greatly enhanced the presence of school social work services in the schools. School social workers identify academically challenged students, assess them along with a multidisciplinary school team, and participate in the decision-making process that involves placement in the least restrictive educational environment. However, school social workers have meaningful roles to play in terms of mainstreaming these students into regular classrooms and activities.

Another major piece of federal legislation that provides opportunities for social workers to be employed in schools is Title I of the Elementary and Secondary Education Act (ESEA) [P.L. 103-382]. This Act provides funding to school systems to raise the academic skills of children who live in low-income communities and who are at risk for school failure.

HISTORICAL DEVELOPMENT OF SCHOOL SOCIAL WORK[1]

School social work practice arose independently in New York, Boston, and Hartford during the 1906–1907 school year. Workers in community agencies initiated contact with the schools in order to link them more strongly with homes and communities (Costin, 1969a). In 1913 the Board of Education in Rochester, New York, financed the first visiting teacher program, the term first used for school social workers (Oppenheimer, 1925). Visiting teachers were placed in special departments under the direction of the superintendent. The first National Conference of Visiting Teachers and Home School Visitors was held in 1916, and the first National Association of Visiting Teachers and Home School Visitors was formed in 1919 by 14 women who were leaders in the field (McCullagh, 1998).

Visiting teachers served primarily as home-school-community liaisons (Oppenheimer, 1925). A concern for the illiteracy of immigrant and American-born children gave rise to the enactment of compulsory attendance statutes, which meant states were forced to educate a variety of children. School personnel looked to new knowledge about individual differences in order to

---

[1]The discussion of the Historical Development of School Social Work is based largely on a similar discussion in Allen-Meares, P., Washington, R. O. and Welsh, B. L. (1996), *Social Work Services in Schools*. Englewood Cliffs, NJ: Prentice Hall.

address the educational needs of students from a wider range of cultural, language, social class, and learning backgrounds. School social workers assumed the role of sensitizing school staff to the life circumstances of students, families, and neighborhoods and they clarified laws, school functions, and student difficulties to parents and families (Culbert, 1916, p. 595).

Social workers also became aware of the opportunity to use education as a vehicle to improve social conditions. For example, social workers in settlement houses (neighborhood-based facilities established in urban centers to develop self-help programs and crime and delinquency-reduction efforts) were expressing the need for schools to relate themselves more closely to the present and future lives of the children (Lide, 1959).

The number of school social workers increased, largely as a result of a series of three-year demonstrations under the auspices of the Commonwealth Fund of New York, which was aimed at the prevention of juvenile delinquency (Oppenheimer, 1925). The Commonwealth Fund gave the National Committee of Visiting Teachers financial support for the placement of 30 school social workers in rural and urban communities throughout the country. During this time, schools became viewed as strategic centers of child welfare. When the Fund withdrew its support in 1930, 21 of the communities continued to finance their visiting teacher programs. Boards of education in other communities had also established visiting teacher programs. By this time, there were about 244 school social workers in 31 states. The National Association of Visiting Teachers grew and focused its efforts on establishing professional standards and direction for its membership.

The literature of the 1920s reflects the beginning of a therapeutic role for school social workers in public schools. The mental hygiene movement brought about an increased emphasis on treating individual children who were experiencing behavioral or emotional difficulties (Costin, 1978). Mental hygiene clinics sprang up in almost every community, and their central purpose was to diagnose and treat nervous and difficult children.

The development of social work services in the schools was greatly retarded during the Depression of the 1930s. Services provided by visiting teachers were either abolished or seriously cut back (Areson, 1923, p. 398). The provision of food, shelter, and clothing preoccupied much of what activity there was. At this time visiting teachers abandoned their earlier roles as attendance officers and home-school-community liaisons, and focused on providing basic needs and emotional support for troubled children (Hall, 1936). Simultaneously, social workers cautioned that not all problems experienced by the "troubled child" were inherent in his or her personality or background. Schools also played a role in the development of student difficulties (Reynolds, 1935).

In the 1940s, social workers called attention to the "appropriate function" of school social work as social casework, referring to direct services to students, parents, and school staff in order to address student difficulties and enable students to take full advantage of their learning environment (Poole, 1949; IASSW, 1974). Tasks associated with social casework methods included identifying and assessing individual students, explaining school problems to parents, referring parents to outside agencies, interpreting students and families to teachers, and explaining their work on behalf of students to parents and teachers (Poole, 1949). A book entitled *Helping the Troubled School Child: Selected Readings in School Social Work: 1935-1955* (Lee, 1959), dealt extensively with the provision of social casework services to different groups of children. Again, the focus on social casework contributed to a clinical orientation. Others alluded to alternative forms of social work intervention, such as group experiences that helped children in their relationships with peers and teachers (Simon, 1955).

Public schools were under attack from all quarters during the 1960s. It was claimed that inequality in educational opportunity existed as a result of segregation, schools reinforced the myth that minority and low-income youth could not perform as well as their white, middle-class counterparts, teachers expected poor performance from these students, and schools were essentially repressive institutions that hindered the development of creativity and the desire to learn. Some parents claimed that they felt alienated from the school and wanted more voice in the education of their children (Lide, 1959).

School social workers continued to work with individual children, even though the literature was calling for a broader view of the school and social work services (e.g., Wessenich, 1972; Willis, 1969). Vinter and Sarri (1965) advocated for the use of group work in dealing with such problems as high school dropout, and viewed student underachievement as a result of both student and school characteristics.

In 1969, Costin assessed the importance that a national sample of school social workers attached to 107 specific tasks, as well as their willingness to delegate tasks to individuals with less training. Costin (1969b) found nine service factors: casework to children and families, case management, interpretation of school social work services to others, clinical treatment of children, liaison between families and community agencies, interpretation of students to teachers, educational counseling, leadership and policy making, and service to teachers. Her findings revealed that the tasks school social workers preferred and performed reflected a continued focus on individual students, and they ranked leadership and policymaking as the least important tasks to perform. Costin called on school social workers to change the model of delivering services to focus more on working with the larger student population and make system-wide interventions. Alderson and Krishef (1973) found that school social workers in Florida ranked interpretation of services and leadership as the most important, indicating that some regional differences existed. Finally, Allen-Meares (1977) replicated Costin's national study and found little shift in the tasks school social workers performed in spite of Costin's call to broaden the goals and services.

The 1970s were a time of great expansion. The number of school social workers increased and more emphasis was placed on family, community team-work with workers in other school-related disciplines, and handicapped students. The focus of a national workshop held at the University of Pennsylvania in 1969 was "Social Change and School Social Work." The workshop was designed to increase innovation and leadership in school social work practice. Proceedings of this workshop and others were later incorporated in a book entitled *The School in the Community* (Sarri & Maple, 1972).

Gottlieb & Gottlieb (1971) believed that school social workers needed to spend less time with individual students and more time with administrators, teachers, community groups, and local agencies. They believed that school social workers could serve as a bridge between the school and community by encouraging educational practices that matched community needs, and also by offering services within the school setting.

The passage of the Education for All Handicapped Children Act (P.L. 94-142) exerted the biggest influence on school social work services in U.S. schools. Social work services were considered an integral part of the assessment and placement of disabled children in the least restrictive environment. Alderson, Krishef & Spencer (1990) found that 50 percent of the national sample of school social workers reported spending at least 75 percent of their time on tasks relating to P.L. 94-142.

During the 1980s and 1990s, considerable educational and legislative movements have affected schools and school social work practice in the United States (for example, P.L. 94-142 and IDEA). As a result, the number of school social workers has continued to increase. In response to the growing needs of this group, NASW held school social work conferences in 1978 in Denver, in 1981 in Washington, D.C., and in 1985 in New Orleans. In addition, NASW provided specialty tracks in school social work at several national annual conferences. These special conferences and seminars focused on expanded roles as well as work with new populations. Constable and Flynn (1982) edited a book titled *School Social Work: Practice and Research Perspectives*, the fourth edition of which was published in 1999 (Constable, Flynn, & McDonald). In 1985 Allen-Meares, Washington, and Welsh published *Social Work Services in Schools* (Allen-Meares, Washington, & Welsh), the first comprehensive text that dealt with this subject matter. A second edition was published in 1996 (Allen-Meares, Washington, & Welsh) and a third edition in 2000 (Allen-Meares, Washington, & Welsh).

Educational legislation continued to play a major role in shaping and expanding school and social work services. For example, school social workers were included as "qualified personnel" in Part H of the Education of the Handicapped Act Amendments of 1986 (P.L. 99-457), Early Intervention for Handicapped Infants and Toddlers (P.L. 100-297), the Elementary and Secondary School Improvement Amendments of 1988, the Individuals with

Disabilities Education Act (P.L. 101-476) and the American Education Act (P.L. 103-227). It is estimated that there are approximately 14,000 school social workers in the United States. It is important to mention that titles such as pupil personnel specialist and visiting teacher are also used to describe the service.

School Social Work Role

Most school social workers in the United States are hired by elementary and secondary school districts. Some spend their time at multiple schools, across multiple age groups within a district. Others are responsible for a particular school or age group. Increasingly, school social workers work in special programs such as infant and preschool programs, or with special populations such as homeless students (Allen-Meares *et al.*, 1996). Social workers in the schools are sometimes employed by consortia that serve multiple districts (Freeman, 1995). For instance, social workers in Iowa are employed by Area Education Agencies that provide services to multiple schools and districts (Johnson, 1987). Finally, a small proportion of school social work services is provided by social workers employed at other community agencies.

In many state offices of education, school social work consultants provide assistance to school social workers and facilitate the development of the services for their respective state. There is a National Council of State Consultants for School Social Work Services. They issued a position statement requesting that more state departments of education hire school social work consultants to coordinate between other agencies and department personnel, provide technical assistance through site visits and training initiatives, participate in program development, evaluate the effectiveness of programs, and link departments of education to professional organizations (Clark, 1991).

The National Association of Visiting Teachers helped to form a professional identity between 1919 and 1930. It was succeeded by the American Association of Visiting Teachers in 1930 and the National Association of School Social Workers (NASSW) in 1943. In 1949, NASSW began to work with other social work associations to identify and support common concerns. In 1955 NASSW, along with six other social work associations, merged to create the National Association of Social Workers (NASW) (McCullagh, 1998; National Association of Social Workers, 1992).

State, regional, and national organizations provide their members with educational opportunities for professional growth, yearly workshops, job networks, continuing education credit, and legislative advocacy. One of the earliest and most visible state associations is the Illinois Association of School Social Workers (IASSW), which was established in 1970. IASSW publishes the *School Social Work Journal* twice per year and hosts an annual conference. Presently, 31 states have associations for school social workers, and contact information can be found on the Internet.

There are four freestanding regional organizations: the Midwest School Social Work Council, the Western Alliance of School Social Work Organizations, the Southern School Social Work Council, and the Northeast Coalition of School Social Work Associations. In 1994, spearheaded by the school social work leadership, a national association of school social workers was formed independently from NASW. The School Social Work Association of America was established to encourage professional development, public policy involvement, communication, research and evaluation, home-school community links, and mentoring for school social workers. The SSWAA Board of Directors is comprised of seven elected members and one delegate appointed from each of the regional groups. In 1997, the SSWAA and the NASW School Social Work Section signed an agreement to work collaboratively to enhance the specialty of school social work. SSWAA publishes a monthly newsletter, advocates for school social work on a national level, and holds a yearly national conference. In April 1999 SSWAA sponsored an International School Social Work Conference held in Chicago, attended by 900 school social workers from 45 states and 21 countries.

In 1978, NASW published the first issue of a special journal, *Social Work in Education* (now called *Children and Schools: A Journal of Social Work Practice*), devoted to social work in educational settings. In 1992 the standards for school social work services, first developed in 1976 by NASW, were revised and included the following sections: competence and professional practice, professional preparation and development, and administrative structure and support. The standards also included appropriate ratios for school social workers and students based upon student population and school needs (National Association of Social Workers, 1992). The NASW Standards are currently being revised and will be available in 2001.

In the United States, school social workers serve two primary functions: assisting in meeting the educational needs of students within schools, and addressing those factors that interfere with students' capacities to realize their learning and educational potential (Freeman, 1995; IASSW, 1974). In relation to the first function, school social workers spend a considerable amount of their time meeting the needs of students, families, and staff in the process of assessment and intervention. Other problems that interfere with maximal use of the educational environment include health problems, substance use, depression and suicide ideation, peer conflict and violence, child abuse and neglect, cultural misunderstanding and conflict, school phobias, difficulties making transitions, poor school climate, detrimental school policies, poverty, and job stress.

As this field has evolved, so have different practice models and approaches. Presently, school social work practice in the United States is informed by an ecological perspective and strengths-based approach that is similar to the emphasis in social work more broadly. In addition, attention to cultural sensitivity and issues of oppression are integrated throughout many interventions. At best, school social workers integrate these theoretical issues and professional objectives, which are largely determined by the political climate, legislation, economic situations, and institutional needs of the schools.

Alderson (1972) describes a "traditional clinical model," which focuses on direct services to individuals and groups of students with social and emotional problems that interfere with their potential to learn (Johnson, 1987). A major assumption of the model is that the individual child or the child's family is experiencing difficulty, and the school provides casework services to address the difficulties (Allen-Meares, 1977; Chavkin, 1985; Fisher, 1988).

The socio-political context of the 1960s gave rise to a new model. Many authors were calling for movement away from individual clinical social casework to a focus on broader systems that impact students, such as peers, teachers, classrooms, administrators, schools, and the community (Gottlieb & Gottlieb, 1971; Radin, 1989).

Alderson (1972) describes three systems-change models. In the "school change model" the target for intervention is the school and its institutional policies and practices. In the "community school model" the focus is on disadvantaged communities where communities are educated about what the school has to offer, there is organized support for the school and its programs, and the dynamics of the community are explained to school officials. The "social interaction model" emphasizes the reciprocal influences of individuals and groups. The target of intervention is the quality of exchanges between children, groups of children, families, schools, and the communities.

An important model that grew out of a demonstration project of a multi-university consortium for planned change in pupil personnel services was Costin's "school-community-pupil relations model" (Costin, 1975; Vargus, 1976). Its primary goal is to bring about change in the interaction of this triad, and thus to modify to some extent harmful institutional practices and policies of the school. Attention is given to the characteristics of groups of pupils and of their school. The focus is on the situation of student groups (such as truants, pregnant teenagers, or dropouts), not on the personality development of individual group members.

In the United States there has been movement toward integrated service delivery (the integration of health, welfare, and education services). In response to the need to avoid service duplication and fragmentation, professionals interested in providing comprehensive health and mental health services to children and adolescents have identified schools as a natural center for prevention, identification, and intervention of student health and mental health needs. Sometimes services are delivered by the school and/or community agencies. School social workers can play a pivotal role in coordinating these services (Freeman, 1995; Lane, 1998). In some cases school social workers coordinate integrative services for the school, while in other cases a school social worker employed by a community-based agency may be the coordinator.

ROLES OF THE SCHOOL SOCIAL WORKER

Direct service to individuals includes assessment and diagnosis of students for special education services, individual counseling with students experiencing mental health difficulties, phone contacts with overburdened parents, or meetings with struggling teachers. Direct services to groups could include running groups for children who have experienced some form of loss, intervening in a classroom by fostering acceptance of mainstreamed students, offering support groups for single parents, or facilitating staff meetings designed to encourage school change.

School social workers are ideally suited to gather information. This includes formal assessments, such as having parents and teachers fill out behavior ratings scales on a student, gathering social and developmental histories on students (Lee, 1987), or observing students in the classroom (Radin, 1989). They also have the expertise to gather information on broader classroom, school, and community characteristics (Allen-Meares *et. al.*, 1996; Anderson, 1974; Costin, 1975; Hare, 1995). This would include knowledge of the climate of the school system, demographic information on the school and community, information about resources, and a sense of the relationship between the school and community (Gottlieb & Gottlieb, 1971; Allen-Meares *et al.*, 1996).

School social workers are viewed as experts in understanding human behavior, mental health issues, relationships, and interventions. In addition, they are expected to know individual students, families, and communities from an in-depth, holistic perspective that includes sensitivity to the strengths, problems, circumstances, and resources present at all levels. School social workers serve as consultants and educators when they advise parents, teachers, principals, schools, and community members about the relationship and mental health issues children and adolescents face (Allen-Meares *et al.*, 1996).

Increasingly, school social workers may be asked to be members of other interdisciplinary teams, such as those at school-based health clinics (Allen-Meares *et. al.*, 1996). To be effective team members, school social workers must be able to define their role, as well as understand and define the roles of other personnel, such as school psychologists, school counselors, and school nurses (Radin, 1989, Gibelman, 1993).

Since its inception, school social work practice has defined the role of home-school-community liaison as one of its major contributions to the education of children (Radin, 1989). School social workers continue to be viewed as links between the major social contexts in the lives of students. They serve as interpreters, clarifiers, informants, and mediators in order to build a trusting, working relationship between families, schools, and communities on behalf of children and adolescents (Allen-Meares, 1990).

With the increase in integrated services (Freeman, 1995), as well as the explicit call for a case manager under laws such as P.L. 99-457 (Radin, 1989), school social workers will likely increase their case management role in coordinating student and family educational, vocational, health, and mental health services.

School social workers can intervene at the individual, group, classroom, family, school, community, policy, and legislative levels. At the individual level, school social workers offer their time and services to distraught students, parents, or teachers. They empower students and parents through the facilitation of support groups. They are catalysts and enablers for change when they advocate for staff time to reflect upon educational practices and needs of the school. They may recognize unmet needs within the community or patterns of unreasonable punishments and suspensions that require policy change at the school level (Radin, 1989).

Normally, crisis intervention involves immediate assistance to return the persons affected back to normal levels of functioning. School social workers often carry this out individually, but they may also be a part of crisis intervention teams, for instance, as participants in a comprehensive suicide prevention program.

School social workers often advocate for individual students, whether in response to misunderstandings, or clear violations of student rights. They also advocate for groups of students who are subjected to individual-, group-, or institutional-level discrimination or outright harassment. Such groups could include ethnic minority students, women, developmentally delayed or physically handicapped students, gay/lesbian/bisexual youth, and students with chronic illnesses such as AIDS. School social workers may approach parents, teachers, principals, school boards, and community agencies to advocate on behalf of any one child or group of children. They may also advocate on behalf of a family, a teacher, an administrator, or for additional community resources (Levine & Mellor, 1988). Finally, school social workers advocate for themselves and the profession through their involvement in local, state, and national organizations (IASSW, 1974).

Poole identified a number of ways that school social workers should attend to the school context. This includes understanding and accepting the function of the school and teachers' responsibilities, identifying the social service needs of the school, developing services that fit within the organization of the school, defining services and their contribution to the school's mission and teachers' goals, coordinating with other personnel to provide integrated services, and collaborating with staff to develop relevant school programs and policies (Poole, 1949). Similarly, Gottlieb & Gottlieb (1971) and Helper (1989) argue that school social workers need to be aware of the organizational constraints on their role.

Based on the school social work literature of the 1990s, it is clear that a model of preventive intervention is being developed in school social work practice, yet such a model has not been formally articulated. Radin (1989) and Lane (1998) identified preventive intervention as one of the major trends in school social work for the 1990s and beyond. Prevention efforts need to be multifaceted and enduring (Muehrer & Koretz, 1992), and are typically aimed at the common antecedents of problematic behaviors (Dryfoos, 1990). School social workers have developed prevention programs that deal with substance abuse, teenage pregnancy, suicide, violence, and child abuse and neglect (Delgado, 1997). There is also a growing body of literature on resilience in childhood and adolescence.

School social workers conduct research and evaluate the efficiency and effectiveness of their interventions through multiple methods. Increasingly, school social workers will need to demonstrate the effectiveness of their interventions and programs to ensure funding and their positions (Hare, 1995).

TRAINING OF SCHOOL SOCIAL WORKERS

States are taking an active role in specifying education requirements for practice in the schools by setting their own requirements for school social work credentials (Torres, 1996). In many states, an MSW with some special coursework and field experience are required. Some states will accept a BSW and additional coursework to qualify for a school social work endorsement. For example, in Illinois, practitioners seeking certification must take two exams and complete an approved graduate social work program that includes special coursework on school social work. One issue is developing reciprocity agreements between states, enabling school social workers to relocate without encountering additional requirements. The National Association of Social Workers, in consultation with Allen-Meares and the Education Testing Service, Princeton, New Jersey, developed the first School Social Work Credential Exam. This exam was first administered in 1992, but has since been discontinued.

Some schools of social work and state offices of education have developed specialized coursework and summer institutes for social work students and practitioners. Training emphasizes knowledge of human development, strategies of institutional and community change, family and community dynamics, organizational theory, multidisciplinary training, networking, diagnosis and assessment, case management, educational legislation, significant litigation, intervention techniques and models of practice, and content on racial and ethnic diversity (Garret and Barretta-Herman, 1995).

ISSUES FOR FUTURE DIRECTION

One of many issues facing school social workers is how to broaden the definition of their services. Studies (Allen-Meares, 1994; Allen-Meares & Dupper, 1998) indicate that approximately 60 to 75 percent of a school social worker's time is spent on services to disabled students. Though practitioners are pleased to contribute to the development of these pupils and the legislative mandate to do so (P.L. 94-142 and IDEA), they see other pressing needs and vulnerable populations. Some complain that administrators' and teachers' expectations, and a view that they should "fix" students, have led to preoccupation with remedial and crisis interventions, rather than interventions that are preventive and systemic in nature. A national study (Allen-Meares, 1994) found that school social workers' preferences were to assess target groups of students, develop prevention and new out-of-school programs, help new staff understand diversity, and facilitate school-community-student relations.

Another issue is that the funding source for the service has been primarily tied to special legislative initiatives. Thus, school social workers serve student populations that are identified in these initiatives. The service then becomes driven by such legislation rather than being empowered by its own vision of goals and objectives. By no means do the authors devalue the contribution such legislation mandates have made to increase the number of school social workers around the nation. It is just that the responsiveness of the service to emerging needs is sometimes limited and new opportunities are ignored.

A major issue in the training of school social workers is that their training takes place in isolation of other school-based disciplines, yet they are expected to function as a member of a multidisciplinary team. Schools of social work, schools of education, schools of nursing, and departments of psychology should develop opportunities for interdisciplinary education at the pre-service level and during the practicum for students.

The emergence of integrated services (which refers to an innovative system of delivering services in which community agencies and schools collaborate to provide a variety of health and social services to children and their families at or near the school site) will redefine the role of the school social worker (Hare, 1995). Major issues that will arise are developing functional working relationships between those workers employed in the schools and those practitioners in community-based agencies in developing a shared philosophy of service, coordinating responsibilities, sharing leadership roles, and accounting for services. Community-based service providers may not fully understand the internal dynamics, and school-based social workers may not be fully informed about community resources.

Evaluations of the effectiveness of interventions implemented by school social workers and more in-depth knowledge of pupil groups and their unique situation are areas warranting attention. There is also a dire need for more demonstration projects and their evaluation to address systematic change in the relationships between and among school, family, and community. School social workers will need to become research consumers. Ideally, before interventions are used the school social worker should review pertinent literature and research on the development of the selected intervention. Practitioners and academics should collaborate on research and evaluation projects, and disseminate outcomes through publications.

In a time of increased record keeping and information systems, protecting student and family confidentiality may pose a challenge, and school social workers may need to advocate around this issue. In addition, although duty to inform laws indicate that mental health professionals such as school social workers must report suspected cases of child abuse and neglect, or intent to harm oneself or others, practices surrounding disclosure of things such as criminal activity and harassment are less clear-cut.

Governing bodies of the educational system will become more localized as a result of site-based management. As decision making about programs and budgets is shifted to local schools, school social workers will need to advocate and market their services at the local level (Streeter & Franklin, 1993). In addition, local governments and universities are also playing a more active role in managing public schools. For instance, in Chicago and recently in Detroit, the city government, headed by the mayor, took over control and management of the local school system. In 1989, a University/Public School Partnership was developed where the university managed the local school system under a 10-year contract (Lane, 1998).

CONCLUSION

The authors are very optimistic about the future development of school social work in the United States as we enter the 21st century. School social workers have expertise with systems, individuals, groups, relationships, organizations, and with theories of change. They will be the leaders needed to facilitate changes in preparing students, families, schools, and communities for a fast-changing world.

REFERENCES

Alderson, J. J. (1972). Models of school social work practice. In R. Sarri and F. Maple (Eds.). *The school in the community.* (pp. 151–160). Washington, DC: NASW.

Alderson, J. J. & Krishef, C. H. (1973). Another perspective on tasks in school social work. *Social Casework, 54,* 591–600.

Alderson, J. J., Krishef, C. H., & Spencer, B. A. (1990). School social workers' role in the implementation of the Education for All Handicapped Children Act. *Social Work in Education, 12,* 221–236.

Allen-Meares, P. (1977). Analysis of tasks in school social work. *School Social Work, 22,* 196–201.

Allen-Meares, P., Washington. R.O., and Welsh. B. (1986). Social Work Services in schools. Engelwood Cliffs, NJ: Prentice Hall.

Allen-Meares, P., Washington. R.O., and Welsh. B. (1996). Social Work Services in schools. Needham Heights, MA: Allyn and Bacon.

Allen-Meares, P., Washington. R.O., and Welsh. B. (2000). Social Work Services in schools. Needham Heights, MA: Allyn and Bacon.

Allen-Meares, P. (1990). Elementary and secondary school improvement amendments of 1988 and the future of social services in schools. *Social Work in Education, 12,* 249–260.

Allen-Meares, P. (1994). Social work services in schools: A national study of entry-level tasks. *Social Work, 39,* 560–565.

Allen-Meares, P. (1996). The new federal role in education and family services: Goal setting without responsibility. *Social Work, 41,* 533–540.

Allen-Meares, P. & Dupper, D. (1998). A national study of knowledge, skills and abilities: Curriculum development for practice in schools. *Journal of Teaching in Social Work, 17,* 101–119.

Allen-Meares, P., Washington, R.O. & Welsh, B. L. (1996). *Social work services in schools (2nd Edition).* Englewood Cliffs, NJ: Prentice Hall.

Anderson, J.J. (1974). Introducing change in school community-pupil relationships: Maintaining credibility and accountability. *Journal of Education for Social Work, 19,* 3–8.

Areson, C. W. (1923). *Status of children's work in the United States.* Proceedings of the National Conference of Social Work. Chicago: University of Chicago Press.

Campaign for our Children (1998). *The Impact of Alcohol and Drugs on Teens.* http://www.cfoc.org/sexdrugs.html

Center for Disease Control (1999). *Some Facts About Chlamydia.* http://www.cdc.gov/nchstp/dstp/chlamydiafacts.htm

Chavkin, N. F. (1985). School social work practice: A reappraisal. *Social Work in Education, 7,* 3–13.

Children's Defense Fund (1996). *Implementing the new welfare law.* http://www/childrensdefense.org/fairstart_implement.html

Children's Defense Fund (1997). *Everyday in America: Facts and figures.* http://www.childrensdefense.org/everyday.html

Children's Defense Fund (1998a). *Children in the States: 1998 Michigan Profile.* http://www/childrensdefense.org/states/data_mi/html

Children's Defense Fund (1998b). *Casting a safety net for our school-age children.* http://www.childrensdefense.org/voice0998.html

Children's Defense Fund (1998c). *Moments in America for children: Facts and figures.* http://www.childrensdefense.org/moments.html

Clark, J. P. (1991). On the need for states to employ school social work consultants: A position statement issued by the Midwest School Social Work Council, the National Council of State Consultants for School Social Work Services, & the National Association of Social Workers Commission on Education. *School Social Work Journal, 15,* 29–31.

Constable, R. & Flynn, J. (Eds.). (1982). *School social work: Practice and research perspectives.* Homewood, IL: Dorsey Press.

Constable, R., Flynn, J., & McDonald, S. (Eds.). (1999). *School social work: Practice and research perspectives.* Chicago, IL: Lyceum Books, Inc.

Costin, L. (1969a). A historical review of school social work. *Social Casework, 50,* 439–453.

Costin, L. (1969b). An analysis of the tasks in school social work. *Social Service Review, 43,* 274–285.

Costin, L. (1975). School social work practice: A new model. *Social Work, 20,* 135–139.

Costin, L. (1978). *Social work services in schools: Historical perspectives and current directions.* Washington, DC: NASW.

Culbert, J. (1916). *Visiting teachers and their activities: Proceedings of the National Conference of Charities and Correction.* Chicago: Hildman Printing Co.

Danziger, S., Sundefur, D., & Weinberg, D. (Eds.). (1994). *Confronting poverty: Prescriptions for change.* New York: Russell Sage.

Delgado, M. (1997). Strengths-based practice with Puerto Rican adolescents: Lessons form a substance abuse prevention project. *Social Work in Education, 19,* 101–112.

Digest of Education Statistics (1995). http://nces.ed.gov/pubsold/D95.html

Dryfoos, J.G. (1990). *Adolescents at risk.* New York: Oxford University Press.

Eccles, J. S., Lord, S. E., Roeser, R. W., Barber, B. L. & Jozefowicz, D. M. H. (1997). The association of school transitions in early adolescence with developmental trajectories through high school. In J. Schulenberg, J. L. Maggs, & K. Hurrelman (Eds.). *Health Risks and Developmental Transitions During Adolescence.* New York: Cambridge University Press.

Faulkner, N. (1999). *Sexual Abuse Statistics.* http://www/prevent-abuse now.com/stats.htm

Fisher, R. (1988). Clinical aspects of school social work. *School Social Work Journal, 13,* 13–22.

Freeman, E. (1995). School social work overview. *National Association of Social Workers 19th Encyclopedia of Social Work.* Washington, DC: NASW Press.

Garrett, K. J. & Barretta-Herman, A. (1995). Missing links: Professional development in school social work. *Social Work in Education, 17,* 235-243.

Gibelman, M. (1993). School social workers, counselors, and psychologists in collaboration: A shared agenda. *Social Work in Education, 15,* 45-53.

Gonchar, N. (1995). College-student mothers and on-site child care: Luxury or necessity. *Social Work in Education, 17,* 226-227.

Gottlieb, B. H. & Gottlieb, L. J. (1971). An expanded role for the school social worker. *Social Work, 16,* 4, pp. 12-21.

Hall, G.E. (1936). Changing concepts in visiting teacher work. *Visiting Teachers Bulletin, 12.*

Hare, I. (1995). School-linked services. *National Association of Social Workers 19th Encyclopedia of Social Work.* Washington, DC: NASW Press.

Helper, J. B. (1989). Utilizing organizational theory to improve the effectiveness of implementing evaluation and intervention programs in elementary and secondary schools. *School Social Work Journal, 14,* 26-35.

Hunte, J. & Schaecher, R. (1987). Stresses on lesbian and gay adolescents in schools. *Social Work in Education, 9,* 3, pp. 180-190.

Illinois Association of School Social Workers (IASSW) (1974). *IASSW's historical beginnings and professional practice. School social work position statement.* http://www.iassw.org/practice.html

Johnson, H. W. (1987). Perceptions of school social worker activities. *School Social Work Journal, 12,* 26-33.

Jozefowicz, D. M. H. (1996). *Dropout prevention in the middle grades: The role of the school social worker.* Unpublished manuscript, University of Michigan, Ann Arbor, MI.

Lane, T. S. (1998). School-linked services in action: Results of an implementation project. *Social Work in Education, 20,* 37-47.

Lee, G. (Ed.). (1959). *Helping the troubled school child. Selected readings in school social work, 1935-1955.* Washington, DC: NASW Press.

Lee, C. (1987). School social work in Louisiana: An analysis of practice. *Social Work, 32,* 442-444.

Levine, R. S. & Mellor, B. K. (1988). Evolving role of a school social worker: A chronology. *Social Work in Education, 10,* 235-243.

Lide, P. (1959). Study of the historical influences of major importance in determining the present function of the school social workers. In G. Lee (Ed.). *op cit.*

McWhirter, J. J., McWhirter, B. T., McWhirter, A. M. & McWhirter, E. H. (1998). *At-risk youth: A comprehensive response (2nd Edition).* Pacific Grove, CA: Brooks/Cole Publishing Co.

McCullagh, J. G. (1998). Early school social work leaders: Women forgotten by the profession. *Social Work in Education, 20,* 55-61.

Muehrer, P., & Koretz, D.S. (1992). Issues in preventive intervention research. *Psychological Science, 1*, 109–112.

National Association of Social Workers (1992). *NASW standards for school social work services.* Washington, DC: NASW.

National Center for Education Statistics (1996). *Dropout rates in the United States.* http://nces.ed.gov/pubs98/dropout/98250-03.html

National Center for Education Statistics (1997). *Digest of education statistics.* p. 65.

National Center for Health Statistics (1999). *National household survey on drug abuse.* http://www.health.org/pubs/nhsda/96hhs/httoc.htm

Office of Non-Public Education (1999). http://www.ed.gov/pubs/servprivate/part1.html

Oppenheimer, J. (1925). *The visiting teacher movement with special reference to administrative relationships (2nd edition).* New York: Joint Committee on Methods of Preventing Delinquency.

Poole, F. (1949). An analysis of the characteristics of school social work. *Social Services Review, 23*, 454–459.

President Clinton's Call To Action (1997). http://www.ed.gov/updates/PresEDPlan

Radin, N. (1989). School social work practice: Past, present, and future trends. *Social Work in Education, 11*, 213–225.

Reynolds, B.C. (1935). Social casework: What is it? What is its place in the world today? *The Family, 16*, 238.

Sarri, R. & Maple, F. (1972). *The school in the community.* Washington, DC: NASW.

Simmon, R. G. & Blyth, D. A. (1987). *Moving Into Adolescence: The Impact of Pubertal Change and School Context.* Hawthorne, NY: Aldine De Gruyter.

Simon, P. (1955). Social group work in the schools. *Bulletin of the National Association of School Social Workers, 27*, p.26.

Steele, B. & Couillard, J. (1994). *Violence prevention/intervention readiness for schools.* Detroit: TLC Institute.

Streeter, C. L. & Franklin, C. (1993). Site-based management in public education: Opportunities and challenges for school social workers. *Social Work in Education, 15*, 71–81.

Torres, S. (1996). The status of school social work in America. *Social Work in Education, 18*, 8–18.

U.S. Bureau of the Census (1997). *Poverty in the United States: Current population reports.*

U.S. Bureau of the Census (1998). *Resident population of the United States: Estimates by sex, race, and Hispanic origin.* http://www.census.gov/populations/estimates/nation/intfile3-1

U.S. Bureau of the Census (1999). *Marital status and living arrangements.* http://www.census.gov/population/www/socdemo/ms-la.html

Vargus, I. (1976). Developing, launching and maintaining the school-community-pupil program. In D.J. Kurpiur & I. Thomas (Eds.). *Social services and the public schools.* Bloomington, IN: Midwest Center Satellite Consortium for Planned Change in Pupil Personnel Programs for Urban Schools.

Vinter, R. & Sarri, R. (1965). Malperformance in the public school: A group work approach. *Social Work, 10*, 38–48.

Wessenich, L.P. (1972). Systems analysis applied to school social work. In R. Sarri and F. Maple (Eds.). *op cit.*, pp. 196–210.

Willis, J. (1969). The mental health worker as a systems behavioral engineer. In R. Sarri & F.F. Maple (Eds.). *The general systems approach: Contribution toward an holistic conception of social work* (pp. 211–244). New York: Council on Social Work Education.

3 SCHOOL SOCIAL WORK IN CANADA: HISTORICAL THEMES AND CURRENT CHALLENGES

Jane Loughborough, Wes Shera, and John Wilhelm

Social Indicators* — Canada	
Population	31,015,000
Percentage under age 15 years	19
Percentage urban	77
Life expectancy at birth	76.2 men, 81.8 women
Fertility rate	1.58 children per woman
Percentage of illiterate adults	Not available
Per capita GDP in $U.S. (1999)	20,822
Percentage unemployed (1997)	7.6

*Social Indicators. From the Statistics Division of the United Nations. Refer to notes on page 249.
Reference: http://www.un.org/Depts/unsd/indicators/indic2a.htm

NATIONAL CONTEXT

Canada is a complex country—it is one of the largest in geographical terms yet least populated in the world. Canada's current population is just over 30 million, and Canada is second only to Australia in terms of area per person at three square kilometers (1.2 square miles) per resident (Statistics Canada, 1996). The majority of recent immigrants come from Asia (primarily India and Hong Kong), Europe, and Africa (Statistics Canada, 1999, CANSIM, Matrix 2). In 1998, there were approximately 8 million residents under the age of 19. In terms of persons of color, Chinese, South Asian, Black Arab/West Asian, Filipino, Latin American, and Southeast Asian are the most predominant groups (Statistics Canada, 1996).

Canadians are respected throughout the world for their humanitarianism, and Canada has been rated on the Human Development Index as the best place in the world to live (United Nations Development Program, 1998). However, it is only fair to say that, from a social justice perspective, not all

Canadians share this quality of life equally. A recent UN report criticized Canada's lack of compliance with the UN Covenant on Economic, Social and Cultural Rights (United Nations, 1998). The major shortcomings identified include: the number of women and children living in poverty; inadequate legal protection of women's rights; the disparities between aboriginal people and the majority of Canadians; reductions in social assistance; the significant increase in homelessness; the 20 percent illiteracy rate; and cuts in services for persons with disabilities. Campaign 2000 (1998), a national anti-poverty organization, claimed that one child in every five in Canada is poor. The province of Ontario has experienced a 116 percent increase in child poverty since 1989, the largest increase in the country. Canada, in comparison to several progressive European countries, exhibits high ambivalence about balancing work and family in its public policies and a low level of support for the state's role in the family (O'Hara, 1998). This ambivalence is evident in the issues confronting school social workers in the education system today.

As an introduction, we provide an overview of Canada's major regions. One method used to comprehend Canada's complexity is regionalization. Driedger (1996) has identified six major regions: the Northlands, the Atlantic Region, Québec, the Bilingual and Multicultural Belt, Upper Canada, and the West. His descriptions of these regions provide a helpful overview of the diversity that is found in Canada. The Northlands comprise four-fifths of Canada; they are sparsely populated and 51 percent of this population is of Inuit (native Indian) origin. Atlantic Canada is underdeveloped economically and has comparatively fewer immigrants. Most of the population is descended from much earlier immigrants from France, England, Ireland, Scotland, and Wales. Québec is one of the most culturally and linguistically homogeneous parts of Canada: 95 percent of the population is of French ethnic origin and more than 80 percent speak French exclusively. The economic sector exhibits a high degree of bilingualism; however, in recent years, with the influence of the Parti Québecois and French nationalists, there has been an increased emphasis on French language and culture.

The Bilingual and Multicultural Belt stretches from Moncton, New Brunswick to Sault Ste. Marie on Lake Huron in Ontario. There are important differences between urban centers, such as Montreal, and rural communities in this region. Driedger (1996) has also noted the high degree of segregation between people speaking different languages and the large number of parallel institutions providing support for the English and French. Upper Canada consists of the remainder of the province of Ontario not included in the Bilingual and Multicultural Belt, essentially southern Ontario. A notable feature is the dominance of settlements along Lake Ontario from Oshawa to Niagara Falls. This area contains more than one-quarter of Canada's total population and it is the core of the country's financial and marketing industries. Support for languages other than English and multiculturalism in general is strong, particularly in Ontario's capital, Toronto, which was recently identified as the most ethnically diverse city in the world (Rees, 1998).

The West consists of the southern portions of the four western provinces (British Columbia, Alberta, Saskatchewan, and Manitoba). This region is very rural with enclaves of various ethnic groups, particularly Asian; no group dominates the region culturally. Although three-quarters of the population report English as their mother tongue, recent immigration has made the area more multicultural.

Michael Adams, in addressing Canadian social values at the end of the 1990s, takes the view that to really understand the situation in Canada we must identify those forces that have changed our values and also appreciate the current "tribes" or clusters of values that make up contemporary Canadian society: "Relative affluence, access to education, travel and information has resulted in growing numbers of Canadians being able to transcend traditional demographic categories of age, gender, religion, social class and ethnicity, and to then define themselves in novel ways. As I see it, this new flexibility, when combined with advanced communications technology, opens up almost limitless possibilities for personal definition and redefinition in the centuries ahead" (Adams, 1998, p. 9).

Key events that have triggered change in the past 20 years include the recession of 1981–1982, the free trade debate of the late 1980s, and the dismantling of the leadership role of the federal government in the area of social programs through the transfer of power and money to the provinces. Much of this change was justified as essential to balance the federal budget and reduce the national debt. The federal government is about to balance its budget, eager to negotiate a new social union with the provinces and significantly reinvest in health care. In the late 1990s, Canadians have been preoccupied with the nationalism of Québec.

As Canadians anticipate the future, it is necessary to move beyond demographics and attempt to comprehend the value diversity and value changes that influence Canadian society. The Canadian quality of life, sense of nationalism, and future depend on it. These value differences can readily be observed in the Canadian education system. Debates around standardized curriculums, parental involvement, students with special needs, and teacher contact time are self-evident illustrations of how values influence our educational system and our children.

EDUCATION IN CANADA

There is no federal educational system in Canada. The Constitution gave exclusive responsibility for education to the provinces and territories to provide a comprehensive, diversified system of education, including public schools, "separate" (Roman Catholic) schools and private schools, designed to be universally accessible and to respond to the bilingual and multicultural character of Canadian society. However, each of the 10 provinces and three territories has developed an educational system reflecting its specific regional concerns and historical and cultural heritage. The provincial and territorial departments of education, each headed by an elected minister, set standards, draw up curricula, and give grants to educational institutions. Responsibility for the administration of elementary and secondary (or high) schools is delegated to local elected school boards or commissions. These boards set local budgets, hire and negotiate with teachers, and shape school curricula within the provincial guidelines.

Public education in Canada is co-educational and free up to and including secondary school. Depending on the legislation in each province and territory, children attend school from the age of six or seven until they are 15 or 16 years old. The age of students completing secondary school also depends on whether the program lasts for four or five years. In Québec, further education is available at the general and vocational colleges (collèges d'enseignement général et professionel), which charge only a minimal registration fee. Approximately 8 percent of Canada's Gross Domestic Product is spent on public-sector education. Canada is second only to the United States in the proportion of the population aged 18 to 24 enrolled full-time in universities, colleges, and technical institutes (Government of Canada, 1999).

Although there are many educational issues that have been of concern historically and which predominate current debates, we have identified four that appear to be prominent in Canadian schools today.

The provision of education programs and services to students with special learning needs continues to be an issue. Many special education models have been developed in the past decade amidst ongoing debate among educators as to the best method of program delivery. One of the primary issues in special education focuses on the total integration of special needs students into a regular classroom versus placement in segregated specialty programs. The majority of school boards continue to provide a range of placements, usually with opportunity for special instruction combined with instruction in a regular classroom program.

Accountability of school boards is a prominent issue in many provinces. Standardized testing of students in selected grades has become the norm in an attempt to measure ability. Perhaps the most dominant controversy regarding standardized tests revolves around whether to include new immigrant students in testing, particularly in areas of high immigration. Urban school boards, which have high levels of immigration, seem to lack clear direction as to how long a student should be exposed to the English language before being expected to complete such a test.

Issues related to funding have arisen within the last decade and are probably the most contentious contemporary concern. During this time many provincial governments have reduced funding for public education, leaving school board administrators to face the dilemma of ensuring an increasingly high-quality education with fewer resources. Accordingly, school personnel often feel pushed to their limits. Disgruntlement and discouragement with government policies is common among school staff.

Student violence in schools is a standard topic in Canadian media. Though the rate of youth violence has actually decreased in recent years, the current rate of youth violence remains substantially higher than that of the mid-1980s. In comparison, the adult rate of violent crimes is decreasing at a greater rate. The greatest growth in the rate of violent crime involved "minor" assaults (Kong, 1997). This increase can be partially attributed to less tolerance of violent youth behavior. However, the genuine increase in youth assault and aggressive behavior among children cannot be ignored. For instance, a 1991 study in Eastern Ontario showed that 22 percent of three-year-olds were unable to control their aggression, which is approximately three times the rate shown by a comparable study undertaken 20 years earlier (Steinhauer, 1995). School social workers and other professionals are faced with the quandary of facilitating school violence prevention programs, whereas the vast majority of their efforts concentrate on crisis management.

HISTORY OF SCHOOL SOCIAL WORK

The history of social work in Canadian publicly funded schools can be traced to two major influences. First, many school social work departments across the country link their own foundations to the expansion of truancy or attendance departments. A brief history of the shift from child labor to mandatory attendance laws and the subsequent emergence of attendance counselors may be useful in understanding the beginnings of school social work. Secondly, school social work in Canada can be directly traced to the 1940s, at which time social intervention programs in schools were facilitated by community mental health practitioners.

During the early 1880s, Canada experienced an industrial revolution that dramatically altered the roles and responsibilities of children. As a result of technological advances during the late 19th century, child labor increased as many jobs that required physical strength and a high degree of skill were replaced by positions requiring only the agility and repetition that an older child could offer. At that same time, the Canadian educational system was being established. Mandatory attendance laws were developed in 1871 and boards of education began to develop attendance regulations (Hurl, 1988). In 1872, the former Toronto Board of Education (now part of the Toronto District School Board) was probably the first school board to employ a truant officer (Grande & McClare, 1983).

The demand for child labor, combined with educational reform, resulted in an increased number of young students attending schools, but a decrease in the enrolment of older students. For example, in the early 1870s in Hamilton, an industrialized city in southern Ontario, the attendance of school age children between the ages of seven and 12 became almost universal, rising to 85.1 percent. This represented an increase of more than 30 percent from 20 years earlier. However, in sharp contrast to the experience of younger children, attendance among children aged between 13 and 16 was only 45.8 percent, a decrease of close to 10 percent from the previous decades (Katz & Dave, 1978). One might deduce from these statistics that educational laws promoted education only as an alternative to labor. It is also true that compulsory attendance was not enforced for families who depended on the earnings of their children (Hurl, 1988).

During the early 1900s, the use of child labor in Canadian industries began to decline in conjunction with several economic, political, and social developments. As factories centralized, expanded, modernized, and developed into specialized, more prosperous industries requiring more highly skilled employees, child labor became less necessary for survival in domestic and worldwide markets (Hurl, 1988).

At the same time, a shift in the entire notion of childhood emerged. During the 1800s, children were viewed as potential adults—hard work and firm discipline was thought to mold children into moral and productive people. By the early 20th century an increasing number of Canadians developed a more sentimental and nurturing understanding of childhood. A generation of middle-class reformers emerged that transformed child welfare in Canada; reformers such as The Society for the Protection of Women and Children joined labor activists in petitioning for protective child labor legislation. Similarly, The National Council of Women supported the Trades and Labour Congress in its quest for increased protection of women and children employed in business and commerce (Sutherland, 1976).

Accordingly, the role of the truant officer evolved, and in 1919 the title was changed to attendance officer to reflect the shift from an authoritarian approach to one of understanding the underlying issues (Martelli, 1988). A more humanitarian approach to school absenteeism emerged as the new attendance officers began to practice social work in schools. Today, the majority of school social workers in Canada continue to address issues related to infrequent school attendance and many hold the dual title of school social worker/attendance counselor. In a 1995 Ontario survey, 69 percent of school social workers reported that they perform some aspect of an attendance counseling function (OASW, 1995a).

The actual title of school social worker did not appear in Canada, however, until the mental hygiene movement in the 1940s and 1950s. It was in this period that psychiatrists began to develop programs for students in schools under the auspices of municipal public health departments. As a result of these initiatives, school social work programs began to emerge throughout the country. School social workers were initially hired in Ontario and Quebec in 1945, Saskatchewan in 1949 (Grande & McClare, 1983), and Alberta in 1957 (personal communication with Marcus Busch, social work consultant, Edmonton, Alberta, Canada, January 15, 1999). Student support staff were officially employed in a social work capacity in Nova Scotia in 1967 (personal communication with Alex Bruce, facilitator, Student Services, Halifax Regional School Board, Dartmouth, Nova Scotia, Canada, January 22, 1999) and in Manitoba in 1968 (personal communication with Hugh J. Curtis, former Area Service Director, Child Guidance Clinic of Greater Winnipeg, January 26, 1999). The first school social worker was hired in New Brunswick in the late 1970s (personal communication with Janet Hunt, school social worker, Department of Health and Community Services, St. George, New Brunswick, January 7, 1999). Although some school boards developed their own internal social work departments, others chose to contract mental health providers from child guidance clinics. The interdisciplinary team approach emerged as school social workers became part of the treatment process, assisting in diagnosis of "nervous" and "difficult" children, as well as implementing interventions recommended by psychiatrists (Grande, 1978).

By 1970, as in the United States, a paradigm shift in the practice of school social work emerged in Canada. It became clear that if a child who was manifesting a problem in school was to be helped, a range of factors must be considered in the problem-solving process: the child; the family; ethnicity and language; religion; class placement; the school and its educational philosophy; teachers; the community; and the interaction of the school with its community. Social workers recognized the importance of engaging and linking the school, the home, and the community in resolving the child's problem, as is promoted in the ecological model (Grande & McClare, 1983).

Hugh Curtis's (1978) study of school social work roles and services in Canada revealed a total of 270 social workers employed in 39 urban school divisions, mainly in the provinces of Ontario and Manitoba. Curtis also noted that in those provinces that relied on external social service resources there was a lack of continuity in the services provided. He identified disciplinary issues, aggressive behavior, academic underachievement, and absenteeism as the main social, emotional, or educational problems for which students received social work services. The majority of Canadian school social workers in Curtis's study were

female with more than two-thirds possessing an MSW degree. Today, the estimated number of school social workers has more than doubled to more than
750 in seven provinces (Ontario Association of Social Workers, 1995a, 1999).

A brief overview of school social work in each of the individual
provinces is helpful in understanding the overall national picture. In British
Columbia, social workers are employed only sporadically in several boards of
education. More often, teachers with specific training fulfill a typical counseling role. Schools also form linkages with community agencies to assist in providing social work services to students. The prairie provinces of Saskatchewan,
Alberta, and Manitoba have a long-standing tradition of employing school
social workers. As early as the 1940s, teachers in Manitoba participated in
social work training to augment their existing role as "visiting teachers," a role
similar to that of an attendance counselor. Approximately 75 percent of school
social workers in these three provinces are employed in fewer than six urban
cities. However, outlying rural boards are also beginning to employ a few social
workers. More than 37 percent of the Canadian population resides in Ontario,
with a marked concentration of residents in a 300-kilometer (approximately
186-mile) band across the south of the province (Statistics Canada, 1999).
Not surprisingly then, the highest number of school social workers is also
located in southern Ontario, where 400 school social workers are employed.
Despite funding uncertainties and rapid changes to the Ontario education system, the overall number of school social workers has remained relatively
unchanged during the past few decades. Some longer-established boards of
education, often in large urban centers, have more recently faced downsizing
and the loss of school social work positions through attrition resulting from
budget cuts. However, newer or expanding boards have been hiring new staff
or contracting for service from local agencies. The use of the title school social
worker is not as exclusive and distinct as practitioners and researchers would
prefer. However, regulation of the social work profession in many provinces is
facilitating a more consistent and meaningful use of the position title school
social worker.

Since the 1970s school social workers in Québec have been based in
local community services centers (Centre Local Services Communitaire),
although school social work existed in the province before that time in a different organizational structure. Usually there is at least one social worker in
each of these health and social service centers to respond to referrals from the
local schools. If local funding allows, social work service to schools can be provided for French, English, or Jewish students and their families. It is as recently
as 1993 that the 32 CLSCs were established in Montreal. Most of the approximately 150 school social workers in Québec have a BSW degree.

The provinces of New Brunswick and Nova Scotia, located in the area of
Canada known as the Maritimes (or Atlantic Region, according to Driedger),
employ school social workers. The Department of Health and Community

Services in New Brunswick has hired social workers to work full-time in schools for more than 20 years. In the more northerly part of this province, French is the predominant language. In the south, school social workers are assigned to both the mainly English speaking rural and urban schools. From 1967 to 1969, mental health workers (former special education teachers) were employed by the school board in Halifax, Nova Scotia. One year later the first two school social workers were hired by a special education coordinator who wanted to make a clear distinction between psychologists who conducted educational assessments of students and social workers who provided counseling but did not address truancy. For many years there have been about 10 school social work positions in Nova Scotia for approximately 60,000 students in 150 schools. Unique to this province is the requirement for school social workers to hold a special license to practice that is issued by the Teacher's Union.

School social workers are not currently employed in Newfoundland, Labrador, Prince Edward Island, or the three territories—Yukon, The Northwest Territories, and Nanavut (constituted in 1999).

In Newfoundland, several proposals outlining the effectiveness of, and need for, such support services have been submitted to the provincial government. The positive outcomes of school-based social work service have been understood and experienced in this province through the placement of social work students in schools for many years.

A recent report highlighting the importance of school social work service comments: "In light of the many social problems in Newfoundland and Labrador, the psychosocial needs of children and youth must be addressed if they are expected to achieve in the educational system .... This goal would be achieved through direct practice with students and their families, and indirect practice with the school and other organizations" (Newfoundland & Labrador Association of Social Workers, 1998).

Native counselors are employed in various areas of native education programs that are being developed in several parts of Canada. As native peoples assume more responsibility for the services on their reserves and in local communities, the number of native counselors involved with students continues to rise. Native peoples continue to develop educational services, resources, and programs that promote cultural awareness. Moreover, native educators are increasingly taking hold of and modifying the educational policies that govern their schools to best meet the needs of their students. Social workers and counselors work with native students to foster an understanding of their cultural roots as well as increase interest in and awareness of educational goals and opportunities (personal communication with John McCree, Native Liaison, Slave Lake, Alberta, Canada, January 5, 1999; personal communication with Terry Needham, February 12, 1999).

SCHOOL SOCIAL WORK ROLE

In Canada, school social workers are mainly employed by school boards, which, in turn, are funded provincially. New Brunswick is an exception to this model, where school-based service is provided by social workers employed by the provincial Health and Community Service Department.

In those provinces that provide school social work service (Alberta, Manitoba, New Brunswick, Nova Scotia, Ontario, Québec, and Saskatchewan), full-time school social workers are assigned several schools for which they provide a variety of services. Generally, all students from kindergarten (age four or five) to grades 12–13 (age 18 or 19) and their families in these schools have access to the school social worker. Many schools also house childcare programs that provide before, during, and after-school care. It is the goal of all staff, including school social workers, in such schools to provide as seamless a day as possible for the students and their families, such that they experience continuity of care and involvement in the school.

A school social worker may also be based in an education center (the administrative building for several families of schools), a local community service center (that houses community social service staff as well as social workers who work in schools) or child guidance clinic, and may travel to a number of schools during the course of a week or two. Regardless of the office location, school assignments for school social workers in Canada are often based on a family of schools model when school social workers will be responsible for one or more high schools (grades 9–10 to 12–13) and their feeder elementary schools. The role of a school social worker in Toronto, Ontario (where the largest school board in Canada, created in 1997, has about 90 school-based social workers for approximately 300,000 students) is much different from fulfilling the same role in rural New Brunswick, where one school social worker undertakes a 90-minute ferry journey to reach an island school.

Many school social workers are paid an annual salary, often negotiated through a trade union, by the board of education, whereas others are paid on the basis of billable hours. In Edmonton, Alberta, individual schools contract with board-employed school social workers for a stipulated number of hours for specific services. With a decline in provincial funding in Alberta, there has been less money available at the local school level. This has resulted both in a decrease in requests for social work services and, at the same time, an effort by social work staff to ensure that their services are effective and valued. The school social workers then have the responsibility to ensure that enough hours per week are requested to maintain the services. It is unlikely that community agencies have experienced an increase in funding to make up for the shortfall in education. We must conclude, therefore, that some children and families who were assisted by school social workers in the past are now receiving a reduced service.

Consultation, coordination and collaboration, and intervention tend to be the main components of the school social worker's role in Canada. With respect to intervention, individual, family, and group counseling and critical incident involvement are required at most schools. As is the case for all social workers, the basic principles of professional practice apply to the school setting: Individuals are respected for their uniqueness, dignity, value, and right to self-determination; confidentiality must be maintained; and informed consent is mandatory to the therapeutic process. Visibility and involvement in the school setting on the part of the school social worker build trust so that children and adults feel safe.

In at least two provinces, Ontario and Québec, guidelines or standards for the practice of school social work have been developed by front line staff in collaboration with the provincial professional organization (OASW, 1995b). These extensive guidelines cover topics from professional identity to organizational context, professional development, role, and ethics.

Referrals to school social workers most often reflect problems in the following areas: family, academic, social functioning, emotional functioning, physical health, mental health, parenting, interpretation, translation, finances, and attendance. In some jurisdictions attendance and absenteeism are the responsibility of attendance counselors who have a very specific mandate to work with those students who are not attending school on a regular basis. Otherwise, the school social worker assumes the role of attendance counselor. Professional school social workers seem to have taken a less-active role in the area of attendance issues in the past couple of decades, possibly the result of an increased emphasis on therapeutic rather than punitive approaches.

Recently, court involvement by frontline school social workers has decreased significantly in some areas, particularly Ontario. At the same time there are a few boards that assign either a part-time or full-time position to court work, often depending on the current practices of the local Family Court Clinic and staffing levels. This court worker may be the liaison worker for attendance cases only or may also be involved with other Family Court matters that require liaison between the student, the family, and school personnel. There are many boards that offer an early-school leaving program for high-school students who would prefer a part-time job in conjunction with school attendance.

Many factors contribute to the ability of students and families to forge an alliance with the school for the purpose of providing the best educational opportunities and outcomes possible. Those same factors (stable housing, financial stability, good parenting, time and energy to be a student, respect for education and educators, and so forth) also contribute to the functioning of the family on a day-to-day basis. As governments, local agencies, and individuals struggle with changing educational, employment, and economic programs, parents and students find themselves caught in a variety of crises. For example, cuts in education funding have reduced financial support for transportation and school supplies for students. With the school setting most often being the best known to the student, after the home environment, school social workers are devoting more time and energy to crisis intervention now than they were 20 years ago. We are now much clearer on the need for recognition at school of critical events both inside and outside of the school building that affect the daily lives of students (for example, the death of a student).

Models of service delivery across Canada consistently include direct service (individual, family, or group counseling), consultation, and some community liaison for referral or planning purposes. In many school boards there is an interdisciplinary team of professionals. For example, a local school team in Toronto meets on a regular basis to discuss a variety of presenting problems with the teacher, student, and parent(s), as well as other interested personnel. An action plan involving one or more goals is often developed and then reviewed later in the school year to evaluate its implementation and effectiveness. In a recent survey, school social workers allocated on average more than 15 percent of their weekly time to local school teamwork (OASW, 1995a).

School social workers provide service to students in special education through assessments and interventions, consulting with teachers and parents, and collaborating with community agencies for external services. In the past decade there has been increased emphasis on the integration of students with special needs into regular classes or at least into a supported classroom setting in the local school. In Ontario, for example, some students with visual, auditory, or physical disabilities attend specialized schools. At the same time, educational/medical assistants are provided for other students with special needs in neighborhood schools so that peer interaction can be more spontaneous and varied. The shift to more integration has changed the role for some school social workers from considerable involvement with the IPRC (Identification, Placement, and Review Committee) process to increased local school class and family support. The IPRC is mandated to identify those students who have special needs in areas of learning disabilities, reading, very high academic functioning, low cognitive functioning, and behavioral, social, or emotional problems. There is a range of services available from the self-contained class to full integration.

In Saskatchewan, each social worker is attached to a behavior program that serves students in a self-contained classroom in a regular school setting. The Calgary Board of Education in Alberta takes a different approach. Students in grades 7-9 who are having problems with behavior, socialization skills, attitude toward learning, home environment dysfunction, and so forth, can be referred to a unique program where a three-person team (teacher, social worker, and educational assistant) provides assessment and counseling as well as an academic program for up to eight students who attend for approximately 20 school days. Individualized student learning plans are developed with the home and school so that the transition at the completion of the program is more successful (personal communication with Allyson Bogoch, social worker, Calgary, Alberta, Canada, December 8, 1998).

Children with new types of special needs, such as paralysis from gunshot wounds, genetic disorders, AIDS, and other new kinds of illnesses, are now entering their local schools. There are increased demands on teachers to work closely with parents and health workers to maximize learning opportunities for these students. For those provinces in Canada that provide a school-based school social work service, the current key social issues are poverty, violence, abuse (especially sexual), parenting, and delinquency. In Winnipeg, Manitoba, gangs are a particular concern at this time. In this relatively young multicultural country, Canadian parents struggle with cultural differences in acceptable social behavior of children and youth, the role of the family members, employment demands and the impact of an advanced technological society. It appears that cell phones, home computers, and video arcades have created a world of communication that is more about electronic interaction than it is about interpersonal contact. It is therefore necessary for school social workers to become knowledgeable about many new situations and work with a wider range of caregivers. Although the role of the school social worker is often that of a generalist, some workers develop specialty knowledge in relation to particular student populations.

Prevention remains a goal for school social workers, despite cutbacks in services both in the community and in school boards. Implementation of prevention initiatives varies from school-wide activities to class or small group programs. The development of class profiles is an example of a preventive program in which school social workers have been involved. In the fall term, teachers use a template developed by their division [such as primary (kindergarten–grade 3), junior, or senior (grades 7 and 8)] to record each child's level in key curriculum areas. This profile easily highlights, at least in a visual way, the areas of strength and weakness so that teaching can be geared to the class as a whole and to students in groups if necessary. School social workers are often part of the team that reviews these profiles, sometimes devoting an hour or two to each class. The class profile process also enables the school to evaluate curriculum needs and resources as well as anticipate future needs for that student population.

The reporting and prevention of child abuse is another key program in many school boards. The development of and training for reporting protocols has mainly been the responsibility of social work staff in most school boards that hire social workers, always in collaboration with Children's Aid Societies, which are the primary investigators. (The Children's Aid Society is responsible for the protection of children under the age of 16 within the mandate of the Child and Family Services Act as well as out-of-home care for children and the development of child abuse and neglect prevention programs. School social workers conduct a variety of prevention programs that are educational in nature, including programs for conflict resolution, stress and anger management, social skills training, bereavement, divorce education programs, and parent education.

Many school boards have worked hard to build a strong relationship with parents, through regular parent/teacher interviews, curriculum nights, focusing on subjects such as math programs, fund-raising activities, and so forth, to promote school-home partnerships in education. Support staff and educators have also recognized the important role the school can play when a crisis or tragedy affects the home or school. School social workers have the training and knowledge to become actively involved in tragic events response teams that work with a school population (students, parents, staff, media, and community agencies) when, for example, a child dies at school, a school bus is involved in a serious accident, a parent commits suicide, or a teacher is suddenly absent from the class. The goal of this work is to recognize and treat the immediate, short-term, and long-term effects of tragic events on children and adults alike.

The balance between the provision of prevention programs and direct intervention work is delicate. It is increasingly difficult for school social workers to do both effectively. As a result, school social workers prefer to have a steady school involvement from one year to the next, not only to develop a solid working relationship with the staff, but also to be able to anticipate service needs and then to respond in an effective and timely manner.

TRAINING OF SCHOOL SOCIAL WORKERS

Many Canadian school social workers maintain membership in one of several associations. Founded in 1926 to monitor employment conditions and to establish standards of practice within the profession, the Canadian Association of Social Workers (CASW) has evolved into a national voice for some 15,000 members by adopting a proactive approach to issues pertinent to social work. This association also provides evaluation of the academic qualifications of social workers who have trained outside North America and who wish to practice in Canada. CASW is active in the International Federation of Social Workers (IFSW), providing leadership within the IFSW Executive as well as within the North American region. By joining the appropriate provincial association (for example, New Brunswick Association of Social Workers/Association des Travailleurs Sociaux du Nouveau-Brunswick), social workers automatically become affiliated with the Canadian Association of Social Workers.

One such provincial organization, The Ontario Association of Social Workers (OASW), has developed a committee specific to school social work. The OASW School Social Work Committee takes a very active role within the province in advocating for and responding to social and educational policy.

Activities of the committee also include research about school social work practice, hosting an annual conference and publishing pamphlets for parents and newsletters for its members.

The Canadian Association of School Social Workers and Attendance Counsellors (CASSWAC) was founded in 1982 in Alberta by a group of school social workers and attendance counselors based in the prairie provinces (personal communication with Bert Halyk, Saskatoon, Saskatchewan, Canada, January 25, 1999). The original intent of this organization was to provide a means by which school-based staff could communicate and exchange ideas through newsletters and conferences. CASSWAC has grown to include school social workers and attendance counselors throughout the country. The Association holds a bi-annual conference and is currently combining efforts with the OASW School Social Work Committee and the Ontario Association of Counselling and Attendance Services (OACAS) in this regard.

In addition to these associations, many school social workers are members of union groups or education-related associations and federations. In most cases, employees within other disciplines such as psychology and speech or language pathology have joined with social workers and other school-based professionals in such unions. These unions are actively involved in advocating for their members, negotiating collective agreements, and attempting to provide better working environments for field staff.

The majority of school social workers in Canada hold a master of social work (MSW) degree, whereas others possess a bachelor of social work (BSW) degree. A three- to four-year undergraduate program is required for a bachelor's degree. Persons who hold a BSW may obtain a master's degree after one year of graduate studies. Those who have a degree in another discipline need to complete a two-year graduate program in social work to obtain the MSW. Most of these programs require the successful completion of one or more terms in a supervised practicum. Social work programs are accredited by the Canadian Association of Schools of Social Work in 36 Canadian universities (CASSW, 1999).

Although many universities offer courses specific to practice modalities and child and family psychosocial development, no specific courses have been developed for social workers in educational settings. Rather, internships or placements in school settings are available to social work students. Further training is obtained through professional development functions organized within specific departments of education or by professional associations and colleges. The OACAS has, in previous years, conducted a course leading to an attendance counselor certificate provided by the government.

In all provinces registration with a provincial association is required to practice social work in any field. The provincial association or college of social workers generally oversees this certification or regulation of social workers in the interests of the public and the profession.

ISSUES FOR FUTURE DIRECTION

The increasing prevalence of family and social problems, the difficult economic climate, and the increasing violence in our society are some of the factors that will continue to place extra demands on the educational system in the future. The decrease in community services and cutbacks in government programs are already the cause of reduced support services to students, their families, and schools. Whether the Canadian student population grows or remains relatively static, the severity and complexity of social problems are likely to continue to increase. Based on historical patterns, it is quite probable that the demand for social work services will continue to expand (O'Neil, 1994).

School social workers in Canada currently tend to practice a case management approach in providing services. This may be the result of necessity rather than of choice or ideal design. School social workers receive an overwhelming number of referrals each year, often preventing the worker from meeting with students and their families on an ongoing basis to provide more intensive service. Also, because crisis intervention is a primary role of the school social worker, efforts to provide ongoing services are often interrupted for prolonged periods. Perhaps more than ever before, school social workers must examine the efficacy of their practices in an effort to determine the best approach to service delivery for their clients. Trying to do all things for all people is impractical and, more importantly, ineffective.

In *School Social Work Practice, Policy and Research Perspectives*, Sabatino and Timberlake (1999) address the need for research and evaluation to ensure accountability of school social workers to themselves, their clients, and their profession. Also, there are growing demands for school social workers to provide evidence to their school boards that they have a positive impact on those for whom they provide service. With shrinking financial resources, school social workers can no longer rely on anecdotal material and goodwill to substantiate the provision of services. Instead, school social workers must direct their interventions using best practice information that is clinically and statistically significant.

Working in one of the largest countries in the world, Canadian school social workers struggle to maintain communication on a national basis. Meetings in person or regular conferences are simply not practical when one could fly from Halifax, Nova Scotia, to Paris, France, more quickly and cheaply than to Vancouver, British Columbia. However, advances in communication technology, such as the Internet, have facilitated connections over such a vast area. School social workers in Canada are beginning to avail themselves of such technology and to take more advantage of the increased communication possibilities. The development of a national school social work website could greatly enhance sharing of best practices throughout the country.

Canadian school social workers have much to be proud of in our history of providing support to students, families, educators, and other stakeholders in the field of education. At the same time, we are taking advantage of opportunities to network internationally and to learn more about the exciting changes taking place globally in this important area of social work practice.

REFERENCES

Adams, M. (1998). *Sex in the snow*. Toronto: Penguin Books.

Campaign 2000 (1998). *Child poverty in Canada: Report Card 1998* [Online]. Available: http://www.campaign2000.ca/rc/

Canadian Association of Schools of Social Work (1999). *Canadian directory of schools of social work* [Online]. Available: www.cassw-acess.ca

Curtis, H. (1978). *School social work roles and services in Canada*. Unpublished doctoral dissertation, University of Utah, Salt Lake City.

Driedger, L. (1996). *Multi-ethnic Canada: Identities and inequalities*. Toronto: Oxford University Press.

Government of Canada (1999). *Education* [Online] Available: www.canada. gc.ca/canadiana

Grande, G. (1978). *A practitioner model for school social work: A systems approach*. Unpublished doctoral dissertation, University of Southern California, Los Angeles.

Grande, G. & McClare, G. (1983). School social work: Strategies for prevention. *Social Work Papers, 17*, 35–42.

Ordre Professionel des Travailleurs Sociaux du Québec (1997). *Guide to the Professional Practice of Social Workers in CLSCs and Schools*. Montreal: Ordre Professionel des Travailleurs Sociaux du Québec.

Hurl, L. (1988). Restricting child factory labour in late nineteenth century Ontario. *Labour/Le Travail, 21*, 82–121.

Katz, M. & Dave, I. (1978). School attendance and early industrialization in a Canadian city: A multivariate analysis. *History of Education Quarterly, 18*, 251–293.

Kong, R. (1997). Canadian criminal statistics, 1996, *Juristat, 17* (8), 1–22.

Martelli, C. (1988). *The formation and development of the social work department within the Metropolitan Separate School Board, 1957–1988*. Unpublished MSW assignment, University of Toronto, Toronto.

Newfoundland & Labrador Association of Social Workers (1998). *Prevention and early intervention through collaboration: A position paper of the Newfoundland and Labrador Association of Social Workers*. St. John's, Newfoundland: Newfoundland and Labrador Association of Social Workers.

O'Hara, K. (1998). *Comparative family policy: Eight countries' stories* (Report No. F/04). Ottawa: Canadian Policy Research Network.

Ontario Association of Social Workers (1995a). *A survey of Ontario school social workers conducted by the School Social Work Committee*. Toronto: Ontario Association of Social Workers.

Ontario Association of Social Workers (1995b). *OASW Guidelines for Social Work Services in Schools*. Toronto: Ontario Association of Social Workers.

Ontario Association of Social Workers (1999). *A survey of Ontario school social workers conducted by the School Social Work Committee.* Toronto: Ontario Association of Social Workers.

O'Neil, M. (1994). *The Social Work Department: Metropolitan Separate School Board present and future needs.* (Document prepared for the Metropolitan Separate School Board). Toronto: Metropolitan Separate School Board.

Rees, T. (1998). *Together we are one: A report on diversity in Toronto.* Toronto: Access and Equity Centre, City of Toronto.

Sabatino, C.A. & Timberlake, E.M. (1999). Research in school social work: Catching up and moving on. In T. Constable, S. McDonald & J. Flynn (Eds.). *School social work practice, policy and research perspectives* (pp. 538–558). Chicago: Lyceum Press.

Statistics Canada (1996). *1996 Census: Nation Tables.* Ottawa: Government of Canada.

Statistics Canada (1999). *CANSIM Matrices* [Online]. Available: www.statcan.ca

Steinhauer, P. (1995). Effects of family stress on children. *Empire Club of Canada Addresses, 1994–95,* February 2, pp. 17–33.

Sutherland, N. (1976). *Children in English-Canadian society: Framing the twentieth-century consensus.* Toronto: University of Toronto Press.

United Nations (1998). *Concluding observations of the United Nations Committee on Economic, Social and Cultural Rights.* (Publication No. E/C.12/1/Add.31.) Geneva: United Nations.

United Nations Development Program (1998). *Human Development Report.* New York: Oxford University Press.

4 SCHOOL SOCIAL WORK IN FINLAND AND OTHER NORDIC COUNTRIES: COOPERATIVE PROFESSIONALISM IN SCHOOLS

Gun Andersson, Tarja Pösö, Erja Väisänen, and Aila Wallin

Social Indicators* — Finland	
Population	5,178,000
Percentage under age 15 years	18
Percentage urban (2000)	67
Life expectancy at birth	74.4 men, 81.5 women
Fertility rate	1.55 children per woman
Percentage of illiterate adults	Not available
Per capita GDP in $U.S. (1999)	25,112
Percentage unemployed (1999)	10.1

*Social Indicators. From the Statistics Division of the United Nations. Refer to notes on page 249.
 Reference: http://www.un.org/Depts/unsd/indicators/indic2a.htm

NATIONAL CONTEXT

In terms of population numbers, all five Nordic countries—Denmark, Finland, Norway, Sweden, and Iceland—are relatively small. In 1998, Denmark and Finland each had a population of approximately 5 million, Norway's population numbered 4.5 million, Sweden's almost 9 million, and Iceland's 270,000. In Denmark, Finland, Norway, and Sweden, children under 15 account for between 18 and 20 percent of the population; in Iceland the proportion is 24 percent. Sweden has the largest proportion of non-nationals, accounting for approximately 6 percent of the population. In Finland the figure is no more than 1.5 percent, less than in any other Nordic country, although the proportion has increased significantly during the 1990s (Feldbaek, 1998).

In discussions of social policy it is quite common to treat the Nordic countries as a single family. One speaks of Nordic welfare policy and Nordic welfare thinking, even of a Nordic welfare regime. The distinctive features of what is thought to represent this model include a broad, publicly organized system of social assistance, support and service mechanisms that are based on principles of universalism, limited means-testing, and an accent on the rights of citizens as users of welfare services.

In many of these analyses a focal concern is with Nordic family policy, centering on social benefits and public services provided for families, considered to be more comprehensive than in most other European countries (Millar & Warman, 1996). One of the basic assumptions of Nordic family policy is that public authorities should provide support to raise and care for children. This support is made available universally for all parents, not only for those in crisis situations. Increasingly, the needs and rights of children are also highlighted; day care services are a case in point. Millar & Warman (1996) state that Nordic social policy is the most advanced in Europe in terms of recognizing children's rights. One example is corporal punishment of children, which is forbidden by law. The basic motive of Nordic social policy may be described as oriented to the defense and protection of the underprivileged. This is clearly evidenced in the case of children, who have very limited influence and power in society. Current policy and practice in Nordic countries protects and values the welfare of children (Pringle, 1998). Child welfare legislation, for instance, is geared to supporting and developing children's welfare and health. Intervention in existing problems is considered a form of reactive child protection, which must remain a secondary option to a policy of preventive child protection. The school system is a key agent in child welfare. Social workers who are active in child protection are just one part of this extensive system of child welfare.

Some commentators, however, are quite skeptical and point out that, despite good intentions, Nordic policies regarding children and the child-oriented welfare system are still clearly focused on adults and on the family (Bardy, 1996; Forsberg, 1998; Riihelä, 1996). Others have said that the emphasis on prevention has meant that child welfare has neglected to develop the tools and competencies needed to deal with acute problems and malpractices that affect children as individuals (Kananoja & Turunen, 1996; Pösö, 1997; Pringle, 1998; Weightman & Weightman, 1995). Finally, research concerned with children and youth has also come under attack for its orientation to adults. For instance, problems and welfare deficits in the lives of children and youth have chiefly been analyzed from an adult vantage point, in the light of questions that are of interest to adults. It is only very rarely that these questions have been addressed from the viewpoint of children and youth themselves (for example, see Kiili, 1998).

EDUCATION IN THE NORDIC COUNTRIES

All Nordic countries have a comprehensive school system, including free education, as well as an extensive day care system for children under school age. The Finnish educational system consists of preschool education that is intended for six-year-olds who will start their compulsory education in the following year. It has been voluntary so far. This is followed by a period of "basic education," which is general education provided for each age group in its entirety. It is intended for children from seven to 16 years of age, and its completion in comprehensive school takes nine years. Upper secondary school provides general education for students who are usually between 16 and 19 years of age and ends with the completion of the matriculation examination. Initial vocational education in vocational institutions is provided in the form of apprenticeship training in virtually all fields. The completion of an initial vocational qualification takes two to three years. Polytechnics provide non-university professional higher education, usually in a multi-field environment, for those who have completed either the matriculation examination or an upper secondary level vocational qualification. Universities provide bachelor's and master's academic degrees and scientific postgraduate degrees, which are the licentiate and the doctorate. In general, completion of a bachelor's degree takes three years and completion of a master's degree takes five years.

All Nordic countries have a comprehensive school system, free education as well as an extensive day care system for children under school age. The education budget accounts for around 8 % of Gross National Product (in 1995 Denmark and Norway spent 8.3 %, Sweden 8 %, Finland 7.6 % and Iceland 5 % of their GNP on education) (Suomen tilastollinen vuosikirja 1998, 646). In Finland the primary school system was set up in the 1860s, but it was not until several decades later that it became genuinely accessible to all people. Even the introduction of compulsory school attendance did not help to achieve full coverage, but by the 1950s all children and adolescents of compulsory school age were attending school (Jauhiainen, 1993, 2). Since the Second World War the aim has been to raise the general level of education and to promote equity among children and youths, i.e. to create equal opportunities for all children regardless of their place of residence, gender, language, or parental income. To this end Finland set up in the 1970s a nationwide comprehensive school system, which is free of charge to all pupils and which has a uniform core curriculum. The system is supposed to cover all children aged seven to 16.

It is indicative of the achievements of the Nordic school system that all Nordic countries are omitted from the global illiteracy statistics in the Finnish Statistical Yearbook (Suomen tilastollinen vuosikirja, 1998). Illiteracy is not a problem in Scandinavia. Indeed, almost from the beginning of the public schooling itself there was recognition that education provided by schools should be complemented by welfare services to support the physical, social, and psychological well-being of students. During the first decades of the 20th century, welfare services in Finland included various subsidies and arrangements to provide physical and material support for schooling (such as school dormitories, kitchens, and summer camps). The next step was to increase health care services in schools, and from the 1970s onward the role of psychologists and social workers has been strengthened (Jauhiainen, 1993). The development of welfare services for school children was closely followed by the expansion of other specialized services, such as a network of child guidance and family counseling centers. With this strengthening of psychosocial welfare services for schoolchildren and the general expansion of the Finnish welfare state, the number of professionals specializing in children and adolescents has also grown quite considerably (Jauhiainen, 1993).

However, the socialization of children and adolescents remains a source of constant concern in Nordic countries as social mores have changed. There is much discussion over appropriate means to socialize children in schools, accompanied by much concern over disruptive students. Neither the schools, nor other support services for children and families, have been able to eliminate anxieties over the rearing of children in a changing world. As children's rights are given more attention in Nordic countries, schools seek new ways to help school children learn to work together in a nonauthoritarian school environment. In the late 1990s there has been increasing concern about the health, mental well-being, and drug use of children and adolescents. However, it seems that the Nordic system of income transfer has at least succeeded in minimizing child poverty. Forssen (1997) has reported that whereas all other OECD (Organization for Economic Cooperation and Development) countries have a growing problem with child poverty, the Nordic countries have kept this problem at bay. In this analysis it appears that income transfer and comprehensive social services are particularly valuable to women and children. Nonetheless, the economic recession that hit Finland in the 1990s has quite obviously affected families with children as well (and particularly sole provider families) and, by the same token, children themselves. Services available for children have been adversely affected. While the number of children who live in poverty is small by international comparison, it clearly must remain a constant concern for social policy in Finland.

The school and the public day care system are among the channels that have a direct effect on children's welfare and play a key role in the promotion of the well-being of children and youth. Social work at school has played its own part in this. While this chapter makes reference to all Nordic countries, it focuses primarily on school social work in Finland and, unless otherwise stated, the descriptions below refer to Finland. One of the reasons for this is that no earlier accounts of school social work exist either in any individual Nordic country or in the Nordic countries as a whole.

The History of School Social Work

The first school social workers were appointed in Norway and Sweden in the 1940s. In Stockholm, social work posts in high schools were initially created on the initiative of municipalities and parent organizations. In the late 1950s, school social work positions were created in the compulsory schools. Between 1966 and 1967, guidelines stated that there should be a school social worker at every high school. In Denmark, school social work was introduced in the 1960s, and in Iceland the first school social worker was employed at a school in Reykjavik in 1977. In Finland the first posts for school social workers were established in the 1960s in Helsinki and in the smaller coastal town of Kotka. Even before this, however, a special schoolteacher had been appointed to a school social work post in Finnish-language schools in Helsinki. Even earlier, some social work had been provided at schools through social services offices and child guidance clinics.

In Finland the school social worker has traditionally been known as a "school curator" ("koulukuraattori"). The Latin origins of "curator" mean "one who cares"; "cura" is Latin for "care" (Salmi & Linkomies, 1967). The term curator was introduced first in Swedish social work terminology, probably in hospitals. Sweden had used the same term ("skolkurator") even before Finland, but also that of "social secretary" ("socialsekreterare"). In Norway school social work is located in the educational psychological service ("pedagogisk-psykologisk tjeneste" or "PPT"), and the title that is used is "social worker in EPS". Denmark has from the outset used the term school social worker. In Iceland the job title is school counselor or, more recently, social worker.

In Finland the system of school social work began to spread during the 1970s. In 1977 there were 85 school social workers in Finland. By 1993 the figure had climbed to approximately 220 in a total of 93 municipalities. In addition, there were some 80 school social workers in vocational institutions. In Sweden the number of school social workers is estimated at 1,500, in Denmark approximately 50, and in Norway 80. In Iceland, the number of school social workers has grown since 1987 as both school counselors and school social workers have been based in schools around the country. At present there are more school counselors (approximately 40) than school social workers (four or five), but the number of school social workers will probably grow because they can handle personal problems rather than just academic problems.

In administrative terms, school social workers in Finland work either under the municipal school department or the social department, sometimes directly under the educational institution concerned (private schools or vocational institutions). The situation is similar in Sweden, but in Denmark all school social workers are employed by the municipal system. In Norway, each local authority provides an educational psychological service with a team consisting of psychologist, special needs teacher, preschool teacher, and social worker.

In Sweden there is no legislation that requires local or central government to provide social work services in schools. Any decisions on opening new posts in this field therefore depend on whether or not there exists the political will to do so. In Finland there have been some moves to incorporate school social work into national legislation, but so far this has come to nothing. The Child Welfare Act, however, had a paragraph added in 1990 which required local authorities to "... provide for students in the municipal school system adequate support and counselling and any other necessary means in order to eliminate social and mental problems related to school and to personal growth and development and in order to improve cooperation between the school and home. To this end the local council may establish posts for school psychologists and school social workers..." (Lastensuojelulaki 7§).

The new law also entitled local authorities to state subsidies to meet the costs of hiring school social workers and psychologists. The decree which specifies the Child Welfare Act says that "... the work of school psychologists and school social workers shall be so organised that it is adapted to local circumstances and to the number of students and the services available. School psychologists and school social workers should do most of their work in schools. In their capacity as experts in their respective fields, the school psychologist and school social worker shall take part in the planning and development of the school community as well as in its educational and guidance work. The school psychologist and school social worker shall work closely with the students, their parents, any other people caring for the students and involved in their guidance, the school community and the education department, the welfare and health authorities as well as other authorities" (Lastensuojeluasetus 2a§).

These steps to incorporate school social work into national legislation were aimed at strengthening the role of preventive social work in schools. However, this never happened. No sooner had the law entered into force than economic recession set in, effectively thwarting ambitions on the part of local authorities to establish any new posts. However, school social work had at least become firmly established and, where it had been started up, it was clearly considered necessary because very few posts were lost. Since the recession the number of school social workers has slowly started to increase again.

Before the Child Welfare Act the majority of school social workers were under the jurisdiction of the education department, but since the introduction of the Act many local authorities decided to transfer responsibility for school social work to the social services department. In 1993 more than one-third of all school social workers were employed by social services departments (Taskinen, 1995). More recent statistical information is unavailable, but we believe the trend toward employment of school social workers by social services departments has continued.

In Finland the establishment and early development of school social work is closely related to the school reforms of the 1970s, which led to the phasing in of the nine-year comprehensive school system from 1972 onward.

The mission for comprehensive schools is to promote the emotional, physical, and social well-being of their students and to foster the growth of children into balanced, healthy, and cooperative citizens. To achieve these objectives for as many students as possible, it was necessary to focus on supporting students in their development and to encourage a climate of open interaction within the school community.

With the launch of the comprehensive school system, steps were also taken to chart the needs for student welfare services. On the basis of its inquiries, the Pupil Welfare Committee (appointed by the Ministry of Education in 1973) proposed a plan for organizing school social work and psychological counseling. The proposal as a whole was geared toward supporting the general educational role of school and integrating social work and psychological counseling into other school work.

The Committee set the following goals for school social work:

- to harness social work to the broader objective of general education;
- to prevent social problem situations;
- to identify and overcome social and economic obstacles to effective school work;
- to encourage and promote collaboration within the school, between the school and parents, and between the school and other organizations;
- to influence planning processes at school and in other sectors of society with a view to facilitating school work both socially and economically. (Oppilashuoltokomitean mietintö 9a, 1974.)

The committee placed particular emphasis on the preventive nature of school social work. In the committee's view school social work should be well-placed to prevent the development of relationship problems by focusing its efforts on promoting human relations and interaction within the school community. The committee drafted a bill for the introduction of a comprehensive network of school social workers and psychologists. However, for various reasons, including opposition from some teachers who perhaps felt threatened by the prospect of a new profession arriving in schools, the bill was never adopted.

Job descriptions for school social workers were initially developed by each municipality. Consequently, job descriptions varied between municipalities, sometimes quite widely. As a rule, the emphasis was on addressing the problems of students who were struggling at school and on helping parents, teachers, and students with their problems. Over the years, the emphasis has shifted somewhat from an orientation on individuals toward a more holistic, community-oriented approach of consultation.

The Finnish school social workers' national association, "Koulukuraattorit – Skolkuratorer," was established in 1973, and it joined the main social work union, the Union of Professional Social Workers, in 1974. Members of Koulukuraattorit – Skolkuratorer must be qualified social workers. In 1998 the association had a membership of 192. Koulukuraattorit – Skolkuratorer has concentrated on the defense of its members' economic and professional interests. It has also taken an active part in public debate on issues concerning children, youth, and families, maintained contact with international organizations, and organized training courses. The association had always had close collaboration with units working with children and youth, and it has also had an active role in the Union of Professional Social Workers. The only specialist school social work publication in Finland is *Curator*, the newsletter of Koulukuraattorit – Skolkuratorer.

School social workers in the Finnish vocational institutions have their own association, which was set up in 1982. This is an independent association that is not a member of any trade organization.

School social work associations also exist in Sweden ("Sveriges Skolkuratorers Förening"), in Norway ("PPT Faggruppe") and in Denmark ("Faggruppen af Skolesocialrådgivere"). In Denmark and Norway the association operates as a branch of the main social workers' union. The Swedish association is not a trade organization, but an ideological association. It also has its own quarterly publication, *Skolkuratorn*.

There is very little research and literature on school social work in any of the Nordic countries. Most of the work consists of reports compiled for decision-makers, short accounts in volumes on student welfare, and diploma projects.

ROLE OF SCHOOL SOCIAL WORK

In Nordic countries, school social work primarily is a municipal service. In Finland most school social workers work within the jurisdiction of school administration, and their immediate superior is the chief education officer or the director of education and cultural services. For school social workers working within the jurisdiction of social services, their immediate superior is the social director or managing supervisor. In the biggest municipalities a senior school social worker will usually be appointed as chief school social worker or chief pupil welfare worker for the whole municipality. School social workers in Finnish comprehensive schools are not accountable to the school's head teacher (principal). In those municipalities where both school psychologists and social workers are employed, the psychologists tend to concentrate in their work on younger children, while the social workers concentrate on older ones. In Sweden many school social workers are also working in the secondary or post-secondary level.

School social workers will typically have their own room and office hours in the schools where they work. This means they are also involved in the school's day-to-day work, for example by taking part in staff meetings. School social workers will usually have responsibility for more than one school, normally between two and four schools, and 10 through 12 at most. This ratio is not, however, strict as only general guidelines exist that state that there should be one school social worker per 1,000 students. There can be marked regional differences although, according to Koulukuraattorit - Skolkuratorer, the guidelines appear to be quite well-met at least in southern Finland.

In some municipalities in Finland, Sweden, and Denmark, social workers from the social services department or a child guidance clinic are charged with responsibility for school social work in addition to their other duties.

In Finland, joint municipal authorities hire school social workers at the upper secondary level. In district-level state administration only one province ever had a provincial school social worker from 1974 onward, but this position no longer exists. In one province there is a provincial school psychologist who is also responsible for school social work. At the National Board of Education, the government department under the Ministry of Education, a senior administrator responsible for pupil welfare monitors the work of school social workers and psychologists.

The school social worker has varied responsibilities at school. However, the job descriptions of Finnish, Swedish, Icelandic, Norwegian, and Danish social workers are very similar to one another. School social workers intervene at the individual, group, and organizational levels, providing casework, group work, consultation, and work for organizational change to meet the needs of students. The emphasis is on helping all students to develop their potential and providing services to those students who have difficulty doing so. The role combines much of both social work and guidance counseling, including both prevention and intervention (Wallin, 1999).

One of the most important jobs of school social workers is to support or help students whose achievement at school is hampered by their social circumstances, for example, through conflicts in the family, alcohol or drug abuse, mental health problems, or domestic violence. Fatigue and truancy are typical indicators of problems. In these kinds of cases the school social worker will usually work closely with the social services department or therapeutic units. Another important task for the school social worker, as an expert in group work methods, is to resolve conflicts between students or other communication problems at school, which easily spill over into bullying or lead to victims being excluded from social circles or the class. In situations when a class does not function properly collectively or when there are problems of disruption, the school social worker may collaborate with the teacher to assess the situation and develop a strategy to help resolve the problem. School social workers are involved in developing ways of working with students and parents to find new ways to socialize children and exert discipline in classrooms. School social workers may also be involved in resolving conflicts between a teacher and a student.

The authorities may also request school social workers to provide various expert statements. For instance, the expertise of school social workers may be used for developing a new curriculum in the school or municipality or for redesigning special-needs education.

Overall the job of school social workers has been moving away from traditional, individualized, face-to-face client work toward developing more collaborative efforts. Whereas teachers would refer directly to the school social worker any "difficult cases" they had, over the years they have learned to tackle the problems themselves and to turn to the school social worker for support and advice. Indeed, in all Nordic countries, school social workers are now seen increasingly in the role of consultants. Today an increasing number of students self-refer to the school social worker rather than being referred by teachers. Many experienced school social workers in Finland specialize in family social work or therapy. Another area of specialization is teamwork, which is particularly useful for facilitating a holistic approach to students' problems.

Schools in Finland have special student welfare groups in which the school social worker is one of the team members. Other members will usually include the head teacher and the deputy head teacher, the school's special needs teacher, school nurse, school psychologist, student counselor (at the upper stages of comprehensive school) and, when necessary, the class teacher or tutor. At its regular (usually weekly) meetings the student welfare group will work out plans for helping individual students or groups of students who need support, develop the school community, agree on a division of responsibilities, and strengthen multidisciplinary skills among the team members. These plans are made in collaboration with the students and their parents.

Special education for students with learning problems, emotional and psychosocial problems, and physical or intellectual disabilities is provided in Finland as comprehensive special education and as special-class, remedial education. (The term "comprehensive special education" is the official English translation used by the National Board of Education to describe temporary teaching provided at clinics for a variety of reasons, including truancy, disruptive behavior, difficulties in the class group, long-term illness, writing difficulties, difficulties with specific lessons, and fear of bullying.) The official decision to transfer a student to a special class group requires negotiation with, and agreement of, the student's parents. In many cases the job of the school social worker is to talk with the various parties involved about the transfer and possibly to provide an opinion on the need for the transfer from a social point of view. However, practices vary widely between different municipalities.

With the implementation of new school legislation in Finland, disabled children have also gained the right to regular schooling in an ordinary school class. Norway has pioneered integration. This can be expected to bring new challenges in the school social worker's job. Supporting students with special needs in vocational institutions is another important aspect of the job of school social workers at the upper secondary level.

Local authorities establishing new positions for school social workers have typically done so in response to a need for corrective action. However, after the initial problems have been resolved, the emphasis then begins to shift toward prevention. The exact contents of preventive work are largely shaped by the specific needs of the municipality, region, or school in question, but in all cases prevention relies heavily on collaboration with teachers and people from the community, including the social services department, child guidance clinics, the youth affairs department, and the police. The preventive effort may be focused on a whole residential area where residents, various authorities, and voluntary workers join forces to try to improve the quality of the area and access to services.

School social workers are often involved in multidisciplinary groups to help set up various kinds of support networks for children and youth. In the school context a typical project may involve arranging a camp to provide teaching and learning outside the school environment. Camps make it easier for new students in a class to get to know one another and also often strengthen the class sense of community.

School social workers have taken a very active part in the ongoing efforts to combat bullying. In Finland one of the strategies adopted has been peer counseling, in which senior students are given appropriate training and are supervised by the school social worker or their teacher to befriend and support younger students.

School social workers have also been consulted in the drawing up of crisis plans for schools in the event of a major accident at school (for example, if someone dies).

Immigrant children and youth arriving in Nordic countries need a great deal of help and support. The number of young immigrants in Finland and Norway is modest by comparison with Sweden and Denmark or many other European countries. Nonetheless, their integration into the school community and school work requires a carefully tailored effort, and the school social worker plays a key part in this.

School social workers have also played an important part in the prevention of substance abuse (see Wallin, 1998), contributing to collaborative programs involving the social services department, the youth affairs department, and the police. Many authorities have set up local working groups in which school social workers are also involved. In Finland heavy alcohol use and the tendency for children to drink at an ever-younger age has been a more pressing problem than drug abuse, but in recent years the use of drugs has been on the increase (Wallin, 1998).

With the ever-accelerating pace of change in modern society and the struggle between the needs and pressures of work life and parenting, many parents have concerns about raising their children. Supporting parents has emerged as an increasingly important role for the school social worker. Many school social workers take part in parents' activities, such as parents' groups in their schools, or arrange discussion groups for concerned parents. School social workers are also often invited to lecture at parent and teacher association meetings on counseling and mental health issues. School social workers do not, however, consider their role there to be primarily as a resource for information and professional instruction, but rather as a facilitator. The main challenge of school social work is to activate parents to become involved in school activities and thereby in the daily life of their children in a new way.

Cooperation between different levels of education is one of the tasks of the school social worker. For example, cooperation between the comprehensive school and upper secondary schools has also intensified in recent years with the growing number of people working in student welfare at the upper secondary level. This is a crucial step in creating a safety net that prevents students from dropping out and becoming marginalized as they make the transition from one level of schooling to the next.

TRAINING OF SCHOOL SOCIAL WORKERS

In Finland, local authorities historically defined the kind of qualifications they required of school social workers. Initially, many school social workers held teaching qualifications. There are no specialist training programs for school social work, although the now-defunct lower academic degree of social worker did include the option of specializing in school social work. In 1983, the qualification requirements for social workers were officially set out in a decree. The current decree, dated 1992, requires a qualified social worker to have completed a higher university degree that includes training in social work or which is complemented by other adequate training in social work. All six universities in Finland offer M.A. degree programs in which the major subject is social work (or social policy) and which require the completion of studies for four to five years. Students can also incorporate in their training program modules from, for example, education, social psychology, or special pedagogics. The program provides the skills and competencies that are needed in client service, planning, research, and supervision in social welfare and health and includes practical instruction, on-the-job training, and visits to various social work units. There is neither statutory protection for the use of the title school social worker nor any universal code for qualification requirements. The Union of Professional Social Workers in Finland has recommended that local authorities and educational institutions recruiting school social workers only hire people who have the appropriate qualifications as social workers. According to the registration files of the Union of Professional Social Workers, currently more than half (54 percent) of school social workers are qualified social workers; 28 percent have an academic degree but do not have formal qualifications; 11 percent have a diploma from a polytechnic; and five percent have completed some other degree in social care.

The situation is similar in other Nordic countries, where there are no specialist training programs for school social work. In Norway, Denmark, and Sweden school social workers need to be qualified social workers. To become a qualified social worker in these countries one needs a university degree, generally a B.A. degree, requiring three or four years study. In Iceland, school counselors require a teacher's certificate in addition to the social work degree, or a B.A. with one extra year of study.

School social workers have traditionally continued their studies and upgraded their qualifications in the areas of family work, therapy, and work counseling. Typically, school social workers have taken short supplementary training courses in certain methods (such as neurolinguistic programming), in legislation, or in the analysis of a certain social phenomenon (such as substance abuse). In the past, before the moves to decentralize the Finnish administrative system, the National Board of Education used to host annual conferences for school social workers on topical issues. During the 1990s the position of the National Board of Education and provincial governments has been very much weakened by sweeping changes in administrative structures, and the training they now offer tends to be sporadic or related to specific development projects in individual schools. Further multidisciplinary training in student welfare is provided by a number of educational institutions.

Professionals engaged in school social work in Finland meet each year at a national conference hosted by Koulukuraattorit – Skolkuratorer. There has traditionally been close Nordic collaboration in the education field; the Nordic conference in school social work has been arranged in rotation in Norway, Sweden, Finland, and Denmark since 1987. Representatives from Iceland have also participated in some meetings. This network will probably extend to Estonia in the near future as school social work is developed in that country (see also Chapter 10, School Social Work in Hungary and Other Countries in Central and Eastern Europe: Supporting Children in Transitional Societies).

Since the founding of Koulukuraattorit – Skolkuratorer there have been calls for special training in school social work or for job induction in Finland. However, it was not until 1996 that the University of Tampere Institute for Extension Studies launched an expert program in school social work, which has been heavily influenced by school social work practitioners. The planning group has included several school social workers, and the program is run by a former school social worker with extensive experience. The program is classified as further training but students do not obtain additional qualifications. The aim of the program is to clarify, strengthen, and expand the school social worker's professional identity and authority; to explore the purpose and content of the job; to assess the quality of one's own input and how it could be improved; and to put one's professional creativity to better use and to try new ideas. The training extends over a period of two years, including six periods of on-site learning, reading, self-directed project work, and a written assignment aimed at professional self-development. The accent in the program is on change, the basic tasks of school social work, collaboration, interaction, and quality. The purpose of on-site learning is to explore the environment of school social work, the opportunities it offers, and the tools and effectiveness of one's work. To date, a total of 44 social workers from all over the country have completed or are currently working in the program. There is a broad consensus of opinion that the program serves its purpose and that it helps to give more depth to the way in which school social work is approached.

Planning is currently underway in Finland for the development of further education provisions for social workers with a master's degree. One area of specialization is work with children and youth, and it is within this area that the needs of school social work should be taken into account.

ISSUES FOR FUTURE DIRECTION

School social work is an area of childcare policy that involves direct interaction with children in their everyday life. This is the main strength of school social work that also aligns it with the recent drive for a new kind of welfare service system designed to meet the needs and interests of children and youth. As we have seen earlier, school social work is not a particularly strong area of social welfare in the Nordic countries. School social work has been moving toward a community-orientated preventive focus, even though the emphasis on the individual student remains. This is the outcome of a long process of change in the broader context of expanding student welfare services. Important developments in this process have been the strengthening of the ideology of comprehensive responsibility in schools as well as the continuing diversification of the expectations and needs attached to the socialization of children and youth.

In the absence of any systematic research on school social work it is extremely difficult to provide a detailed account of what it actually involves in practical terms. All schools are different with respect to their pedagogic methods and social makeup, and on this basis it is reasonable to assume that the actual practices of social work also vary. This assumption is supported by the prevailing view that social work is an expert's job for which no norms need, nor can, be set externally. It is, nevertheless, essential that the research effort be stepped up: this is one of the main challenges for the future.

There are growing calls in social work today for specialized expertise in certain specific areas such as health care, child protection, probation, and after-care. These areas, it is believed, should be strengthened so that they can complement general expertise in social work. If this trend continues, we can also expect to see school social work develop into a stronger specialty in its own right. School social work is already treated as a separate, independent sector both in further training and in professional organization.

In the future we can expect to see school social work becoming an increasingly important partner for the school, students, parents, and others. For some time now, children and youth with the most severe problems have been referred from school to external specialist services such as psychiatric care. However, the availability of social welfare and health care services has not increased at the same rate as the need for care and services. Therefore, in the future school social work will probably have to strengthen and to some extent redefine its role as a service that addresses and resolves problems. This may well involve redefining the role of school social work. Some commentators believe that the established, preventive, and constructive working methods of student welfare will have to be replaced by more problem-centered approaches (Jauhiainen, 1993). For others, the restructuring of social services concerning children and families, due to the changes and cuts in the welfare and education system, mean a positive challenge for the preventive and ecological approach to school social work. However, in the past, school social work has shown that it is capable both of responding to changes and of influencing the course of those changes. This is crucially important to the future of school social work, for it to continue to develop as a strong and distinctive area of professional social work.

REFERENCES

Bardy, M. (1996). *Lapsuus ja aikuisuus - kohtauspaikkana Emile*. Helsinki: Stakes.

Feldbaek, I. (Ed.). (1998). *Nordic Statistical Yearbook 1998:1, 36*. Copenhagen: Nord.

Forsberg, H. (1998). *Lapsen vai perheen tähden?* Helsinki: Lastensuojelun Keskusliitto.

Forssen, K. (1997). Lapsiköyhyys ja perhepolitiikka OECD-maissa. In K. Salavuo (Ed.), *Onko sosiaalipolitiikalla vaikutusta* (Julkaisuja 23) (pp. 37-89). Helsinki: Sosiaali- ja terveysministeriö.

Jauhiainen, A. (1993). *Koulu, oppilaiden huolto ja hyvinvointivaltio. Turun yliopiston julkaisuja* (Sarja C. Osa 98) Turku: Turun yliopisto.

Kananoja, A. & Turunen, M-M. (1996). *Tähän suuntaan lastensuojelu* (Aiheita 4). Helsinki: Stakes.

Kiili, J. (1998). *Lapset ja nuoret hyvinvointinsa asiantuntijoina* (Työpapereita 105). Jyväskylä: Yhteiskuntatieteiden ja filosofian laitoksen yhteiskuntapolitiikan laitos, Jyväskylän yliopisto.

Lastensuojelulaki 5.8.1983/683. Muutos 9.2.1990/139. Suomen Säädöskokoelma 1990.

Lastensuojeluasetus 16.12.1983/1010. Muutos 15.6.1990/546. Suomen Säädöskokoelma 1990.

Millar, J. & Warman, A. (1996). *Family obligations in Europe*. London: Family Policy Studies Centre and The Joseph Rowntree Foundation.

Oppilashuoltokomitean mietintö 9a (1974). *Komiteamietintö 1973:151*. Helsinki: Valtion painatuskeskus.

Pösö, T. (1997). Finland: Child abuse as a family problem. In N. Gilbert (Ed.), *Combatting child abuse: International perspectives and trends*. Oxford: Oxford University Press.

Pringle, K. (1998). *Children and social welfare in Europe*. Buckingham: Open University Press.

Riihelä, M. (1996). *Mitä teemme lasten kysymyksille?* (Tutkimuksia 66). Helsinki: Stakes.

Salmi, J.W. & Linkomies, E. (1967). *Latinalais-suomalainen sanakirja*. Helsinki: Otava.

Suomen tilastollinen vuosikirja (1998). Helsinki: Tilastokeskus.

Taskinen, S. (Ed.) (1995). *Miten käy lasten palvelujen?* (Aiheita 6). Helsinki: Stakes.

Wallin, A. (1998). *Oppilashuolto mahdollisuutena ehkäisevässä päihdetyössä*. Helsinki: Stakes.

Wallin, A. (Ed.) (1999). *Koulukuraattori arkityössään. Koulun sosiaalityön asiantuntijaohjelman lopputyöjulkaisu* (Julkaisusarja A 2/99). Tampere: Tampereen yliopiston täydennyskoulutuskeskus.

Weightman, K. & Weightman, A. (1995). Never right, never wrong: Child welfare and social work in England and Sweden. *Scandinavian Journal of Social Welfare, 4*, 75-84.

5 SCHOOL SOCIAL WORK PRACTICE IN GHANA: A HOPE FOR THE FUTURE

Marie-Antoinette Sossou and Theresa Daniels

Social Indicators* — Ghana	
Population	19,734,000
Percentage under age 15 years	40
Percentage urban (2000)	38
Life expectancy at birth	56.0 men, 58.5 women
Fertility rate	4.22 children per woman
Percentage of illiterate adults (2000)	19.7 men, 37.1 women
Per capita GDP in $U.S. (1999)	400
Percentage unemployed	N/A

*Social Indicators. From the Statistics Division of the United Nations. Refer to notes on page 249.
Reference: http://www.un.org/Depts/unsd/indicators/indic2a.htm

NATIONAL CONTEXT

Ghana, a former British colony, is located on the south coast of West Africa a few degrees north of the Equator. Ghana has a roughly rectangular area of 238,537 square kilometers (approximately 92,105 square miles), which is approximately the size of the United Kingdom. Its southern boundary is a coastline of 554 kilometers (approximately 344 miles) on the Gulf of Guinea. The Greenwich meridian runs close to its eastern border. It is bounded by Togo in the east, Burkina Faso in the north, and Côte d'Ivoire in the west. Ghana achieved independence on March 6, 1957.

According to 1997 estimates, Ghana has a total population of approximately 17.7 million people and an annual growth rate of 3 percent. Nine million (51 percent) of this population is under the age of 18 years (UNICEF, 1998). The rapid growth of Ghana's population has been the result of the interplay of a declining mortality rate, persistently high fertility, and migration.

In 1990, an estimated 70 percent of the population lived in the rural areas of the country. The remaining 30 percent live in the urban areas and are concentrated along the coast and in the 10 administrative regional capitals of the country (UNICEF & Republic of Ghana, 1990).

Present-day Ghana is ethnically very diverse, with more than 100 identifiable ethnic groups and more than 50 languages and dialects, contributing in various ways to this diversity (Roe, Schneider, & Pyatt, 1992). Among the main linguistic groups are the Akans, which are made up of the Fantis along the coast and the Ashantis in the forest region north of the coast. The Guans are found around the plains of the Volta River. The Ga and the Ewe-speaking people are found in the south and the southeast part of the country. The Moshi and Dagomba ethnic groups are mostly found in the northern and upper regions of the country. Apart from a number of isolated ethnic conflicts in the northern section of the country, there are no major ethnic divisions or conflicts among the people. English is the official language used in schools, government, large-scale businesses, and national media. Akan, Ewe, Ga, Nzema, Dagbane, and Hausa are the local dialects used in radio and television broadcasting in the country. In terms of religion, 43 percent of the population are Christians of various religious denominations, approximately 38 percent are traditional believers, and 12 percent are Muslims. There is complete freedom of religion and expression of religious beliefs.

The main inequities between different ethnic groups in Ghana are related to geographical location and access to natural resources. Social class differentials are based on differences in education, personal achievement, and professional qualifications. There is, however, an emerging middle class, which cuts across ethnic origin and is the result more of higher education and professional qualification rather than having been born into a particular ethnic group.

Since independence in 1957, various parliamentary and military governments have engaged in efforts to improve the material and social conditions of Ghana's citizens, with varying degrees of success. The present government came to power on December 31, 1981, as a military one. Following international and domestic pressure for a return to constitutional rule, the ban on party politics was lifted in 1992 and presidential and parliamentary elections were held. In January 1993, a fourth republican government was inaugurated. The constitution establishing the fourth republic declares Ghana a unitary republic with sovereignty residing in the Ghanaian people. Executive authority is established in the office of the president together with the council of state. The president is the head of government, and commander-in-chief of the armed forces. The president is also responsible for the appointment of the vice president. Legislative functions are vested in parliament, which consists of a speaker and 200 members of parliament who are popularly elected by universal adult suffrage for a period of four years.

The country is divided into 10 regions for administrative purposes. The various regions are: Greater Accra, Western, Central, Eastern, Ashanti, Brong Ahafo, Volta, Northern, Upper East, and Upper West. The political head of each region is a regional minister who is responsible for the administration and coordination of the various activities of the districts forming the region.

Each region is divided into districts or counties. These districts constitute the focal points in the decentralized administration of the country. Presently, there are 110 districts and three of these districts, Accra/Tema, Kumasi, and Sekondi-Takoradi, have been designated as metropolitan areas. A district chief executive responsible for the daily administrative activities heads each district.

Economically, by West African standards, Ghana has diverse and rich natural resources. However, agriculture is the main economic activity, representing 45.5 percent of the gross domestic product. The services and industrial sectors constitute 39.5 percent and 15 percent of GDP, respectively. Production of goods and services is based on traditional labor-intensive techniques in all spheres of the economy, although some large enterprises have adopted modern capital-intensive technologies. The economy is open to world markets and the major exports are cocoa, gold, diamonds, manganese ore, bauxite, timber products, and processed agricultural products.

Culturally, as in most parts of Africa, social and kinship bonds play a very important role in the lives of Ghanaians. The traditional extended family system used to form a complex network of rights and obligations, which was responsible for day care and welfare for its members in time of need. This family system also served to redistribute resources between rich and poor members and, in the absence of social security, provided mechanisms for the survival of its weaker members. The extended family system has, however, come under severe strain as a result of the harsh economic crisis affecting developing countries and the introduction of economic structural adjustment programs to achieve transition from a planned and centrally dominated economy to a liberalized and decentralized market-oriented economy.

The structural adjustment program supported by the World Bank and the International Monetary Fund (IMF) has increased the hardship experienced by some vulnerable groups in the country. There is increasing incidence of poverty and female-headed single-parent families, resulting from out-migration of able-bodied men from the countryside in search of employment in the cities and urban centers. The numbers of unmarried mothers, orphaned children, street children, child labor, and problems experienced by older people have also increased both in the urban areas and smaller towns of the country.

EDUCATION IN GHANA

The Ministry of Education is the overall national department for education in Ghana. It is responsible for making all educational policies for the country. The Ministry aims to provide: basic education for all; education and training for skill development with emphasis on science, technology, and creativity; higher education for the development of middle and top-level manpower requirement, and to provide facilities to ensure that all citizens are functionally literate and self-reliant. The Ghana Education Service and the National Council on Tertiary Education are the implementation agencies responsible for all levels of educational system in Ghana from primary schools to university or tertiary institutions.

Article 39 of the Fourth Constitution provides a constitutional right to free and compulsory primary and junior secondary school education for every child of school age. Primary education begins at age six and lasts for six years. Under educational reforms implemented in 1987, children continue their education into junior secondary schools for a further three years. At the end of this period students who pass the basic education certificate examination may progress to senior secondary schools for a further three years. Students who pass their final examination may gain admission into one of the country's five universities through a selection or entrance examination. In 1996, the government initiated free, compulsory, universal basic education (FCUBE) for all children of school age. This is an improvement on the old educational policy of the country. The main difference between the 1987 and the 1996 reforms is that the former was founded on an experimental basis and covered a limited number of regions. The latter provides universal coverage for the whole country. As many school-age children are competing for a limited number of school places, a "shift system" was introduced. As a result, one group of children attends school in the morning, from 8:00 A.M. to 12:00 noon, and a second group of children attends the same school from 12:30 P.M. to 5:00 P.M.

UNICEF (1998) data highlight gender differentials in uptake of education and literacy rates. Enrollment in primary education is 76 percent (83 percent of all boys and 70 percent of all girls); enrollment in secondary education is 37 percent (45 percent of all boys and 29 percent of all girls). The total adult literacy rate is 65 percent (76 percent of males and 54 percent of females).

There are a number of special schools under the supervision of the Ghana Education Service that provide basic education to students with sensory and intellectual impairments. There are no special schools for physically disabled children. They are therefore integrated into the normal public school system and receive physical education and vocational training at orthopedic centers and other state rehabilitation centers. There is, however, no effective provision for helping students with learning problems. The teachers in the classrooms with children with learning disabilities tried to devise appropriate remedies based on experience more than on scientific information.

MAJOR SOCIAL PROBLEMS EXPERIENCED BY CHILDREN

The welfare of children in Ghana has recently become the subject of growing concern. A key problem affecting children's quality of life is child labor. The International Labor Organization (1979) defines child labor as the engagement of children under the age of 15 in economic activities, other than light domestic and agricultural work, which is perceived to be detrimental to the development of the child and hinders the child's proper preparation for his or her adult roles and responsibilities. Traditionally, young children in Ghana and in many other African societies have contributed their labor to the family economy in the home and on family farms as a form of socialization. Child labor has now taken the form of any kind of work that is carried out for economic gain, subjecting children to exploitation by employers. It is, however, difficult to obtain reliable statistics on the number of children at work, although a survey conducted by the social administration unit at the University of Ghana found at least 1,000 children from different ethnic groups working in Accra alone (Apt *et al.*, 1992). In Ghana, child labor exists in both rural and urban areas, but more so in urban areas. In addition, there is an increasing number of children of school age roaming the streets, market places, lorry parks, beaches, and video centers during school hours. These children are referred to as "street children" because they spend virtually all or a significant part of their time on the streets, including sleeping. Precise statistics of the number of street children in Ghana are not available, although children from broken homes, orphans, emigrant children, and children whose parents are unemployed or are poor, are thought to be at particular risk (Ghana National Commission on Children, 1990). These children are usually undernourished and lack adequate health care and social and mental development. The most significant cause of nonattendance and school dropout is poverty—the inability of parents to pay for their children's school supplies, or in the worst cases, to provide food and shelter for their children.

Several studies have highlighted additional problems facing children in Ghana. In research conducted by the Centre for Social Policy Studies (1997), a number of school children were asked to discuss child abuse, its causes, and consequences and to give recommendations for curbing the problem. The children defined child abuse as lack of parental care and affection, physical molestation, excessive punishment, sexual abuse, denial of basic human rights, and mental injury. Among the causes identified for the alarming rate of child abuse in Ghana are economic hardship and poverty, breakdown of the extended family system, and the matrilineal system of inheritance. In the matrilineal system, the upkeep and the maintenance of children are the sole responsibility of their mother and her relatives, specifically their maternal uncles, and not their father as practiced in the patrilineal system. When the mother and her relatives are unable to provide adequately for the children because of financial difficulties or other family obligations, these children have to fend for themselves. Other causes of child abuse are: unreasonable expectations of children; parental immaturity stemming from teenage parenthood; step parent problems; belief that the child is "possessed" through witchcraft; divorce, and domestic violence (Centre for Social Policy Studies, 1997). All these problems are endemic in the social fabric of society, but there are no reliable statistical data on their prevalence or intensity. They are, however, of great concern to researchers, policy makers, and legislators, and attempts are being made to formulate substantive policies and legislation for the protection of the rights of children and to ensure their proper development. A step in this direction was the enactment of a new Children's Act by parliament in 1998. The problems of children in Ghana, therefore, posed a major challenge to school social workers as they are confronted with both social and economic problems in the school environment.

THE HISTORY OF SCHOOL SOCIAL WORK

Before the advent of colonialism, the problems of suffering, deprivation, want, deviance, and poverty in the traditional Ghanaian family systems were normally taken care of by individuals, families, and tribal groups. Concern for other people was a key value of traditional Ghanaian society (Drake & Omari, 1962). Nevertheless, the slave trade and colonization brought major changes and disequilibrium to the traditional family system. New social problems emerged with which traditional resources were neither familiar nor able to cope.

The beginning of social work in Ghana in particular, and in Africa in general, can be traced to the activities of three major groups: Christian missionaries; voluntary agencies; and tribal societies. These groups, working closely with ethnic societies, established various charities for families in need (Gold Coast, 1944-1954). They pioneered social work and urged the colonial government to lend its support. Social work then assumed an official status under the Colonial Development Act of 1940, which marked its transition from the private sector to the central government (Gold Coast, 1944-1954).

In 1943, a secretary of social services was appointed and entrusted with social policy and coordination of all existing welfare activities in the country. Expatriate and indigenous social workers trained overseas formed the nucleus of the administration. In 1946, the Department of Social Welfare and Housing was created (United Nations, 1957). In 1951, Social Welfare was separated from Housing, and a Ministry of Education and Social Welfare was formed.

Since independence, social work practice has experienced many structural changes and has also intensified, expanded, and assumed other dimensions, of which school social work is one. There have been advances in disaster relief, community organization and development, and the training of social workers. There has also been improvement in services to women and children, people experiencing behavioral or relationship difficulties, and people with physical or intellectual impairments (Drake *et al.*, 1962).

The Department of Social Welfare, the state organization responsible for the general welfare of children and families, initiated school social work in the early 1950s. Although there were no officially designated school social workers, trained social welfare personnel were assigned to carry out this program in addition to other social work activities. School social work activities took the form of providing social and rehabilitative services to young delinquents and also, by forming and running parent-teacher associations in schools, of helping both parents and teachers maintain, improve, and deal with problems connected with the education of children.

However, before the official introduction of school social work activities, the Ghana Education Service, the state organization responsible for educational programs in Ghana, employed teachers who visited schools in the country to ensure that good academic standards as required by the education service were being maintained.

The introduction of the shift system in schools resulted in an increase in juvenile delinquency and other social problems because it became an excuse for truancy. The period after the first successful military coup in 1966 also witnessed agitation and riots in schools (Salakpi, 1997). These problems were too much for the limited staff members of the Department of Social Welfare to handle alone; hence, in 1967, the Ghana Education Service established its own social work service, the School Welfare Service.

The main responsibility of the school welfare program as designated by the Ghana Education Service is to help prevent or minimize the negative effects of social adjustments, change, and development, and to ensure that children stay in school and take advantage of the best that the school environment has to offer them.

The rationale behind the establishment of the school welfare program is based on the understanding that no school curriculum can be effectively delivered unless the psychological and social needs of the children who are to absorb it, and the teachers who are going to implement it, are taken into consideration. A school social work program staffed with trained school social workers with an emphasis not only on treatment, but also on prevention, is seen as an indispensable service within the education system. In addition, the pioneers of school social work believed that the school system plays a major role in the developmental process of children. Hence, if child welfare and other child-centered programs are to have the desired effect, then they should be embodied in the school programs. The school is seen to be a convenient place for child-related programs because children assemble in large groups for a number of hours every day. According to Ferguson (1963), given that all children enter school at an early age and continue in school until their late teens, the school is in a unique position to discover early any indication of a child's unhappiness or maladjustment, whether this is social, economic, psychological, or emotional.

The first officers, who were all trained teachers, but had no professional social work background, were given the title of school welfare officer. The head of the welfare unit held a two-year diploma in social administration from the University of Ghana, but had no specialized training in school social work.

Initially, the school welfare program made slow progress. This was a consequence of skepticism within parts of the Ministry of Education, resulting from the novelty of the new welfare program and confusion and doubts about both its actual functions and usefulness within the educational system. Six years after the establishment of the program, there were only 10 school welfare officers responsible for school welfare programs in the whole country. In 1974, a new Director General of Education called for improvement and extension of the program to cover not only school children and parents but all personnel of the Ghana Teaching Service. He argued that the welfare of school children should not be viewed in isolation from the general welfare of parents, teachers, and other school personnel. As a result, a four-week, intensive in-service training program in aspects of social work practice was organized for selected classroom teachers, who were later posted to the various regions of the country as school welfare officers. The trainers were drawn from the Departments of Sociology and Psychology of the Universities of Cape Coast and Ghana, respectively. The total number of welfare officers subsequently increased to 131. There are now approximately 163 school welfare officers throughout the country, with the Ashanti region having the greatest number at 24. The welfare officers, who are all trained teachers, also hold various types of social work certification, ranging from a diploma given to candidates after a two-year course in social administration at the University of Ghana, to a degree in social work.

THE ROLE OF SCHOOL SOCIAL WORK

Social work in the education system is part of an interprofessional approach to understanding and providing help for school children who are unable to use their learning capacities to the full extent, including those school children whose problems require special services to enable them to make full use of their educational opportunities. In addition, the service also deals with the emotional, psychological, social, and sometimes financial problems of teachers and other staff members of the Education Service.

School welfare officers perform four main services. These are: providing social services to school children; providing social services to teachers and nonteaching staff members; developing collaborative services between the home and school; and developing partnerships with community agencies and establishing parent-teacher associations.

Under the function of services to school children, the welfare officer is responsible for developing tangible solutions to help solve the social, emotional, and physical problems that compromise the educational development of the child in the school environment. Some of the problems identified are extremely poor academic performance, irregular school attendance, lateness, persistent tiredness, deprivation, neglect, and strained pupil and teacher relationships. There are also problems of lack of parental care and supervision, criminal behavior and exposure to physical and moral danger, malnutrition, and other feeding problems such as children coming to school hungry or without money to purchase food at school. School welfare officers also work with children who have been unjustly dismissed from school; children engaged in prostitution; youth addicted to alcohol, drugs, or gambling; bullying; and students with disabilities. Substance abuse and bullying are among the emerging problems in secondary or high schools. They are prohibited in these institutions, and offenders are severely punished with suspension or outright dismissal. In extreme cases, school social workers are called to intervene by offering professional services to both students and parents.

School welfare officers act as nutrition officers under the school meal program, inspecting school feeding arrangements to ensure that food sold or provided to school children is well-cooked and kept under hygienic conditions to help prevent contamination and outbreak of disease. The school meal program was introduced by the school social work unit following a survey of students in elementary and primary schools in Accra that revealed many school children were malnourished. The program was therefore introduced to help provide school children with at least one balanced meal each day and to make sure the food is prepared under hygienic conditions.

School welfare officers are also responsible for hearing grievances from school children in cases of agitation and school disturbances and demonstrations.

Under services for teachers, school welfare officers believe that a competent and happy teacher is an asset to the nation. They therefore try to help teachers solve any social, emotional, financial, and psychological and accommodation problems. The school welfare officer has the responsibility of helping newly appointed teachers to a new environment find suitable accommodation and school places for their own children, and ensure their salaries are paid to them on time to avoid financial hardship. School welfare officers also help in organizing meetings and seminars to educate teachers and nonteaching staff members on their duties, obligations, and rights in the service. They provide information on salary increments, eligibility for promotion, retirement procedures, and working conditions and benefits of the Ghana Education Service. They also make routine visits to schools and offices to find out about problems likely to affect the efficient discharge of the duties of any staff member, and develop appropriate problem-solving strategies.

School welfare officers are also responsible for holding occasional seminars for teachers to promote the exchange of ideas on the most effective techniques of observation and detection of simple psychological problems of school children.

In addition, school social workers facilitate home-school collaboration. The school welfare officer makes home visits and assists parents in becoming more active in their children's education, meeting their needs and resolving problems affecting them at school and at home. The welfare officer also provides parents with techniques and strategies to encourage positive behavior in their children, and also develops and facilitates parental education through group activities and family life education programs. The family life education program began in 1976, following increasing recognition of the family as the center of the child's well-being. The family life education program involves the imparting of relevant knowledge in relation to social, health, psychological, developmental, moral, cultural, and civic issues to help young people develop positive and responsible relationships toward their families, communities, and society as a whole.

School welfare officers act as a link between parents and special schools for children with physical and intellectual impairments, to encourage parents to enroll their children in school. They also participate in the admission of physically disabled children to orthopedic and state rehabilitation centers.

The collaborative services performed by school welfare officers take the form of liaising between schools and other human services agencies to help foster mutual cooperation and understanding that is needed for the development of children. School welfare officers therefore work collaboratively with the Department of Social Welfare, the juvenile correctional system, hospital welfare officers, rehabilitation centers, the Ministry of Health, youth employment centers, public or community health units, dental clinics, and nutrition centers. School welfare officers serve as educators in the community to enhance common knowledge of school and community issues and community environmental sanitation.

The formation of parent-teacher associations is another service performed by school welfare officers. The main purposes of the associations are: to bring parents together to identify their common interest in the development of their children; to help promote proper understanding of the needs of children and to draw the attention of school authorities to children issues and to any problems they may be experiencing; and to provide a forum for joint parent-teacher discussions of problems in schools and at home and to foster home-school liaison.

School welfare officers also refer parents with other related social problems such as child support issues, juvenile delinquency, and marital problems to the appropriate community agencies responsible for handling these issues. The welfare officer clarifies to parents educational policies, procedures, and any relevant issues affecting schoolchildren's education goals and development.

In summary, the majority of the services provided by the school welfare officers in Ghana are geared toward preventive interventions. For example, the parent-teacher associations, the home and school collaboration programs, and family life education activities are designed to provide the necessary information, skills, and services available to help parents, teachers, and schoolchildren prevent school-related problems.

TRAINING AND PROFESSIONAL DEVELOPMENT OF SCHOOL SOCIAL WORKERS

At the inception of organized school social work practice within the Ghana Education Service in 1967, the need for formal education and training of the newly recruited officers was recognized to ensure the effective and efficient delivery of school social services to school children. On recruitment, new school welfare officers, who are trained and certified teachers, are given orientation courses in the basic scope, principles, and practice of social work.

In 1975 the Ghana Education Service entered into an agreement with the social work unit of the University of Ghana to provide professional training in social work and administration for the welfare officers. Since 1975, the University of Ghana has taken responsibility for training both school welfare officers and other professional social workers.

Training is provided through a two-year diploma course in social administration, which has been designed to train experienced social workers and middle-level personnel from the Departments of Social Welfare, Community Development, Prison Service, and industrial establishments. During the training, students undertake a 10-week mandatory fieldwork placement within both state and private human service organizations.

After the two-year programs, students are awarded a diploma in social administration, which is recognized by the state and the International Council for Social Work Education.

At the commencement of the 1989–1990 academic year, a three-year undergraduate course in social work was introduced at the University of Ghana. So far, a number of school welfare officers have undertaken this program.

There is a proposal to develop and upgrade social work professional training at the University of Ghana to the master's level. The intention of this program is to provide extra skills and in-depth professional training to social work students to help improve services.

The social work unit of the University of Ghana is also contemplating the establishment of a school of social work as an exclusive professional training institution. When realized, this plan will help expand programs for training specialist social workers, such as school social workers, medical social workers, and geriatric social workers. Until these plans are put into operation, school welfare officers will continue to be trained in both the diploma program and the undergraduate degree program with a special emphasis on school social work activities.

The Ghana Education Service and the Ghana Association of Social Workers have been responsible for organizing refresher courses, in-service training, symposia, seminars, and workshops for all categories of social workers, including school welfare officers. The purpose of these activities is to update, renew, develop, and evaluate social work activities and programs. A number of school welfare officers have also benefitted from a number of overseas short courses, training, seminars, and meetings sponsored by the government and other private agencies.

The Ghana Association of Social Workers is the professional organization for social workers in Ghana, but there are also associations for those working in community development and in schools. In 1975, school welfare officers inaugurated a Ghana Education Service Welfare Officers Association, whose aims were to promote the ideals of school social work, to raise the educational standards and practices of the school welfare officers, and to protect the interests of the new profession. The association is currently undergoing change to make it more active, professionally competent, and internationally recognized. The association is also in the process of developing a professional school welfare journal to inform and educate the Ghanaian public about the needs and importance of school welfare services. The association has proposed legislation to establish a national board of social work for the purpose of licensure of social workers. The proposed board would standardize the training and regulate the practice of all social workers, including school welfare officers, in Ghana and would also liaise with professional licensure bodies for social workers in other countries so that international standards are maintained.

ISSUES FOR FUTURE DIRECTION

The future of school social work in Ghana looks very promising and at the same time very challenging. This is in view of the national goals and aspirations of the country as a whole as far as education and social development of Ghana are concerned. Despite initial problems, the school social work program is accepted as a good preventive mental health program for schoolchildren, parents, and teachers. It is a program that is meant to help maintain equilibrium between the child's world in school and in the community so as to minimize the negative effects of social change and its related social problems.

The free, compulsory, universal basic education (FCUBE) is a very ambitious pre-tertiary education program in terms of cost, infrastructure, and human resources. The school social work program, therefore, has a major role to play in the school system to ensure proper intellectual, social, and emotional development of children.

The establishment of the school welfare program has ensured some measure of recognition in the country and among some schools. All kinds of problems, ranging from vandalism and violence to emotional and other interpersonal problems are referred to school welfare officers. The methods mostly used in solving these problems are problem-solving techniques and group and individual counseling procedures. Preventive school programs are also developed through the use of parent-teacher associations and community groups to encourage active local participation in schools.

Nevertheless, the school social work program in Ghana is still struggling with both professional and nonprofessional problems. These problems need to be addressed to enhance the future development and efficiency of the school welfare program.

The first major problem facing school social work in Ghana is the lack of professional recognition of the school welfare officers. In most cases, they are regarded first and foremost as teachers and, in situations of a shortage of teachers, they are among the first group of people to be deployed into the classroom to teach instead of providing social work services to school children and their parents. This situation poses a threat to the general welfare of school children because there are no other specialist services. A way out of this dilemma could be through the employment of school social workers who are not also qualified teachers so that they could be solely responsible for school welfare issues and problems.

There is also the need for effective public social education on the needs and importance of school social work. This process could go a long way to inform and educate the general public, parents, and schoolchildren about the services available in schools for the general welfare of schoolchildren.

In the area of research, the social work unit of the University of Ghana has conducted a number of research studies on street children, family and child welfare, and teacher education. Collaborative international agencies are UNICEF, Plan International, and the British Overseas Development Agency (Agarwal *et al.*, 1994).

However, because school social work is relatively new in the country, there is a need for more school-related research to be undertaken. So far, a research and information-management unit has been set up under the Department of Social Welfare to collect statistical data in collaboration with the

Save the Children Fund. The Save The Children Fund is an international non-profit organization with branches in 70 countries including Ghana. This organization works to create a better world for children in the world's most impoverished communities. The Save the Children Fund in Ghana is committed to helping children by listening to children, learning about their lives, hopes and views. The Fund also supports practical projects which involve children and their families in improving their day-to-day-lives. This program is expected to facilitate the identification of areas in need of assistance, as well as provide information on sustainable policies. The program is concerned primarily with problems of delinquency, child labor, and teenage pregnancy, which threaten the total development of children. There is therefore a need for effective collaboration between the Ghana Education Service, the Department of Social Welfare, the social work unit of University of Ghana, and international agencies.

In their professional training, school social workers are exposed to the ethical issues and obligations guiding social work practice as a profession. The principles of confidentiality, self-determination, and respect of clients are therefore strictly adhered to in practice. The Ghana Association of Social Workers has a code of ethics, adapted from the international code of ethics, but there appears to be no formal mechanism for addressing issues relating to violations.

In terms of the country's vision to become a middle-income nation by the year 2020, a national development program has been introduced. The reintroduction of the free compulsory and universal basic education for all children is part of this program. An important aspect of the reintroduction of the free compulsory education for all children is that it is now a legal offense for parents to refuse to send their children to school. This poses a great challenge to the social work profession as a whole and to school social workers in particular. In addition, the emergence of a new political administrative structure in Ghana supported by district assemblies to effect a decentralized political administrative policy, grass-roots democracy for promoting local initiatives, and self-help attitudes toward local development pose a greater challenge to school social workers in the various districts. At the district level, school social workers would be expected to collaborate and coordinate activities with helping professions such as health, nutrition, community development, and social welfare and the District Assembly. These professions are expected to investigate and determine the social needs of the districts and to provide guidance for the local district assemblies. They are also expected to plan comprehensive programs and strategies to help the people in the districts, including schoolchildren. The assessment of community needs and human potential in the districts will provide data to assist the assemblies in developing social policies to better meet the needs of people in communities. School social workers would therefore be very helpful in investigations into the causes of child delinquency, crime, child abuse and neglect, teenage pregnancies and parenthood, and drug abuse among the youth in the districts.

Whereas school social work's contribution to social work practice in Ghana is relatively new, it is likely that practice will improve in the immediate future. School social workers would become part of the professional team that will continue to be involved in all major sectors of the social welfare system in Ghana. However, there is the need for effective organization by the professional association of social workers in Ghana so that the profession may secure professional identity and national status.

REFERENCES

Apt, N.A., Blavo, E. Q. & Opoku, S.K. (1992). *Street children in Accra*. Accra: Save the Children Fund.

Agarwal, A.M., Attah, A., Apt, N.A. & Grieco, M. (1994). *Bearing the weight: Kayayoo, Ghana's girl-working child*. Accra: Response.

Centre for Social Policy Studies (1997). *Child abuse: Situational analysis*. Legon: Centre for Social Policy Studies.

Drake, St. C. & Omari, P.T. (Eds.). (1962). *Social work in West Africa*. (Report of the seminar on social work in West Africa). Legon: University of Ghana.

Ferguson, E. (1963). *Introduction to social work*. Englewood Cliffs, NJ: Prentice Hall.

Ghana National Commission on Children (1990). *Annual report, 1990*. Accra: Ghana National Commission of Children.

Gold Coast (1944–1954). *Annual reports*. Accra: Gold Coast Government Printer.

International Labor Organization (1979). *Standards on the work of child and young persons*. (Supplement to Report 11) International Year of the Child (IYC) Discussion papers. Geneva: International Labor Organization.

Roe, A., Schneider, H. & Pyatt, G. (1992). *Adjustment and equity in Ghana*. Paris: Development Center of the Organisation for Economic Cooperation and Development.

Salakpi, V.P.K. (1997). *The impact of University of Ghana trained welfare officers on schools of Greater Accra Region*. Unpublished dissertation. Legon: University of Ghana.

UNICEF (1998). *Country report on Ghana*. New York: UNICEF.

UNICEF & Republic of Ghana (1990). *Children and women of Ghana: A situation analysis*. Accra: UNICEF & Republic of Ghana.

United Nations (1957). *Report on the world social situation*. New York: United Nations.

SCHOOL SOCIAL WORK IN ARGENTINA: THE CHALLENGE OF STATE REFORM

Graciela Tonon

Social Indicators* — Argentina	
Population	37,487,000
Percentage under age 15 years	28
Percentage urban (2000)	90
Life expectancy at birth	70.6 men, 77.7 women
Fertility rate	2.44 children per woman
Percentage of illiterate adults (2000)	3.1 men, 3.2 women
Per capita GDP in $U.S. (1999)	7,735
Percentage unemployed (May and October 1998)	12.8

*Social Indicators. From the Statistics Division of the United Nations. Refer to notes on page 249.
 Reference: http://www.un.org/Depts/unsd/indicators/indic2a.htm

To understand school social work in Argentina, it is necessary to view it in the context of the historical, political, and social life of the country. Rapid social change and the transition from military rule to democracy in the 1980s and 1990s have produced corresponding changes in the lives of children and families. In addition, state reform during the last decade of the 20th century has created economic conditions that have resulted in a large increase in poverty among children, with associated consequences for their education. These changes present a challenge to school social workers as they help prepare children for life in the new millennium. School social work faces its own challenges in defining its identity and determining its own future path.

NATIONAL CONTEXT

Argentina is a republic of 23 diverse provinces and a Capital District, Buenos Aires. With a surface area of 3,761,274 square kilometers (1,452,315 square miles), it is the eighth largest country in the world. In contrast, the population density of 11.7 people per square kilometer (4.5 people per square mile) is many times smaller than that of the industrialized countries of northern Europe. From north to south the country is 3,694 kilometers long, with widely varying features including the broad grassy plain known as the Pampas, a subtropical tableland, Meseta Subtropical, and the cold mountains and arid plateaus of Patagonia.

The most recent census (INDEC, 1991) showed a population of approximately 32,608,560, with 87 percent living in towns of more than 2,000 inhabitants. It is estimated that the population has grown rapidly since 1991, reaching approximately 38,000,000 in 1999. Thirty-four percent of the total population lives within the Capital District (Buenos Aires city) and the surrounding region of Greater Buenos Aires. Thirty-one percent of the population is under 14 years of age, 60 percent between 15 and 64 years old, and 9 percent older than 65 years. The proportion of young people in Argentina is considerably higher than in European countries and North America (United Nations, 1999a).

The different regions of the country have varied demographic dynamics reflecting the origins of their population groups. After the conquest by the Spanish in 1492, the area was part of the Spanish Empire until independence in 1816. During the 19th century, many immigrants from Spain, Italy, and other European countries settled in the country, and most Argentineans are the descendants of these European immigrants. Only approximately 150,000 aborigines, organized in 700 communities, remain in Argentina. The only surviving tribes are the Collas, Tobas, Matacos, Tehuelches, and Mapuches, each with their own language in addition to Spanish. For the most part these tribes live in remote rural areas subsisting on agriculture, hunting, and fishing, attempting to maintain their culture, and avoiding integration into the mainstream Argentinean culture. Some of the original tribes, such as the Querandies and Onas, have not survived.

Following World War II, Argentina experienced a long period of Peronist dictatorship, followed by military junta rule and, finally, a period of democratization, starting with democratic elections in 1983. Political and economic reforms during the 1990s produced drastic changes affecting every aspect of social life in Argentina. The purpose of state reform was to democratize the state and thereby to change its role in political, social, and economic issues. The main objective of reform has been structural change in the major state functions of justice, national security, exterior defense, international relations, and administration. The administration of education, health, and social security, together with relationships between government and nongovernmental agencies, has also undergone structural change. Federal legislation has been passed, affecting the operation of all of these state functions. The National Economic Emergency Law (1989, Ley de Emergencia Económica) deregulated the economy, privatized many public enterprises, and transferred social services to provincial administration. The National Law of Convertibility (1991, Ley de Convertibilidad) introduced parity between the Argentine peso and the American dollar (the one-for-one principle). The National Regime of Social Security (1991), National Constitution (1994), and the Federal Education Law (1997) are the other major pieces of legislation of state reform.

Argentina continues to have a larger middle class and higher per capita income than other South American countries, with an average per capita income of U.S. $10,300 (United Nations, 1999b). However, there has been a sharp increase in poverty in the last few years. Statistics for October 1998 showed that one in three adults and one in two children are poor. It is calculated that 13,000,000 people in Argentina currently are below the poverty line (INDEC, 1999). The poverty line is calculated on the price of the "family basket," reflecting the number of calories needed daily to feed a family of two parents and two children. In Argentina the "monthly family basket" is approximately 480 pesos/U.S.$.

The increase in poverty is a result not only of falling employment rates, but also of a drop in salaries. Unemployment is at 14 percent with 1,700,000 unemployed people, in addition to 1,800,000 underemployed people. Three hundred thousand people work in short-term (six months) national community programs for a monthly salary of 200 pesos/U.S.$. At the same time, 100,000 people receive federal unemployment benefits (INDEC, 1999).

It is estimated that 4,500,000 children below the age of 14 years (45 percent of the total) are poor (INDEC, 1999). A similar number of children are without necessary health care, and this situation has resulted in an increase in preventable illnesses. There has been a 40 percent increase in the prevalence of infantile diarrhea and a 150 percent increase in pulmonary tuberculosis in the last decade (INDEC, 1999). The infant mortality rate was 22 per 1,000 for the years 1995–2000 (compared to seven per 1,000 in the United States for the same period) (United Nations, 1999c).

Although unemployment and poverty, with the associated lack of health care, are the major hardships affecting families in Argentina today, there are several other growing social problems including domestic violence, alcoholism and drug abuse in teenagers and families, and teen pregnancy.

The new economic model produced many changes for the middle class. The privatization of public enterprises and the reduction in the number of public sector employees resulted in many people losing their jobs. Although inflation disappeared, unemployment is higher and the number of people living in poverty has increased. Whereas there was a large middle class, now the gap between rich and poor has grown and the polarization of social classes more closely resembles that in other Latin American countries. There are many changes in the welfare system resulting in inadequate services to children, especially poor children.

The reduction in the role of the public sector also resulted in loss of social services, which had provided for various needs. Private agencies, including the Catholic Church, have stepped in to help meet the needs of poor families. The Catholic Church occupies an important place in the lives of families in Argentina. Statistics for 1996–1997 (Conferencia Episcopal Argentina, 1996–1997) show that the church distributed U.S. $1.7 million (35 percent of its income) in various forms of social assistance, including food, housing, health care, and education.

The other important process that started in the 1990s is the foundation of a new regional economic system, MERCOSUR (Mercado Común del Sur), an economic agreement between Argentina, Brazil, Uruguay, and Paraguay with the goal of integrating the region through the establishment of free trade, elimination of tariffs, and institution of common pricing.

Although the main purpose of this process is economic, the member countries also signed agreements relative to education. These include a 1991 proposal to integrate all levels of education in the member countries, a 1995 agreement to allow post-graduate students to study at any national university in the four countries, and a 1997 agreement allowing employment of professors in any of the national universities. These accords will ultimately affect not only the educational systems in the MERCOSUR countries but also their individual cultural identities.

To date, the effects of the MERCOSUR on education and employment are limited, as a university degree does not yet provide accreditation to practice a profession in another country. However, Argentina is proposing a system of mutual accreditation in the professions for the four MERCOSUR countries (Nicoletti & Tonon, 1999).

In summary, there are currently two major factors affecting social change in Argentina— internal State reform and the MERCOSUR. There has been an uninterrupted period of democracy since 1983. It has been a time of turmoil and rapid change with profound repercussions for families and children. A new president was elected in October 1999, and there will inevitably be new public policies that will again change the picture in this young democracy. As the state changes, the role of social workers also changes, and the profession must reexamine its role and methods in the new political and social environment.

The major problems affecting children and families in Argentina are rooted in the turmoil of the last half-century and the economic crisis of the last decade. Beyond the basic statistics relating to poverty, unemployment, and health there is little research available about the types of social problems faced by children and youth and how these affect their education. The following study conducted by the author in 1999 through the Social Work Department of the Universidad Nacional de la Matanza, a public university 20 kilometers (12 miles) outside the Capital District, is a first attempt to document the lives of school-aged children and youth in a poor community and identify obstacles preventing them from benefitting from their education.

MARIANO ACOSTA: A CASE EXAMPLE OF CURRENT PROBLEMS IN A POOR COMMUNITY

In the absence of national statistics about social problems, the study illustrates the typical problems affecting the school population and reflects the issues with which school social workers are involved. Social work students conducted the study as part of their coursework. The students interviewed school directors and school social workers at all the schools in the community of Mariano Acosta.

Mariano Acosta is a semi-rural community 40 kilometers (25 miles) from the Capital District in Buenos Aires Province. Unemployment and associated problems are the basis of many of the social difficulties affecting school children. The roads in the community are unpaved; there is no sewerage system and no community water system. The homes are simple wooden structures with metal roofs. They all have electricity, but residents must pump their own water. The majority of adults are now unemployed, as are students on leaving school. Thirty-five percent of the students qualify for free school lunches on the basis of their family being below the poverty line. The children either walk to school or travel free by public bus. There are seven primary schools in the community, each serving between 850 and 1,200 students, for a total of 6,404 students.

Informants for the study indicated their views that, in rank order, the problems affecting children and youth were teenage pregnancy, substance abuse, poor living conditions, child abuse, child neglect, and lack of resources for youth. In the absence of statistics regarding the prevalence of most of these problems, the study undertaken was qualitative and indicates the need for more quantitative research.

Teenage pregnancy was ranked as the first concern by those interviewed. Typically the young mother keeps her child and remains living with her parents, who help her to support the infant. Teenage parents typically do not marry and there are no school or other community programs to help meet their educational or social needs.

Substance abuse by youth (usually starting at 12 to 13 years of age) was reported as consisting primarily of inhaling commonly available solvents, with marijuana and alcohol use also common. There has been a rapid increase of substance abuse in the last decade, although there are no treatment or prevention programs in either the schools or the community. Substance abuse is associated with the lack of resources for young people, including recreation, employment, preventive programs, and treatment facilities. Juvenile crime is also increasing, including theft and gang activity, both tending to be associated with drug use.

Child abuse and neglect was described as consisting of physical, psychological, and sexual abuse by parents or adult caretakers. School social workers and other community professionals must report cases of abuse to the Children's Court, and a judge determines whether the child will remain at home or go to an institution. There is no system of foster care in Buenos Aires Province, although foster care is available in the Capital District. There is no organized system for assisting families following abuse or neglect, nor service provision to prevent further abuse.

EDUCATION IN ARGENTINA

The Argentinian education system is administered by the individual provinces, although the Federal Education Law (1993, Ley Federal de Educación) has introduced a more uniform model as part of the overall government reforms. There are two systems of education in Argentina. In Buenos Aires Province, a new law, which was implemented in 1997, extended compulsory education (educación general básica) from seven to nine years. Children enter primary school at six years of age until the age of 14 and then transfer to high school for a further three years. In the remainder of Argentina, primary education lasts for seven years (from six to 12 years) followed by a five-year period of high school education. Ninety-six percent of children attend elementary school (first through seventh or ninth grade, depending on the province), 54 percent attend secondary school, and 14 percent attend a university. In addition, 73 percent of children attend a kindergarten, which is part of the public school system. The provincial government in Buenos Aires gives poor students a stipend of 100 pesos/U.S.$ per month to continue their education at the high school level. Four percent of adults are illiterate.

Special education serves children with special learning needs, specifically children who have visual and auditory disabilities and those with developmental disabilities. There are some special schools for children with disabilities, although there are few in certain parts of the country. All special schools in Buenos Aires Province and the Capital District have school social workers, although this is not the case for the rest of the country.

HISTORY OF SCHOOL SOCIAL WORK

School social work originated in Argentina in the 1960s. Until 1997, school social work existed only in Buenos Aires Province and in the Capital District. After the passage of the Federal Education Law, several other provinces decided to make social work support available to children in primary schools, even though there was no legal obligation to do so. However, not all parts of the country are currently served by school social workers.

Before 1997, social work in the schools was practiced in Buenos Aires Province under the job title school social worker ("trabajador social escolar" or "trabajador social de escuela"). In that year, the government changed the title to social assistant ("orientador social") and extended eligibility for employment in these posts beyond social work to include such disciplines as sociology and anthropology. In the Capital District, the job continues to be called school social work and only a professional in possession of a social work degree can occupy the position. School social workers in Buenos Aires Province and the Capital District must hold both a social work degree and also a teaching certificate in primary education. Some school social workers have a professional license in addition to academic qualifications. However, possession of the professional license is not a requirement for social workers in schools.

Professional licensing is administered by national and, in some cases, provincial laws. The National Law for Professional Practice (1986) regulates professional activities, describes the rights and obligations of social work, and includes a code of ethics. These laws apply to all social workers irrespective of their field of practice. The professional social work license is called the "matricula profesional" and is obligatory for social workers in Argentina, although there is no mandate or law specifically for school social workers.

In Buenos Aires Province, all primary schools and special education schools must have at least one school social worker. The number of social workers is based on a formula, requiring one social worker per 500 primary school students or one social worker for each special education school. Schools of more than 1,000 students may have two school social workers if they serve large numbers of students who are at risk because of poverty or other adverse social conditions. School social workers covering kindergartens and high schools may be assigned to two or three schools.

School social workers are employed during school hours only, that is, for about four hours a day, either from 8:00 A.M. through 12 noon or from 1:00 P.M. through 5:00 P.M. during the school year, which runs from March through December. Because the hours are limited and because school social work is perceived an entry-level job, school social work salaries are the lowest social work salaries in Argentina. Consequently, many school social workers must also hold another job to generate an adequate income.

SCHOOL SOCIAL WORK ROLE

In all schools, school social workers are part of a multidisciplinary team, called a school orientation team, which includes a psychologist, pedagogue, and teacher or a special education teacher. The school social work role is designed for teamwork, although there are special functions specific to school social work.

The team must evaluate the school as a social community, assess the needs of the individual class group, work with individual students, and organize educational programs for the prevention of social problems in the community.

In evaluating the needs of the school community, the school social worker studies the history of the school, the special needs of families in the school community, the varied groups in the school, and the relations between school and community. Assessment of classroom groups includes characterizing the nature of the group, identifying the children's social needs that influence their learning, and understanding the relationships between children and between the children and the teacher. Individual work includes work with children with learning and/or behavior problems, poor attendance, various health problems, alcohol or drug problems, and teen pregnancy.

The school social worker provides a social and family history to assist the team in resolving school problems. The social history includes many aspects of family life including health, family relations, family values, and any problems experienced by the family. Although casework and work with the school orientation team occupy most of the school social worker's time, some prevention programs are also organized in an effort to prevent social problems such as drug and alcohol abuse, domestic violence, and teen pregnancy.

TRAINING OF SCHOOL SOCIAL WORKERS

Social workers in Argentina graduate with a social work degree following a five-year program at a public or private university. Before 1997, those seeking employment as a school social worker were required to hold general social work qualification in addition to a teaching qualification in primary education from a teacher training college.

Because the social work degree program does not include any coursework specific to social work in schools, school social workers obtain their knowledge of work in schools from on-the-job training and from interdisciplinary, post-graduate courses designed for school professionals.

School social work in Argentina does not yet have a firm identity as an individual specialty. While there is a national association for social workers, Consejo Profesional de Graduados en Servicio Social y Trabajo Social, several provinces have an association for social workers to protect their professional rights and administer professional licensing. However, there is no dedicated association for school social workers. Rather, school social workers view themselves as part of a school team. Their professional conferences are designed for the school orientation teams, and professional activities such as presenting papers at conferences and writing professional papers are carried out in conjunction with other team members. Such activities are carried out from a team perspective, rather from the perspective of a school social worker. Articles in professional journals are therefore typically articles about the role of the team, rather than about the school social work role specifically.

ISSUES FOR FUTURE DIRECTION

As Argentina has moved forward with the state reform process, social work has also changed. There are new fields of practice, changing needs in the client population and also the potential for new methods and programs to respond to rapidly changing social situations.

School social work has been one of the traditional fields of practice in Argentina and continues to be one of the dominant areas of social work intervention. A survey of social work employment in the Capital District and Buenos Aires province indicated that approximately 25 percent of social workers were employed in schools (Krmpotic *et al.*, 1997). Although, as indicated above, such a concentration would not necessarily be representative of the country as a whole, this gives an indication of the potential of school social work to develop into an effective agent for change in the lives of Argentinean school children. School social workers are well-positioned to intervene in the lives of children, schools, and families. Theoretically, they are also positioned to undertake preventive work in the schools. The rapid pace of change in Argentina clearly calls for preventive activities to help prepare children to live in a changing society. Given that school social workers are the only helping professionals who are in contact with all children, they are in a position to conduct programs to provide the material, educational, and emotional support necessary for success in school. Prevention programs for the entire student body, for marginalized populations of students, and those at risk of educational failure are needed. However, there are few such programs. Because of the current economic situation and the attendant stress for families, school social workers' efforts are currently focused on intervention in existing social problems, rather than on prevention. The dilemma of whether to focus resources on prevention or intervention points to the need for the profession to develop its own identity and priorities.

The expected effect of the recent change in government regulations that allows non-social workers to work as "social assistants" is that it will undermine the progress of school social work as a strong profession with a clear identity firmly based on social work knowledge and skills. The recent change in the job title from school social worker to social assistant is a major problem for the profession. Neither the public nor the social work profession understands the importance of social work in schools, and consequently school social work remains a low-status profession with little recognition. In the future there will be fewer jobs available for social workers in schools as other disciplines enter the field. However, the social work profession has not challenged the administrative ruling that has essentially removed the professional basis of school social work. Because the change in the position title and qualifications are recent, it is not yet possible to analyze how school social work will be affected in the immediate future and on a long-term basis.

As reforms continue in Argentina, the need for social work to expand into new roles and to consider as-yet unidentified activities is imperative. This carries implications for training. Specialized training for school social workers is needed to prepare social work graduates to deal more effectively with the complex problems they will find working in a school setting. Social workers will need new skills to deal competently with the realities of present and future social problems. The most urgently needed skills are for social workers to be able to adapt flexibly to change and to intervene using effective methods. Social work training must prepare practitioners who can work in teams, organize programs, obtain and use data for planning effective strategies, and use technology.

Social work is a profession that must be defined by the needs of the client. These needs are both multifaceted and constantly evolving, mirroring the complexities and rapid changes of life in Argentina. The practitioner must be able to deal with this complexity and uncertainty, and be competent to make decisions involving ethics and policies as well as being able to use technical knowledge and skills. The lack of literature focused on social work in schools and ways of dealing with the needs of school children is a hindrance to the progress of school social work into a mature profession that is seen as effective and necessary in the school system.

Several factors affect the development of school social work, including the inadequate number of professionals in schools, the low status of the profession and the lack of specific training, informed by specialized research and publications in the field. It is a young profession developing in conjunction with the progress of a young democracy. The number of school social workers is insufficient to satisfy the needs of school children, and many areas of Argentina have no school social workers, particularly rural areas. For many school social workers, the position is the first job after graduation. Although this situation provides a young work force with characteristic energy, the school social work profession as a whole may have less experience and standing in the education community.

School social work has much to contribute to the process of social reform in Argentina, in particular in helping the next generation prepare to participate fully in a democracy. It faces its own challenges to make it an effective agent of change. Specialized university courses, research and professional literature, and a strong professional organization are needed to help school social work determine its identity and to raise its status. The effectiveness of school social work in Argentina depends on how it responds to these challenges in the new century.

REFERENCES

Conferencia Episcopal Argentina (1996–1997). *Informe Bianual de la Colecta Nacional Más por Menos*. Buenos Aires: Conferencia Episcopal Argentina.

INDEC (1991). *Censo Nacional de Población*. Buenos Aires: INDEC.

INDEC (1999). *Censo Nacional de Población*. Buenos Aires: INDEC.

Krmpotic, C., Tonon, G., Allen, I. & de la Fare, M. (1997). *La inserción actual de los Trabajadores sociales en el mercado laboral*, Buenos Aires.

Ley Nacional 23.77 (1986). *Ejercicio de la Profesión de Servicio Social o Trabajo Social.*

Ley Nacional 24195 (1997). *Ley Federal de Educación.*

Nicoletti, R., Tonon, G., Meza, M., Reitano, S. & Nicoletti, J. (1999). *MERCOSUR: la integración en su dimensión universitaria, Investigación*, Universidad Nacional de La Matanza, Programa Nacional de Incentivos, 1998–1999.

United Nations (1999a). *United Nations indicators on youth and elderly populations*, Statistics Division [Online]. Available: http://www.un.org/Depts/unsd/social/youth.htm

United Nations (1999b). *Indicators on income and economic activity*, Statistics Division [Online]. Available: http://www.un.org/Depts/unsd/social/inc-eco.htm

United Nations (1999c). *United Nations indicators on health*, Statistics Division [Online]. Available: http://www.un.org/Depts/unsd/social/health.htm

7

School Social Work in Germany: Help for Youth in a Changing Society

Wilfried Wulfers

Social Indicators* — Germany	
Population	82,008,000
Percentage under age 15 years	15
Percentage urban (2000)	88
Life expectancy at birth	75.0 men, 81.8 women
Fertility rate	1.29 children per woman
Percentage of illiterate adults	Not available
Per capita GDP in $U.S. (1999)	25,749
Percentage unemployed (April 1999)	8.8

*Social Indicators. From the Statistics Division of the United Nations. Refer to notes on page 249.
Reference: http://www.un.org/Depts/unsd/indicators/indic2a.htm

National Context

The creation of the Federal Republic of Germany on October 3, 1990, resulting from the reunification of East and West Germany, has been followed by much social, political, and economic change. Germany has grown by nearly one-third in terms of land area, and now covers 356,733 square kilometers (137,743 square miles). Its population has grown from 61 to 82 million people. The ever-growing immigrant population now numbers approximately 8 million, which is approximately 10 percent of the total population. There is considerable social tension related to immigration policies, with an increase in prejudice against foreigners. Among the migrant population, Turks (1.91 million) and citizens of the former Yugoslavia (1.23 million) make up the largest groups. Almost 80 percent of the German population associate themselves with the Roman Catholic or Protestant churches. Unemployment continues to increase steadily, and there are now approximately 4 million unemployed people, equaling roughly 10 percent of the employable population. Germany has the lowest birth rate in the world, with only 1.3 children born per woman, and there are more people over the age of 60 than under 15 years of age.

Germany is a federal democracy consisting of 16 provinces. The state Constitution provides a mandate for a multiparty parliamentary democracy, guaranteeing German citizens specific basic rights, including the right to life, the right to freedom from bodily harm, and the right of freedom of the person. The head of state is the federal president, elected to a five-year term by a federal assembly (the Bundesversammlung). The chancellor presides over the federal government. The federal parliament (comprising a "lower house," the Bundestag, and an "upper house," the Bundesrat) and the provincial parliaments hold legislative power. Provinces participate in legislation and administration through the federal council. Since 1961 no single political party has been able to win an absolute majority of seats in the federal parliament, necessitating coalition government.

EDUCATIONAL STRUCTURE

The literacy rate in Germany is 99 percent, and compulsory education lasts between nine and 10 years depending on the province. Under the federal constitution, the 16 provinces are responsible for education, so there is considerable variation in education provision.

The German educational system is divided into four levels. The first level, kindergarten, serves children from age three to six and is optional. Primary education ("Grundschule") lasts from six to 10 years of age for grades one through four. Secondary school is divided into two stages, and students can take the first general education qualification or school-leaving certificate after the first stage at tenth grade. The second stage of secondary school lasts from age 15 through 18, ending at grade 13. For the most part, students opt for vocational training, which requires attending a vocational school after the first stage of their secondary education. Alternatively they study at a "gymnasium" roughly equivalent to an American high school, selecting a specific course of study. On leaving school, students receive a leaving certificate that shows the qualification received.

At the tertiary level of education, there are universities and technical and trade schools. There are more than 300 institutions of higher education in Germany, including 104 independent universities.

Special education is provided in special schools for students with intellectual, sensory, language, and behavioral handicaps. Psychologists and other specialized personnel, rather than school social workers, make decisions about educational placement of students with special needs. Educating students with disabilities in separate public-sector schools is controversial, as some believe that they would be better served being educated alongside the general school population. There is a movement to include disabled students in regular classes, but only a few integrated classes are currently operational.

Social Issues

The social landscape in Germany has changed dramatically during the last three decades, affecting children and youth in particular. Many of these changes reflect changes in the structure of the family. In general, the family alone can no longer bear the responsibility of raising children, as would have been unquestionably its task in the past. Many children now grow up in households headed by a single parent and without siblings. Socialization that in earlier times occurred within sibling groups has become less common among today's children and youth, with the increase in single-child families. Furthermore, divorce and remarriage have led to an array of different familial situations. Increasingly, even mothers of small children are in paid employment outside the home. On the other hand, the range of organized play and learning activities has grown considerably, as has consumerism among children, especially in the area of television and computers. The everyday life of the child has changed dramatically with the widespread availability of entertainment and information media. Television programs, video equipment, and computer games occupy more and more of adolescents' time.

Changes in the makeup of German society are also affecting children and youth. Children have much more daily contact with people of non-German descent. However, insufficient advantage is taken of the opportunity this presents to promote intercultural understanding. On the contrary, there are increasingly one-sided, negative portrayals of foreigners in the media and growth in right-wing extremism that contributes to prejudice and xenophobia.

Economic and technical changes have transformed production and work processes and have led to new qualification requirements for workers. Furthermore, reduction in funding for social programs from the state and communities is leading to a serious reduction in social services, leading to increased exclusion of groups who are unable to compete in the new economic reality. Growing unemployment and difficulty in finding apprenticeships also affect youth, contributing to increasing anxiety and disaffection among adolescents. In the context of youth and unemployment, there are several key factors to consider. Each year more than 8 percent of German students leave the general education school without receiving a diploma; 15 percent of this age remains unqualified for entry-level work and, depending on the region, 14 to 25 percent of youth under the age of 25 are unemployed (Christe et al., 1996).

The availability of illegal drugs through organized criminal activity is growing steadily in Germany, and, at the same time, the tendency among youth to abuse addictive substances is growing. Legal and illegal drugs are a significant and increasingly dangerous part of the lives of young people and children.

Teachers alone are ill-equipped to deal with these social issues, which are increasingly affecting schools. School social work professionals have expertise not only in educational and pedagogical matters, but can also intervene in the family and with the social issues described above. Today they have a crucial role to play in German schools to help students with personal, family, and school problems.

HISTORY OF SCHOOL SOCIAL WORK

The origins of school social work in Germany can be traced back to 1970 when the introduction of full-time social pedagogues into secondary educational institutions in West Berlin resulted in the integration of socio-pedagogical measures for a majority of students (Kath, 1973). Social pedagogy is a traditional profession in Europe that existed before school social work and provided services to a variety of clientele in different settings. It includes a range of care, counseling, and advice for families and youth. For example, it has traditionally included helping clients with social skills, interpersonal relations, and personal growth. Social work itself developed at the beginning of the 20th century and dealt primarily with care for the poor and other marginalized populations. Now social work and social pedagogy have increasingly been blended together, and the term school social work includes elements of both social work and social pedagogy. School social work can be regarded as an extension of the work of social pedagogues in schools, adding elements of social work to provide a more complete service.

Today, more than 25 years later, school social work has established itself in most states and in many schools, although it is still far from being generally considered an "institutionalized form of cooperation between school and youth welfare" (Gewerkschaft Erziehung und Wissenschaft, 1994, p. 1). Given that the states have autonomy in educational matters, there is considerable variation in the extent and nature of school social work from state to state. Moreover, there is still much discussion about what is included in the concept of school social work, with many differences of opinion reflecting differing sociopolitical and conceptual views. The German term for school social work ("Schulsozialarbeit") is a direct translation of the term used in the United States. In the provinces of the former West Germany around 1970, this type of work was understood purely as the performance of social pedagogy within schools. In the interest of differentiating social pedagogy, which was practiced within schools, from services offered outside schools, the designation Schulsozialarbeit came into use (Abels, 1970). School social work was introduced with the expectation that underprivileged children could receive help in their socialization and adjustment in school.

Despite differences in terms of content and definitions, there is broad agreement among all authorities on the subject that school social work should be regarded as a link between the school and external social work services. Stickelmann (1981) presents his definition of school social work:

School social work is the attempt individually or through social group work with children and youths to intercept the social problems and tensions to which children and youths from underprivileged, and often incomplete, families are especially prone and that above all arise in school settings. The purpose is to break down tendencies to stigmatize, and to work against the exclusion of specific children, youths, and groups in schools. Through these methods, school social work approaches the situation of children and youths with alternative learning and experiential offerings (p. 405).

I have used the term school social work as an umbrella term that includes: all activities appropriate for dismantling conflicts and discrepancies between students, teachers, and parents in the school or related to the school on the basis of sound social work methods. In this way, the child's classroom, social, and psychological situation is improved. The chosen activities should contribute to an opening up of the school toward both inside and outside opportunities, while at the same time effecting an improvement in school life. Collaboration with other public and private entities working in this area is indispensable (Wulfers, 1996, p. 28). The term school social work is now well accepted in Germany. Although there are as yet no unified vision, goals, or methods in this relatively new field of social work, identification of target groups among the clientele, specific methods, and goals for school social work have begun to crystallize. In principle, school social work exists to cater for the full range of issues that affect the whole student population. However, there are insufficient resources to allow for work with the entire student body, and so the available service is provided primarily to targeted groups of students exhibiting problems in their adjustment to school.

In summary, it can be said that the clientele of school social work are children and youth who:

- are at risk through alcohol and drug use and involvement in criminal activity;
- demonstrate behavior or discipline problems; and
- experience particular psychological difficulties.

Problems in the school environment, rather than in the students themselves, also contribute to the need for school social work. For example, there are conflicts between students and teachers, the curriculum stresses purely cognitive content and often does not reflect the needs or interests of students, and there is excessive emphasis on achievement, leading to anxiety both for present performance and for career and life prospects. The large size of schools and the rigidity of the school system contribute to student stress and to difficulty in resolving student concerns. School social work is needed to help schools respond to the stress experienced by students, rather than to promote conformity.

Resolving the problems of these target groups of students requires contact and collaboration with parents and with institutions and agencies outside of school. School social workers focus on the needs of the child, and when the child's needs are in conflict with the school, parents, or other authority figures, the school social worker helps to work out these conflicts to meet the needs of the student. School social workers focus on the social and emotional needs of the child, whereas teachers emphasize the academic needs, and all of these needs must be met to help the child adjust to school. Rothe (1990) points out that:

Social work must be present in the schools to unburden teachers. To alleviate disruptions, individual children cannot be sent home, only to wander about because they have no place to go. The root causes of the child's anxiety and aggression in the home, in schools, and in the social arena should be discovered and when possible eliminated through cooperation with the family and social group, with teachers, with youth assistance entities, with work internships and employment positions, through the participation of children and adolescents and parents in school and community responsibilities (p. 270).

CHILD AND YOUTH WELFARE LEGISLATION IN GERMANY

Local authorities are responsible through their youth welfare departments for a range of youth services, including preventive, recreational, and therapeutic work. Legislation has brought these youth departments into a closer relationship with schools in an attempt to improve services to young people. At the time of reunification in 1991, a new Child and Youth Welfare Law was passed that encouraged the development of school social work. This law legitimized the "person-in-environment" principle (referring to providing service to the client in the natural environment), which became officially recognized by public youth welfare agencies ("Jugendhilfe"), resulting in acknowledgment that the school is an important environment for children and youth (Lorenz, 1991). Secondly, Sections 13 and 18 of the Child and Youth Welfare Law are especially important in regard to school social work because they provide the first mention in legislation that young people should be offered special social pedagogical help to promote their education in school, their transition from school to employment, and their social integration. Although the law does not specifically mention the term school social work, it facilitates the service by recognizing that support should be given to children and youth in their natural environment. Furthermore, public youth welfare agencies are required to collaborate more effectively with other individuals and institutions whose activities affect the well-being of young people and their families. This legislation laid the legal groundwork for increased collaboration between youth welfare and schools, and many communities made this a starting point for embarking on new collaborative initiatives.

THE SCOPE OF SCHOOL SOCIAL WORK IN GERMANY

It is difficult to quantify the number of people working in school social work in Germany. School social work is well-established in various types of schools in some provinces. For example, there are approximately 1,000 permanently employed school social workers or social pedagogues working in schools (including preschools, primary schools, and comprehensive schools) in the former West Berlin (population 2 million). In the province of Nordrhein-Westfalen school social work is represented by approximately 1,500 school social workers. Contrarily, in Hamburg and Niedersachsen relatively few school social workers have been hired because of measures to limit public expenditure.

School administrators in other provinces do not hire school social workers at all, as a result of a rigid division of tasks, called in Germany the "subsidiary principle." Explained simply, this sociopolitical principle requires that superior entities (for example, city governments or schools) only take responsibility for activities that subordinate entities (especially the family) are not in the position to handle. Thus, the responsibility and right to raise children is seen as belonging to the family. This regulation is strictly enforced in the province of Hessen (population 6 million). However, even with the restrictions required by this regulation, there are approximately 80 projects in Hessen, employing almost 300 people, dealing with school social work (GEW-Hessen, 2000). The tradition of social work is strong, despite restrictions because of the subsidiary principle, and the profession is growing steadily.

ROLE OF SCHOOL SOCIAL WORK

Rademacker (1992) writes: "school social work and youth welfare have always had the goal of improving the clients' chances of success in school alongside the goal of helping them overcome social marginalization . . . School social work developed from these goals, that is from the goal of developing school-related benefits for children and adolescents and their families. However, school social work in no way implies a limitation to the school as the field of action" (p. 14).

The primary activity of school social work is not only the treatment of individual symptoms, but much more the attempt to achieve a holistic approach to problem-solving that addresses the needs of students not only in school but also in the totality of their environment. The involvement of public youth welfare services and other agencies that serve children and young people is an integral part of school social work. The general goals of school social work would include the following five goals: First, it would prevent behavioral problems in schools. Students who stand out because of violent behavior or conduct problems in school often become clients of youth welfare later. It follows, then, that school social work should take measures to address these problems by working with both student and school system. The second goal is the promotion of social competence of children and youth through targeted action. Fostering collaboration between agencies serving youth is the third goal. The fourth goal is to determine priorities for social work intervention in conjunction with school administrators. Finally, school social work should inform parents of students requiring assistance of available support provided by statutory and community agencies and encourage parents to take advantage of these services.

Currently, it is not possible to present a binding, narrowly defined catalog of activities undertaken by school social work. This inability to define school social work is due to variations in emphasis in different regions and different schools, differences in the strengths of the worker, and differences also in the requirements of school administrators. There are many student and school problems that need social work attention and the worker is always faced with the necessity of choosing the most important on which to concentrate. Many of the tasks performed by school social workers relate to improving students' behavior and adjustment in school. They provide individual and group counseling, and work with the students' parents and teachers to help resolve problems. They also provide homework groups where students can learn independent study skills and improve motivation. Voluntary participation and confidentiality are essential components of the service; otherwise there will be little trust between students and workers. School social workers also bring in outside speakers to the classroom to open up the school and increase student motivation.

Other tasks relate to the students' life outside class; for example, school social workers are involved in the students' leisure activities, including student clubs and student unions. They also offer opportunities for groups of students to discuss specific topics, such as the integration of foreign students. The transition from school to work is another area in which social work expertise is called for. It is increasingly difficult for students to find work or apprenticeships, and social workers are providing help with career orientation and job placement.

In addition to these specific tasks, the work of bringing teachers and school social workers together to broaden each other's perspective through continuing education is essential. Such activities help the two professions to work together collaboratively and to foster both the students' academic progress and social development. Some observers consider the relationship between teachers and social workers in German schools to be fraught with contradictions. Because teachers already have responsibility for the social development of students, the introduction of social workers may be interpreted as a criticism of teachers' handling that aspect of education (Lorenz, 1992).

The establishment of new positions for school social workers does not always occur without friction. Teachers sometimes view the role of school social workers as solving crises with students and returning them to the classroom ready to learn. School social workers sometimes perceive teachers as only interested in conveying subject matter to students without considering the development of the student as a whole person. There can be much skepticism about working together to resolve problems through interdisciplinary collaboration. An important function of school social work practice therefore is to establish a partnership with teachers in which the knowledge and skills of both professions are respected and used to benefit the child. Because school social work is relatively new to the German school system, the development of collegial working relationships is a fundamental and important goal for the profession.

THE WIESBADEN MODEL

School social work is a relatively new and still-developing field in Germany. Research and publications about this young profession are growing, although there are as yet no journals or professional associations specifically for school social work. There are journals for social pedagogues, but not specifically for social pedagogues working in schools. Hence, it is still difficult to offer a comprehensive view of school social work practice in Germany. The following description of the Wiesbaden Model, described by Kersten & Wulfers (1999), is offered here to give a more concrete picture of the development of school social work in one city.

School social work in the city of Wiesbaden, the state capital of Hesse, is an independent field under youth welfare, a government agency responsible for providing youth services. The school social work service started in 1977 and has expanded to 18 citywide locations, with two school social workers at each location. These 18 programs have been amalgamated into a School Social Work Division, serving a total student population of 4,000, under the auspices of the Department of Youth in Wiesbaden.

The concept of school social work was first developed in Klarenthal, a district of Wiesbaden. Following the successful implementation of the service in Klarenthal, it was extended to other locations under a contract with the schools.

It should be noted, and this is of the greatest importance for the success of the work, that the parameters were set before school social workers were introduced into the schools. In addition, six conceptual guidelines for the service were agreed:

1. Teachers and school social workers would work closely together on a daily basis.

2. School social workers were assigned to work with students in specific classes or age levels.
3. Students would participate on a voluntary basis.
4. School social workers would participate in developing programs for the entire school, such as all-day services and community use of the school building.
5. School social workers would link up with a network of social services for youth in the city.
6. School social workers would provide assistance for students with basic needs such as food, clothing, and emotional support.

Since the introduction of school social work services in Wiesbaden, there have been positive results in several areas. Feedback from teachers and parents indicates that the school social work service was beneficial for the academic success of students. Students with family and personal problems improved their attendance, returned to school after dropping out, and received their diplomas after successfully completing school. Other students improved in their social skills and learned to cooperate with others, resolve peer group conflicts, and improve in their attitude to school work. Other successful activities involved helping students make the transition from school to employment.

Since 1990, school social workers in Wiesbaden have been involved in the expansion in the number of "supportive elementary schools" in the city to a total of eight. Supportive elementary schools provide care for students from 7:30 A.M. to 4:00 P.M. Each school accommodates 36 students in the after-school program, which provides lunch when school finishes at 12:00 noon, followed by activities until 4 P.M. The program relieves working mothers of the necessity of taking their children to day care centers after 12:00 noon when classes finish. The children in the school area are able to remain at school during the afternoons and can play with their friends. The school becomes a place for social relationships as well as education and becomes a more important part of the children's lives.

In 1998 the program "Bridges to Education," which is coordinated by school social workers, was established. Through this program, all schools with school social work would provide high school students with career orientation and assistance in securing apprenticeships. In addition, school social work and various youth organizations in the region would offer supplementary courses, projects, seminars, and individual assistance with career choice and job application.

The program in Wiesbaden has broadened the pedagogical repertoire to include a much greater consideration of all aspects of the children's lives. In particular, family life and the emotional needs of the children are receiving more attention in schools through the work of school social workers. The schools have become a more significant part of the community, because they are now open in the afternoons and provide support services and extracurricular activities for the community. Provision of leisure activities for children and youth in areas where previously there was a lack of such services has alleviated the problems that arise when young people spend their time unsupervised. The assistance that students have received in graduating from school and finding apprenticeships has helped to provide some stability in their life, and has established a foundation for them to pursue independent lives. The transition from school to work has presented a major problem in recent years with the growing unemployment rate. Providing services to young people at this stage of their lives helps to avoid serious repercussions in their transition to adulthood.

TRAINING OF SCHOOL SOCIAL WORKERS

Social work training in Germany requires three years at a technical college ("Fachhochschule"), followed by a practicum of one year in an approved social agency. While there are many opportunities for general social work training in the provinces of the former West Germany, there are no specialized qualification programs for school social workers, although the year-long practicum can take place in a school setting to allow the student to gain experience in school social work.

Raab and Rademacker (1982) wrote that education for school social workers lacks professional development in the field. Additionally, the social work profession did not exist in the former East Germany, so there are few trained social workers in the East, making it especially difficult to find qualified social workers for schools in this part of the country. For school social work to develop and become an effective agent in schools and communities, the social work curriculum needs to be developed to ensure that its content is relevant for practice in the school setting. In 1983, the German Youth Institute discussed the issue of the qualifications needed for school social workers. It concluded that general social work training with a concentration in school social work with sociopedagogical knowledge was the best training for social workers who would ultimately work in schools (Proj. SSA, 1984). The curriculum should include psychology, sociology, pedagogy, and methods suited to children and youth in schools, as well as preparation for teamwork with teachers.

The relatively undeveloped state of knowledge of the field of school social work in Germany adds to the difficulty of providing specialized courses at this stage. Research into the present status of the field, effective methods, the host setting of the school and its role in socializing children, and collaboration between youth agencies and schools is needed so that the curriculum content for the specialty can be based on it. Preparation for school social work should provide a broad multidisciplinary training in both social work and social pedagogy. There are several technical colleges where social workers and social pedagogues train together for the first two years, providing a suitable educational milieu for the blending of the roles of these two professions into school social work. Given that school social work requires application of theory to practical problems, the training should involve students in projects reflecting the type of problem-solving required in the field.

For school social workers already employed in the field, opportunities for continuing education (including specialized conferences) have been available, but more are needed to prepare social workers with generalist training for work in schools (Wulfers, 1994). School social workers need opportunities to exchange experiences with other school social workers, supervise their work, extend knowledge of new projects, and improve collaboration with teachers and organizations outside of school. Self-reflection and career support should be offered in an ongoing group-discussion atmosphere. As such, this idea is not geared toward continuing education, but rather consists of a reciprocal support system, perhaps in conjunction with an impartial expert supervisor, for the discussion of problems that arise in school social work.

ISSUES FOR FUTURE DIRECTION

At the beginning of the 21st century, German society faces great social and economic changes that profoundly affect the lives of children and families. More than 3 million children live with unemployed parents, and young people themselves face an uncertain future because of dwindling apprenticeship positions and career opportunities. In addition, many German young people find school to be a stressful experience and question the relevance of their education.

School social work is a relatively new field that holds the promise of support for students who demonstrate their stress and disillusionment by developing social, psychological, or cognitive problems in school. The school social worker is someone students can turn to at school who is not seen as part of the administration. Parents value the school social worker as a neutral person who can mediate problems at school. Teachers also can share their concerns with a colleague who is distanced from internal school problems. Through links to the wider community, school social work also helps to open up the school to the local neighborhood and society at large.

School social work has an important role in school reform, both by helping schools respond to the differing needs of students and by developing programs in schools that give students opportunities to solve their problems. Involving parents and community organizations in creating a more open school environment is an important part of school social workers' contribution to school reform. The challenge for school social work is to foster and strengthen the collaboration between youth welfare and schools. Such collaboration will provide opportunities for developing alternative philosophies and alternative forms of education that can prevent social and psychological problems developing in young people and improve their chances of success in school. School social work must develop a clearer profile, determine its goals, and identify its target groups to fulfill its role in such a partnership with schools.

Training for those entering the field and continuing education for school social workers already practicing in schools is crucial. Because of its short history in Germany, much remains to be done in establishing training opportunities, developing standards, documenting effective strategies, and establishing a research base in school social work. The needs of young people are changing rapidly, and schools must change to meet these needs. School social work today is an essential partner in helping schools prepare young people for their future.

REFERENCES

Abels, H. (1970). *Schulsozialarbeit. Soziale Welt, 21/22,* 347–359.

Christe, C. *et al.* (1996). *Schulversagen und Übergangssystem in der Bundesrepublik.* Oldenburg: BSI.

Gewerkschaft Erziehung und Wissenschaft (1994). *Informationen Schulsozialarbeit.* Beschlossen vom GEW Hauptausschuß am 18. September. Frankfurt: GEW.

Gewerkschaft Erziehung und Wissenschaft-Hessen. (2000). *Gewerkschaft Erziehung und Wissenschaft-Landesverband Hessen: Totalerhebung: Einrichtungen zur Schulsozialarbeit in Hessen.* Frankfurt: GEW.

Kath, B. (1973). Vom Elend der Sozialpädagogik in der Schule. *Betrifft:Erziehung, 6,* 70–72.

Kersten, B. & Wulfers, W. (1999). Wenn wir die nicht hätten: Schulsozialarbeit heute und was sie in Wiesbaden bewirkte. *Pädagogisches Forum, 27,* 92–96.

Lorenz, W. (1991). The New German Children and Young People Act. *British Journal of Social Work, 21,* 329–339.

Lorenz, W. (1992). School-based social work in Germany. *Journal of Education Social Work, 1,* 47–52.

Proj. SSA. (1984). *Schule:Arbeitsplatz für Lehrer und Sozialpädagogen.* München: DJI.

Raab, R. & Rademacker, H. (1982). *Schulsozialarbeit in der Bundesrepublik.* München: DJI.

Rademacker, H. (1992). Schulsozialarbeit: was ist das? *Erziehung und Wissenschaft, 44,* 12, 14–15.

Rothe, M. (1990). Familienorientierte Schülerhilfe. *Zentralblatt für Jugendrecht, 77,* 269–274.

Stickelmann, B. (1981). Schulsozialarbeit. In Petzold, H-J. & Speichert, H. (Eds.), *Handbuch pädagogischer und sozialpädagogischer Praxisbegriffe* (pp. 405–408). Reinbek: Rowohlt.

Wulfers, W. (1994). Wir stehen erst am Anfang: Ein Rahmenkonzept für die Aus- und Weiterbildung zur Schulsozialarbeit. *Pädagogisches Extra, 22,* 45–48.

Wulfers, W. (1996). *Schulsozialarbei: Ein Beitrag zur Öffnung, Humanisierung und Demokratisierung der Schule.* Hamburg: AOL.

8

SCHOOL SOCIAL WORK IN HONG KONG: CONSTRAINTS AND CHALLENGES FOR THE SPECIAL ADMINISTRATIVE REGION

Sammy Chiu and Victor Wong

Social Indicators* — China (Hong Kong SAR)	
Population	6,960,000
Percentage under age 15 years	16
Percentage urban (2000)	100
Life expectancy at birth	77.3 men, 82.8 women
Fertility rate	1.17 children per woman
Percentage of illiterate adults (2000)	3.5 men, 9.8 women
Per capita GDP in $U.S. (1999)	23,579
Percentage unemployed (1997)	6.3

*Social Indicators. From the Statistics Division of the United Nations. Refer to notes on page 249.
Reference: http://www.un.org/Depts/unsd/indicators/indic2a.htm

INTRODUCTION

School social work is one of the key components of personal social work among young people in Hong Kong. It originated in 1971 as a pioneer project, with the aim of helping primary and secondary school children overcome difficulties arising from their learning and social environment and obtain optimum benefit from their schooling experiences. Since 1971, school social work services have expanded considerably. In the 1997–1998 school year, there were 286 school social workers, with the great majority coming from 18 nongovernmental organizations serving 435 secondary schools (Working Group on Review of School Social Work Service, 1999).

THE BIRTH OF HONG KONG SPECIAL ADMINISTRATIVE REGION

Hong Kong was leased to Britain in 1841 as a result of the Opium War, becoming a British colony. After more than 150 years of British rule, it was restored to the People's Republic of China (PRC) and was made a Special Administrative Region (SAR) under the principle of "one country, two systems" in 1997.

In the early 1840s, Hong Kong was a small fishing port in South China with slightly more than 30,000 inhabitants. By 1997 the total population had reached 6 million, and Hong Kong was widely recognized for its remarkable economic performance with Gross Domestic Product (GDP) per capita over U.S. $22,000, comparable to the GDP of many western societies (Hong Kong SAR Government, 1998).

The Joint Declaration signed by the British and Chinese governments in 1984, which governed the restoration of Hong Kong to China, provides for the Hong Kong SAR to be subject to the authority of the PRC while, at the same time, enjoying a high degree of autonomy (with the exception of foreign and defense affairs). The PRC further elaborated in Annex 1 of the Joint Declaration that "Hong Kongs [*sic*] previous capitalist system and life-style [*sic*] shall remain unchanged for 50 years." This undertaking was formalized by the Basic Law enacted and promulgated by the National Peoples Congress of the PRC that has, since July 1, 1997, become the mini-constitution of the Hong Kong SAR. The Basic Law stipulated the preservation of independent jurisdiction, free economy, civil liberties, and social welfare that the people of Hong Kong had enjoyed under British rule, thus largely preserving existing social welfare systems and provision despite the change of sovereignty.

THE LEGACY OF THE COLONIAL WELFARE SYSTEM

One of the major characteristics of Hong Kong's colonial social welfare system can be understood as the supremacy of selective, but minimal, state intervention (Chiu, 1991). Chan, R. (1997) notes that, from the outset, the Hong Kong colonial government had refrained from playing a proactive role in providing social services and had restricted its role in the redistribution of wealth, even though poverty and substandard housing were acute in the 1950s and 1960s.

Limited state provision was further legitimated in the 1970s when the concept of positive non-interventionism, a virtual synonym of laissez-faire government, was formally adopted as the government strategy in managing economic and social affairs. Belief in positive non-interventionism justified the government's provision of inadequate social services, even when the economy was experiencing continuous growth. Positive non-interventionism was translated into several social strategies. First was the low taxation rate. The colonial government saw tax basically as an evil, necessary only when it could not be avoided. Consequently, tax rates have always been kept to the minimum possible. In 1975, the profit tax rate for corporations was 15 percent. In 1995, it was increased to 16.5 percent, representing only a marginal increase during 20 years. The standard rate of income tax was 15 percent in 1975, and it has remained unchanged up to the present time. At different times the government reiterated its view that revenue generated from taxation should only support essential and modest public expenditure. Accordingly, the use of taxation as a means of redistributing wealth and promoting social justice was seen as neither necessary nor possible (Hong Kong Government, 1977a).

The second major characteristic of social welfare in Hong Kong is its minimal provision. Belief in the limited role of the state in welfare provision has been virtually unchallenged since early British rule, and has resulted in a severe restriction in government-provided welfare services. As a result, social work and social security have been restricted to playing a residual and remedial function, even during the booming economy of the 1970s and 1980s (Chiu & Wong, 1999). Since 1975, total government expenditure as a percentage of Hong Kong's GDP has been held below 20 percent, which is among the lowest in southeast Asia and much lower than many western industrialized countries with comparable economic performance. Before 1995, government spending on social welfare, including social security, services for elderly people, services for families and young people, rehabilitation, and other social work services, had been kept within the region of 5 percent of GDP. Social security expenditure has begun to increase in recent years because of an increasing aging population and rising unemployment.

In 1999 the SAR government implemented an "Enhanced Productivity Programme" (EPP), which imposed a 5-percent funding reduction over three years on every government department and all nongovernmental welfare organizations funded by the government. School social work, together with other social work services, such as services for families and for older people, will have to be provided under even more stringent resource allocation with the implementation of the EPP.

The third characteristic of the social welfare system in Hong Kong is the emphasis on the traditional Chinese concept of welfare. Some argue that the western concept of welfare stressing the notion of rights is incompatible with the Chinese culture that places more emphasis on the concept of obligations (Tao, 1991). It is believed that the people of Hong Kong have their "cultural roots deeply engrained in the long enduring tradition of Confucian moral values and beliefs" (Tao, 1991, p. 24). The locus of this philosophy is that the self in Chinese culture is seen as a relational being rather than an independent entity. What culture thus suggests is not, therefore, a fulfillment of individual rights, but primarily a fulfillment of one's own role obligations. The call for recognition of the uniqueness of Chinese cultural and ethical consideration in social policy in general, and in youth service in particular, has received enthusiastic support from the SAR government (Tung Chee Hwa, 1997).

The family has always been regarded as the most fundamental unit in Chinese society. Confucian teachings, which form the cornerstone of Chinese relational ethics, suggest that familial relationships were the prime set of interpersonal relationships that linked individuals and the emperor state. The central role of the family in social welfare has always been a subject of social construction of the colonial government. First, satisfaction of social service needs had been construed primarily as a personal and family responsibility. The colonial government assumed that needs with regard to poverty, old age, delinquency, and natural disaster, were all personal matters, and it is culturally appropriate that these be dealt with within the family (Hong Kong Government, 1965a). Hence, the state would only have a responsibility when the family failed. Second, there was the assumption that the Chinese family remained intact and its caring function effective (Hong Kong Government, 1977a).

The Working Party on Rehabilitation Policies and Services (1992) stated that high values continue to be attached to the family unit in Hong Kong to an extent that cannot be matched by any other institutions. Third, owing to the first two assumptions, the primary objective of the government in social welfare was not to provide services to replace the function of the family, but rather to preserve and to strengthen family functioning. Preservation of family function was not only desirable socially but equally, if not more so, economically, helping not only to minimize government intervention in social welfare but, more importantly, to sustain social control that the colonial government much needed.

SOCIAL ISSUES AND YOUTH PROBLEMS

Hong Kong is largely a Chinese society, with some 94 percent of the population born of Chinese ethnic origin. However, Hong Kong is also a society made up of immigrants. With the constant arrival of new immigrants, most from Mainland China, the Hong Kong-born Chinese have remained at some 60 percent of the total population (Census and Statistics Department, 1996). To prevent large-scale immigration from Mainland China, the former British Hong Kong and the Chinese governments agreed that no more than 150 immigrants per day would be allowed into Hong Kong. This quota is now being reviewed by the Hong Kong SAR and the Chinese central governments for the purpose of speeding up family reunion, but a final decision is still pending. The second largest ethnic group is the British, at more than 2 percent of the population. Filipinos, most of whom work as domestic helpers, form the third largest, at approximately 2 percent of the population. The welfare and salary of foreign domestic helpers has been one of the issues of concern to the minorities living in Hong Kong. To date, relations between ethnic groups have been relatively harmonious, though some hidden tensions have been reflected, for example, in new immigrants from China being victimized by local people as welfare dependents. This victimization is rather subtle and only surfaces at times of economic recession. In recent years, the SAR government has provided funding for community centers to run induction and extension courses for the new immigrants. The primary objects of these courses are to help new immigrants to learn about Hong Kong and to prepare young immigrants for the local education system. In addition to new immigrants from China, Hong Kong has absorbed some 15,000 Indo-Chinese people since the late 1970s, most of whom have now migrated elsewhere. At the end of 1998, there were 1,026 Vietnamese refugees, 638 Vietnamese migrants, and 577 Vietnamese illegal immigrants staying in Hong Kong (Hong Kong SAR Government, 1998). Effective January 9, 1998, new Vietnamese immigrants arriving in Hong Kong by boat or by other illegal means are no longer treated as refugees, but as illegal immigrants who are subjected to repatriation.

In addition to other adjustment and adaptation problems, many new arrivals found it difficult to use the Cantonese dialect, the most popular spoken language used in Hong Kong. Moreover, the new arrivals are often under pressure to pick up some basics of English for schooling or employment. At present, the Hong Kong SAR government is emphasizing the use of Chinese as the language of instruction and education. Thus most of the primary and secondary schools now use Chinese as a written language and Cantonese dialect as a spoken language for their teaching purposes. However, exemptions are given by the government to approximately one-fifth of some 500 secondary schools to continue to use English as their medium of instruction. These are mainly prestigious schools that often admit students with better examination results. Many parents and students are critical of the exemption policy because it implies that other schools that are not exempted are of inferior status. Furthermore, this seems to contradict the government's policy of promoting wider use of the Chinese language and giving it higher status in schools.

As in many other developed countries, the marriage rate is falling and the divorce rate is increasing. Between 1989 and 1998 the crude marriage rate in Hong Kong fell from 6.8 to 4.7 per 1,000 population, representing a decrease of 45 percent over 10 years. During the same period, the divorce rate has increased from one in every 8 marriages to one in every 2.5 marriages (Census and Statistics Department, 1999). The sharp increase in divorce has resulted in more single-parent families, many of which are in poverty. Statistics provided by the Social Welfare Department show that the number of single-parent families receiving social security assistance has increased more than fivefold between 1988 and 1998, and a total number of 17,161 single-parent families received social security assistance in 1998 (Census and Statistics Department, 1999).

Marriage and family life have also been affected by the increase in cross-border exchanges between China and Hong Kong following the introduction of economic reform in China in the late 1970s. Because of the growth of trade, business, and transport between the borders, approximately 2.3 percent of Hong Kong laborers (or approximately 80,000) have been working in China since the early 1990s (Census and Statistics Department, 1992). One result of increased commuting between Hong Kong and China has been an increase in extramarital affairs, which has contributed to marital and family relationship problems (Young, 1996).

Various youth problems have attracted the attention of government, policy makers, and helping professionals since the 1970s. For example, the rate of crime committed by young persons aged between 7 and 20 increased from 1,185 per 100,000 in 1976 to 2,722 per 100,000 in 1996 (Census and Statistics Department, 1997; Vagg et al., 1995). Alarmingly, the figures of reported violent crimes in 1996 show that among all cases of rape, indecent assault, and serious assault, the proportion committed by young persons aged below 21 are 42 percent, 27 percent, and 36 percent, respectively (Hong Kong Police Force, 1997). Another problem attracting growing media attention is the increase in suicides among young people. Lai (1997) estimated that the suicide rate for teenagers aged between 15 and 19 has increased from 4.4 per 100,000 in 1993 to 7.93 per 100,000 in 1994. This increase reflects, to a certain extent, the tremendous stress faced by young people and the lack of support available to them. However, the overall suicide rate of 12.4 per 100,000 in 1994 indicated that suicide of young people is still much less frequent than among the older population (Yip, 1995).

According to official figures, the number of newly reported young substance abusers under age 21 has shown a decreasing trend, from 52.6 percent in 1993 to 42.4 percent in 1998 (Narcotics Division, 1999). However, there is a concern that there is serious underreporting of substance abuse. Front line social workers and youth workers have observed a growing popularity of a variety of substances including amphetamines, cough medicine, and other psychotropic substances (Har, 1999). From 1990 to 1998, the mean age of initial drug abuse for all newly reported cases has decreased from 26.3 to 24.5. Newly reported female drug abusers are comparatively younger than their male counterparts, as their mean ages were respectively 22.8 and 24.9 in 1998 (Narcotics Division, 1999).

Teenage unwed pregnancy has also become one of the major concerns of youth workers in Hong Kong. Although there are at present no official statistics, a study conducted by the Hong Kong Federation of Youth Groups (1995) shows that teenage pregnancy is increasing, and that it is as likely to occur in higher as in lower socioeconomic groups. Notwithstanding the concern among youth workers about teenage pregnancy, the absence of territory-wide data means that it is impossible to ascertain the true seriousness of the problem. However, according to a survey conducted by the Hong Kong Family Planning Association, 7 percent of secondary school respondents admitted that they had sex during dating (Hong Kong Family Planning Association, 1996). Another survey by the Hong Kong Federation of Youth Groups also shows that 60.9 percent of the youth respondents approve of premarital sex (Hong Kong Federation of Youth Groups, 1998). According to Mother's Choice, a non-governmental organization targeted to help young girls with unwed pregnancy, requests for assistance have been on the rise, and there were more than 1,500 requests for help in 1997 (Hong Kong Federation of Youth Groups, 1999). At present, termination of pregnancy is illegal unless approved by two registered medical practitioners on specified grounds, such as that the continuation of pregnancy would involve risk to the life of the pregnant woman, or that the pregnant woman is under the age of 16, or that the pregnancy is a result of incest, rape, or other involuntary intercourse (Lee, 1991).

EDUCATION IN HONG KONG

The development of the education system in Hong Kong can be traced to the post-World War II years. Similar to other areas of social service, such as health care and social welfare, education was mainly provided by religious and charitable organizations funded by local and overseas donations. From 1949 to the early 1950s, Hong Kong received a large influx of immigrants from Mainland China as a result of the civil war between the Chinese Nationalist and Communist Parties. To meet the needs of a predominantly young and rapidly growing population, the then-colonial government saw the need to expand the school system, with the provision of primary school places as the most urgent priority (Hong Kong Government Secretariat, 1981). In the first colonial education White Paper, titled "Education Policy," the government set "primary education for all" as the immediate goal for Hong Kong (Hong Kong Government, 1965b). As a result, massive school building programs were launched and primary school places were greatly expanded. In 1971, the objective of providing free primary education for all was achieved, and attendance at primary school for children aged between 6 and 11 was also made compulsory. In line with the expansion of primary school places, the government further stated its plan to provide three years of free junior secondary school education for all primary school leavers by the year 1979 (Hong Kong Government, 1974). In 1980, the right of young people to enjoy nine years of free education up to the age of 15 was further safeguarded by the Attendance Order of the Hong Kong Education Ordinance (Lee, 1991).

At present, education in Hong Kong is organized into four tiers. They are, respectively, pre-schools and kindergartens, primary schools, secondary schools, and post-secondary colleges and universities. Voluntary and private

bodies serving children aged from three to five operate pre-schools and kindergartens. As of 1999, there were a total of 744 kindergartens in Hong Kong with
a total enrollment of 175,073 preschool-age children.

Primary schooling starts at the age of six and lasts for six years. At
present, most primary schools are bi-sessional schools, where students attend
either the morning or the afternoon session within the same building.
Though the government encouraged primary schools to be converted to
whole-day schools, the progress of conversion has been very slow because of
insufficient funding. The most recent interim target set by the government
is to enable 60 percent of primary school places to be provided on a
whole-day basis in 2002–2003 (Hong Kong SAR Government, 1998). In the
1998–1999 academic year, there were 856 primary schools in Hong Kong
enrolling a total number of 466,507 students (Hong Kong Education
Department, 1999).

Secondary schools are divided into three main types according to their
curriculum: grammar schools that provide academic (contrasted with technical) courses, technical schools, and pre-vocational schools, all providing five
years of secondary education leading to the Hong Kong Certificate of
Education Examination (HKCEE). Students are allocated to different schools,
after completing primary education, according to their schooling performance, academic aptitude, and parental choice. At present, 90 percent of secondary schools are grammar schools (Hong Kong SAR Government, 1998).
With the provision of nine years of compulsory education, the first three years
of junior secondary education is free. Recent government statistics show that
100 percent of children aged between 6 and 14 were in primary and junior
secondary education, 85 percent of young people aged between 15 and 16
received secondary level or technical education. Up to one-third completed 13
years of formal education, with approximately one-third of these entering universities or post-secondary colleges.

Finally, there are 62 special schools providing places for students with
physical handicaps, visual impairments, hearing impairments, mental handicaps, and students considered to be "maladjusted". In addition, the Hong Kong
Red Cross operates hospital schools in which lessons are provided for
convalescing children to facilitate their resumption of schooling following
their recovery. In 1999, hospital schools existed in 16 public hospitals
providing small classes for a total of 422 primary and secondary students
(Hong Kong Red Cross, 1999). Special support is also given to secondary
schools that admit primary school leavers whose academic performance falls
within the lowest 25 percent of primary school leavers in a particular year.
These students are designated as academically low achievers (ALAs), and mostly study in the ALA (so-called "Band 5") schools. In the school year 1998–1999,
approximately 20,000 children designated as academically low achievers
were admitted into 154 secondary schools in the territory (Hong Kong

Education Department, 1999). Following the recommendations of the Working Group on Support Services for Schools with Band 5 Students (1993), the government started to reduce the normal class size for ALAs from 40 to 35 to enable teachers to provide students with more attention. There are fewer academic subjects in the ALA school curriculum, and the selection of subjects such as humanities, cultural, practical, and technical subjects is based on students' interest.

THE ORIGINS OF SCHOOL SOCIAL WORK IN HONG KONG

School social work was initiated in Hong Kong in 1971 as a pilot project without government funding when six nongovernmental welfare organizations, mainly family service agencies with a religious background, extended their work into affiliated schools to help students deal with any emotional and social problems that might hinder their academic achievement. School social work was seen primarily as both an extension of family service and an application of social work principles and methods in schools (Lo, 1981). The assumption behind this pioneer project was that schooling problems among youngsters were symptoms of personal malfunctioning, itself rooted in family problems such as inadequate parenting and relationship conflict. An implied objective of early school social work, therefore, was that intervention with students in schools would help the family resolve its problems and regain normal function. The school was primarily regarded as a setting for social work practice. The underlying assumption is that school merely provided a necessary, neutral, and perhaps problem-free, environment for the growth of children and young people, whereas the targets of intervention were the students and their families. That school social work was pioneered by family service agencies also determined the method of intervention given that casework, which focused on personal and interpersonal changes and appeared to be the main method of intervention practiced by family service agencies in Hong Kong.

School social work received a further boost following publication of a report in 1975 on government-commissioned research into juvenile crime in Hong Kong (Ng, 1975). Ng concluded that the weakening of social bonding and emotional attachment to conventional institutions such as school and the family among young people was the main cause for the upsurge of youth crime. Ng recommended that social work focus on helping youngsters facing difficulties in attachment to, or at risk of dropping out of, the school and their family to resolve these difficulties. Ng's report seemed to be well-received by the government. Two years later, the government announced its plan to set up a school social work service in primary and secondary schools (Hong Kong Government, 1977b).

In addition, the government also planned to set up outreach youth work teams in nine districts of Hong Kong to help youngsters considered to be on the margin of delinquency. The plan to launch school social work was formalized in the Social Welfare White Paper entitled "Social Welfare into the 1980s", in which the government would provide subvention (financial assistance) to nongovernmental welfare organizations for a school social work service to all primary and secondary schools in Hong Kong (Hong Kong Government, 1979). School social work in primary schools was to be provided by student guidance officers, who were mostly teachers equipped with some counseling and social work knowledge and skills, and in secondary schools by social work graduates. The objective of school social work, as stated in the government plan, was "to identify and help pupils whose academic, social and emotional development is in jeopardy for whatever reason, to assist pupils to make the maximum use of their educational opportunities, to develop their potential to the fullest possible extent and to prepare them for responsible adult living" (Social Welfare Department, 1984, p.125).

The Social Welfare White Paper marked an important watershed in the development of personal social work among young people in Hong Kong. Not only did school social work begin to receive government funding, but outreach work to youth as well as youth center provision were also fully funded to form an integrated framework for services to youth. However, notwithstanding the development in the scope of the youth service, the objectives and content of school social work have remained more or less the same as before. The long delay in the government launching school social work in all primary and secondary schools in Hong Kong once again reflected its nonintervention welfare ideology. In 1981 when the service was fully operational the government estimated that 2 percent of students in the age group six through 16, and 1 percent of those aged 17 through 20, might experience personal problems and require the assistance of the school social work service (Hong Kong Government, 1982). On the basis of this estimate, student guidance officers were allocated to primary schools at a ratio of 1:3,000 students in urban areas and 1:2,000 students in rural areas. In addition, student guidance officers were supported by student guidance consulting officers (social work graduates) at a ratio of 1:30,000 students. In secondary schools, one qualified social worker was provided for every 4,000 students. According to this calculation, each school social worker was to serve a maximum of four secondary schools, whereas the actual number of schools served varied according to the school size. In the early 1980s there were 93 student guidance officers serving 477 primary schools, and another 91 social workers serving 297 secondary schools (Hong Kong Government, 1982).

Growth of School Social Work

In a study revealing that 7.8 percent of the student population in Hong Kong was in need of the school social work service, the Hong Kong Council of Social Service (1977) highlighted the insufficiency of the service's resources, recommending that the government improve staffing levels, in five phases, from one school social worker serving 4,000 students (1:4,000) to 1:1,000, that is, one school social worker serving one school. Because of resource considerations, the government did not accept the entire recommendation. Although acknowledging the effectiveness and contribution of school social work, the government only pledged to improve the provision to one social worker serving 2,000 students (approximately two schools) by 1996 (Hong Kong Government, 1991). As for the ALA schools, the government promised to provide one school social worker to 1,000 students. Despite the reluctance of the government to improve the funding for the school social work service, the number of school social workers continues to grow alongside the increase in the student population. In the 1997–1998 school year, there were 282 school social workers serving a total of 435 secondary schools, among which 154 ALA schools are being served at the ratio of one school social worker to 1,000 students (Working Group on Review of School Social Work Service, 1999). The most recent policy address delivered by the Chief Executive of the Hong Kong SAR announced that the government will permit the school social worker to student ratio to be improved to 1:1,000 from 2000–2001 (Hong Kong SAR Government, 1999). However, no additional government funding will be given to the nongovernmental organizations for improving the ratio. In other words, these organizations will have to cut existing services or seek new funding to pay for the additional resources required by the improvement in the school social work service.

Objectives of School Social Work in Hong Kong

As stated above, school social work was specifically designed to identify and help students whose academic, social, and emotional development were in jeopardy, to assist them to make the maximum use of their educational opportunities, to develop their potential to the full and to prepare them for responsible adult living (Hong Kong Government, 1982). The general objectives set by the government were translated into three specific dimensions (Wong, 1983):

- to help and to enable students to benefit from their educational opportunities, and to prepare them for full adult lives;
- to collaborate with school teachers and other related professionals to improve the education system; and

■ to help students develop positive social and moral values so as to reduce and prevent juvenile crime.

Although social workers may regard the improvement of the education system as one of the objectives of school social work in Hong Kong, it is nevertheless important to note that this is not the government's intention (Hong Kong Government, 1979). Given that the general social welfare framework was to support, if not reproduce, the status quo, there was no intention on the part of the government to use school social work as a tool to promote system change. This was illustrated by the guidelines for school social workers, when 60 percent of their working time should be devoted to helping individuals based on casework methods, 20 percent with small groups, and the remaining 20 percent on mass programs through which developmental youth work was delivered (Ko and Wong, 1990). Furthermore, a survey conducted by the Hong Kong Council of Social Service showed that, of 332 school personnel interviewed, 68.4 percent perceived counseling students with problems related to development and adjustment to school life as the top priority of the school social work service, whereas only 0.6 percent viewed improvement of the education service with equal importance (Hong Kong Council of Social Service, 1986). Although improvement of the education service was only taken to imply matters related to teaching and the syllabus, it would be hard to imagine how improvement and changes in the whole education system would receive wide support from the education sector. So, beyond good intentions, school social work seemed to have inherited the legacy of the pioneer project where remedial work remained the main focus of activity.

SCHOOL SOCIAL WORK ROLE

Most school social workers are employed by nongovernmental welfare organizations, although a few are employed by the government's Social Welfare Department to work in the school setting. They are not employees of the respective schools, but remain employees of the welfare organizations with which the schools have contracted for service. Although there is no direct line of accountability between the school administrator and the social worker, school social workers usually maintain cooperative relationships with the principal of the school through the support of the discipline or guidance teacher. A survey on the future development of school social work conducted by the Hong Kong Council of Social Service (1986) revealed that school personnel tend to identify the primary role of school social workers as helping students rather than teachers, with 88.6 percent of respondents regarding the prime contribution of school social work as the promotion of the well-being of students through direct service. Only 3 percent acknowledged the contribution of school social work to the provision of professional knowledge and advice to teachers, and 13 percent recognized the role of mediation between the school and students. Students appear to have similar views about the role of school social work. Respondents in Ko & Wong's (1990) survey of 2,200 students attending 40 different schools in Hong Kong expected school social workers to perform tasks related mainly to solving personal difficulties such as emotional, behavioral, and family problems; improving relationships such as conflicts with peers, family members, and school teachers; as well as strengthening personal functioning in society, such as participation in social affairs and improving interaction skills. According to the Clientele Information System of the Hong Kong Council of Social Service, the main problems faced by young people who received help from the school social work service in the 1995–1996 school year were, respectively, behavioral and emotional problems (25.4 percent), schooling and problems relating to studying (23.5 percent), family problems (22.9 percent), and peer relationship and developmental adjustment (22.8 percent) (Working Group on Review of School Social Work Service, 1999).

As far as the mode of service delivery is concerned, most schools adopt the "stationing mode," whereby school social workers are stationed in the school for a certain number of days each week. A review of school social work services has shown that one-third (32 percent) of school social workers spend most of their time performing the role of a counselor and one-fifth (19 percent) serve as an enabler (Working Group on Review of School Social Work Service, 1998). According to the guideline on school social work service issued by the Social Welfare Department in 1994, the role of an enabler is to "help and encourage students to devise proper means in meeting their needs and to work out solutions to their own problems related to their developmental process and adjustment to school life and to use more effectively the resources available to them" (Working Group on Review of School Social Work Service, 1998). Both roles, as reported by the school social workers, are focused on helping students solve their behavioral and emotional problems, meeting their developmental needs, and adjusting to school life. The review also showed that casework was considered the most important approach adopted by school social workers and, not surprisingly, almost all school social workers interviewed (97 percent) indicated satisfaction with their work in providing guidance and counseling to students.

Although the objectives of school social work neither dictate a remedial focus nor discourage school social workers from engaging in preventive services, few school social workers see prevention as their major task. At the same time, for the reasons suggested earlier, few school social workers attempt to mobilize the collective participation of students and teachers to advocate for improvement in the education service, either within the individual school or the education system as a whole (Chan, C., 1997; Liu, 1997). Consequently,

school social work has seemingly become student social work, largely emphasizing remedial work and individual adjustment to the school environment
rather than promoting environmental change.

In spite of the mainstream practice focused on individual counseling and
guidance, some school social workers have developed a more proactive role
that both promotes school-based prevention and facilitates student participation in the school environment rather than seeing students as merely targets of
social work intervention (Ling Chow, 1996; YMCA School Social Work Branch,
1997). Other school social workers have placed more emphasis on working
with other community-based helping professionals and mobilizing support and
resources from the wider community. (This will be discussed in more detail
below when we consider issues for the future direction of school social work.)

School social workers who are aware of the organizational dimension of
service provision and delivery would no doubt consider school managers and
teachers as working partners. Nevertheless, the relationship between the
school and school social workers is not entirely unproblematic. Teachers and
school social workers work in different sectors: the former in the education
sector, the latter in the welfare sector. Teachers often complain about their
heavy teaching load and schools are given few resources to cope with the
demands of both teaching and the personal needs of students. Furthermore,
the concerns of teachers may not always coincide with those of the students
themselves. For example, some underprivileged young people have, at least
partially, questioned the relevance of educational goals and school curriculum
in Hong Kong (Wong & Shiu, 1998). This is particularly true for those students
who have become alienated from the schooling process and for those who do
not recognize schooling as necessary for their future career development.
More often than not, the school may resort to power and moral hegemony to
maintain effective control over those "marginal" students in the course of education. It is not unusual for school management to "counsel out" problematic
students in junior secondary classes, despite their entitlement to nine years'
compulsory education. Some school social workers may find themselves
caught between protecting the welfare of marginal students and maintaining a
good working relationship with the school. The best way to resolve this
dilemma is to work out a "win-win" solution. However, because of mistrust of
the marginal students, and in view of the power held by the school, this is often
easier said than done.

It is not an easy task to resolve this potential role conflict between
schools and school social workers. However, three points are worth highlighting here. First, it is important to promote better communication and understanding between school personnel and school social workers. Competent
school social workers cannot afford to overlook the organizational dimension
of the services they provide. Second, there is a need for school social workers
to understand the meaning of marginality defined by school personnel. For

example, to what extent is the phenomenon of marginal students something constructed in terms of moral values, behavior, academic competence, appearance, or social life, or a mix of all of these? In an empirical study conducted by the authors, teachers showed particular bias against the moral values and behavior of their marginal students (Chiu, Wong & Chiu, 1995). Consequently, school social workers need to understand how the process of marginality is constructed within the school setting and to promote better understanding and acceptance of marginal students by school staff. Finally, school social workers have to be sensitive to the meanings students attach to their noncompliant or antisocial behavior and values.

TRAINING OF SCHOOL SOCIAL WORKERS

School social workers typically hold a recognized degree in social work and are required to register with the Hong Kong Social Workers Registration Board to be eligible for employment as a social worker. Following implementation of the Social Workers Registration Ordinance in June 1997, the board not only enforces registration and adherence to a code of practice, but also serves as an accreditation body determining the suitability for registration purposes of both local and overseas social work training programs.

At the undergraduate level, both diploma and degree courses in social work are generic in nature, designed to equip students with necessary basic and general knowledge and skills essential for practice in a variety of social work settings. However, some courses enable students to undertake options on social work with young people, and there are opportunities for students to undertake fieldwork practice in school social work settings. Although such training opportunities are no doubt an advantage for students considering employment in the school social work service upon their graduation, specialized training in school social work at the pre-service level is not required in Hong Kong.

In addition to orientation programs provided by employers, the Hong Kong Council of Social Service and the Lady Trench Training Centre of the Social Welfare Department provide induction courses for newly recruited school social workers, and also organize seminars and in-service training programs especially for school social workers. Given that school social work is integral to social work with young people in Hong Kong, many other seminars and workshops on topics such as empowerment practice with youth, working with marginal youth, and youth and popular culture are also available for school social workers. Moreover, four universities in Hong Kong now provide specialized social work courses at postgraduate level. Although some of these programs may take youth as one of the specialties, there is, as of yet, no specialized school social work program.

Issues for Future Direction

Rather than upholding the rhetoric of reform and advocacy, the objectives of school social work are now redefined to better reflect the service orientation of school social work in helping students in relation to their developmental process and their adjustment to school life. They are as follows:

- to help students develop their full potential, achieve healthy personal growth, attain adequate and proper school education, establish harmonious human relationships, and elicit their concern for the community;
- to help students with any personal, family, and interpersonal relationship or schooling problem; and
- to strengthen the linkage among students, families, the school, and the community.

According to the guidelines on school social work service, school social workers are expected to play eight important roles. These eight roles are enabler, counselor, social educator, consultant, mobilizer of resources, researcher, advocate, and mediator (Working Group on Review of School Social Work Service, 1998). However, a survey conducted by the Working Group in April 1997 concluded that these roles are not equally emphasized (Working Group of Review of School Social Work Service, 1998). Although many school social workers prefer to act as counselor, enabler, and social educator, fewer prefer to play the role of mobilizer of resources, researcher, or advocate. The findings confirm that the role of advocate is essentially rhetoric, and one that school social workers perform rarely.

To strengthen support to students, the working group proposed to redefine the existing eight roles of school social workers into four: counselor, consultant, coordinator, and community and social educator. According to the working group's definition, the consultant role is to provide a consultation service to school personnel, parents, and students on ways of addressing the needs of students. The coordinator role is to coordinate and mobilize community resources for the benefit of students, families, and schools. The role of community and social educator is to enable students and their families to develop positive social values and attitudes in facing life situations, to promote harmonious family relationship through running and supporting students' and parents' groups.

It remains to be seen whether such a redefinition of objectives and roles of school social work will enable school social workers to strike a balance between individualist practices and school-based and community-oriented practices. Undoubtedly, school social workers who rely on a casework approach are unlikely to be able to meet the future challenges of school social work. School social workers must at the same time seek support from their potential working partners, whether by means of "reaching in" to professionals and administrators at the school level, or "reaching out" to other helping professionals or agencies/organizations at the community level. Most important of all, such an orientation should not be confined to the instrumental task of mobilizing human resources, but should also address the needs and difficulties experienced by the students in their own context. It is not only about mobilizing untapped resources, but also concerned with promoting necessary social, and perhaps structural, changes.

In recent years, some school social workers have started to collaborate with community-based youth services in meeting the needs of students. For example, student associations, such as a federation of class monitors and school prefects as well as other student committees have been organized with the object of encouraging students to participate more actively in school affairs. Further examples are evident in other schools where school- and community-based social workers collaborate in advocating for an "alternative curriculum" to meet the diverse needs of students. Although these are small-scale pilot projects, they have received positive feedback from school personnel.

On the other hand, with the early onset of students' problems and with the increasing rate of juvenile delinquency, there is an obvious need to strengthen cooperation between primary school student guidance officers and the secondary school social workers. Establishing a proper mechanism for a mutual referral of cases is necessary. Looking ahead, there is a need to strengthen both formal and informal collaboration and exchanges between the two parties.

Cooperation between family and school is another issue being emphasized by the government in recent years. In promoting cooperation between the school and the family, however, it seems that the focus has been placed primarily on promoting responsible parenting and positive family values, whereas parents, and working parents in particular, seem to have been left unsupported. As a bridge between students and parents, school social workers may need to consider using more advocacy and community-organizing measures to better address parental needs.

Finally, the recent change of the funder/provider relationship between the government and the welfare sector may also affect school social work service. Under the new funding and service agreement (FSA) imposed by the government, each school social worker is required to handle 70 active cases, close 23 cases, conduct 40 group/program sessions, and provide a total of 380 consultations to school personnel or parents within a year. The worry is that to satisfy the required quantitative output school social workers may be largely bound to be more oriented toward casework and less toward school-based work. There is little room for innovative service and community-based projects, and even less so for services to be critical or advocacy-oriented.

151

Apart from the FSA, service quality assessment has been introduced to enforce closer and stricter monitoring. With an increasing emphasis placed on the role of monitoring, the quality assessment exercise and the FSA may excessively increase the bureaucracy of service provision and management (Chiu & Wong, 1999). There is an urgent need for school social workers to keep an eye on the challenge of managerialism, lest the service be tempted to take management and monitoring measures as a panacea for all the difficulties confronted by practitioners and users.

CONCLUSION

School social work in Hong Kong has witnessed some 30 years of development. In view of the growing complexity of student needs and the rapidly changing societal context of Hong Kong SAR, there is an urgency to adequately address the structural, community, and organizational dimensions of the school social work service. A challenge for school social workers in Hong Kong is to critically appreciate the increasingly managerial context of the service, and yet advocate policy reforms and initiate innovative ideas so that support and participation from both students and parents, and the school and community at large, can be further enhanced.

REFERENCES

Census and Statistics Department. (1992). *Hong Kong residents working in China* (General Household Surveys: Special Topics Report No. X). Hong Kong: Government Printer.

Census and Statistics Department. (1996). *1996 population by-census: Summary results*. Hong Kong: Government Printer.

Census and Statistics Department. (1997). *Hong Kong annual digest of statistics: 1996 edition*. Hong Kong: Hong Kong SAR Government Printing Department.

Census and Statistics Department. (1999). *Hong Kong annual digest of statistics: 1998 edition*. Hong Kong: Hong Kong SAR Government Printing Department.

Chan, C. T. (1997). Reconstruction of Theory for School Social Work Practice in Hong Kong. In YMCA School Social Work Branch (Ed.), *Collection of essays on school social work* (pp. 19-38). Hong Kong: YMCA.

Chan, R. (1997). *Welfare in newly industrialised society: The construction of welfare state in Hong Kong*. London: Avebury.

Chiu, S. (1991). Towards Universal Social Policy in Hong Kong. *Journal of Policy Viewers, 1*, 1-8.

Chiu, S. & Wong, V. (1999). Confucian welfare: A new legitimation for social welfare in Hong Kong Special Administrative Region? In B. Lesnik (Ed.), *International perspectives in social work: Social work and the state* (pp. 75-85). London: Pavilion.

Chiu, S., Wong, V. & Chiu, T.C. (1995). *In the eyes of the helpers and the general public: Perceptions and stereotypes towards marginal youth in Hong Kong* (Working Paper Series No. 9505). Hong Kong: Faculty of Social Sciences, Hong Kong Baptist University.

Har, H.M.K. (1999). A critical review on youth substance abuse: Looking for a new Paradigm. *Journal of Youth Studies, 2*, 199-210.

Hong Kong Council of Social Service. (1977). *An exploratory study on the existing school social work programme in Hong Kong*. Hong Kong: Hong Kong Council of Social Service.

Hong Kong Council of Social Service. (1986). *Opinion survey on school social work service: A report*. Hong Kong: Working Group on Future Development of School Social Work, Hong Kong Council of Social Service.

Hong Kong Education Department. (1999). *Fact sheets*. Hong Kong: Government Printer.

Hong Kong Family Planning Association. (1996). *In-school youth*. Hong Kong: The Family Planning Association of Hong Kong.

Hong Kong Federation of Youth Groups. (1995). *Teenage pregnancy: The services and policy options*. Hong Kong: Hong Kong Federation of Youth Groups.

Hong Kong Federation of Youth Groups. (1998). *Indicators of youth values*. Hong Kong: Hong Kong Federation of Youth Groups.

Hong Kong Federation of Youth Groups. (1999). *Hong Kong youth trends analysis*. Hong Kong: Hong Kong Federation of Youth Groups.

Hong Kong Government. (1965a). *Aims and objectives of social welfare in Hong Kong*. Hong Kong: Government Printer.

Hong Kong Government. (1965b). *Education policy.* Hong Kong: Government Printer.

Hong Kong Government. (1974). *Secondary education in Hong Kong over the next decade*. Hong Kong: Government Printer.

Hong Kong Government. (1977a). *Services for the elderly: A green paper.* Hong Kong: Government Printer.

Hong Kong Government. (1977b). *Personal social work among young people in Hong Kong: A green paper*. Hong Kong: Government Printer.

Hong Kong Government. (1979). *Social welfare into the 1980s*. Hong Kong: Government Printer.

Hong Kong Government. (1982). *The five year plan for social welfare development in Hong Kong - review 1981*. Hong Kong: Government Printer.

Hong Kong Government. (1991). *Social welfare into the 1990s and beyond*. Hong Kong: Government Printer.

Hong Kong Government Secretariat. (1981). *The Hong Kong education system*. Hong Kong: Government Printer.

Hong Kong Police Force. (1997). *Annual report of Hong Kong police force 1997*. Hong Kong: Hong Kong SAR Government Printing Department.

Hong Kong Red Cross. (1999). *Annual report 1998-99*. Hong Kong: Hong Kong Red Cross.

Hong Kong SAR Government. (1998). *Hong Kong - A new era - Annual report 1998*. Hong Kong: Government Printer.

Hong Kong SAR Government. (1999). *Chief Executive's policy address 1999*. Hong Kong: Government Printer.

Ko, G. & Wong, P.Y. (1990). *Secondary school students in Hong Kong: Expectations and perceptions of school social work and guidance teachers services*. Hong Kong: City Polytechnic of Hong Kong.

Lai, K.H. (1997). Teenage drugs subculture: Implications for preventive strategies in social work practice. *Hong Kong Journal of Social Work, 31*, 1-17.

Lee, C.N. (1991). *Everyday law compendium for Hong Kong*. Hong Kong: Commercial Press.

Ling Chow, H.Y. (1996). New challenges of school social work service in the turn of the century. In Children and Youth Division, Hong Kong Council of Social Service (Ed.), *The challenges, transformation and development of children and youth service* (pp. 101-110). Hong Kong: Writers' and Publishers' Co-operative.

Liu, E.S.C. (1997). School social work in Hong Kong: Task analysis and its implications for future development. *Hong Kong Journal of Social Work, 31*, 35-48.

Lo, M.F. (1981). The review and the prospect of school social work service in Hong Kong. *Hong Kong Council Quarterly, 78*, 1-5.

Ng, A. (1975). *The social causes of violent crime among young offenders in Hong Kong*. Hong Kong: Social Research Centre, Chinese University of Hong Kong.

Narcotics Division. (1999). *Annual report of the central registry of drug abuse.* Hong Kong: Hong Kong SAR Government Printing Department.

Social Welfare Department. (1984). *Social welfare five years plan - Review.* Hong Kong: Government Printer.

Tao, J. (1991). *The moral foundation of welfare: A comparative study of Chinese Confucianism and deontological liberalism: A case study of Hong Kong.* Unpublished PhD dissertation, University of East Anglia, Norwich.

Tung Chee Hwa. (1997, December). Speech by Mr Tung Chee Hwa, the Chief Executive, at the Conference on the Review of the Implementation of the Charter for Youth. *http://www.info.gov.hk/ce/speech/ccesp-20.htm*

Vagg, J., Bacon-Shone, J., Gray, P. & Lam, D. (1995). *The final report on the social causes of juvenile crime.* Hong Kong: Fight Crime Committee.

Wong, L.K. (1983). The situation of school social work in a secondary setting. *Hong Kong Council Quarterly, 84,* 29–32.

Wong, V. & Shiu, W. (1998). The structural is personal? Re-examination and re-development of youth work in Hong Kong. *Journal of Youth Studies, 1,* 196–207.

Working Group on Review of School Social Work Service. (1998). *Draft report on review of school social work service.* Hong Kong: HKSAR Government Printer.

Working Group on Review of School Social Work Service. (1999). *Report on review of school social work service.* Hong Kong: HKSAR Government Printer.

Working Group on Support Services for Schools with Band 5 Students. (1993). *Final report on support services for schools with Band 5 students.* Hong Kong: Government Printer.

Working Party on Rehabilitation Policies and Services. (1992). *Green paper on equal opportunities and full participation: A better tomorrow for all.* Hong Kong: Government Printer.

Yip, P.S.F. (1995). *Suicides in Hong Kong 1981-1994* (Research Report, Department of Statistics, No. 94). Hong Kong: Department of Statistics, The University of Hong Kong.

YMCA School Social Work Branch. (Ed.). (1997). *Collection of essays on school social work.* Hong Kong: YMCA.

Young, K.P.H. (1996). Social work with families and children. In I. Chi & S. K. Cheung (Eds.), *Social work in Hong Kong* (pp. 11–23). Hong Kong: Hong Kong Social Workers Association.

9 | SCHOOL SOCIAL WORK IN MALTA:
EMPOWERING CHILDREN FOR CITIZENSHIP
Godwin Pace

Social Indicators* — Malta	
Population	392,000
Percentage under age 15 years	20
Percentage urban (2000)	91
Life expectancy at birth	75.9 men, 81.0 women
Fertility rate	1.77 children per woman
Percentage of illiterate adults (2000)	8.6 men, 7.2 women
Per capita GDP in $U.S. (1999)	9,349
Percentage unemployed (Dec. 1999)	5.3

*Social Indicators. From the Statistics Division of the United Nations. Refer to notes on page 249.
Reference: http://www.un.org/Depts/unsd/indicators/indic2a.htm

NATIONAL CONTEXT

The Maltese islands are a small archipelago of six islands and islets in the Mediterranean Sea, situated 97 kilometers (60 miles) south of Sicily and approximately 223 kilometers (138 miles) from the nearest point in North Africa, encompassing an area of only 246 square kilometers (95 square miles). Their population is 376,513 (Central Office of Statistics, 1999).

Malta, the largest island from which the archipelago takes its name, is the cultural, administrative, industrial, and commercial center of the whole archipelago. It is well-served with harbors, the most important of which is the Valletta Grand Harbour. Malta's capital city, Valletta, was built by the Knights of Malta under Grand Master Jean Parisot de la Valette, after the Great Siege of Malta in 1565.

Malta has a long history, with the first evidence of settlement dating back to at least 4000 B.C. Because of its location, Malta has always been occupied by various civilizations dominating the Mediterranean. Throughout the ages, the islands have been occupied by the Phoenicians, the Carthaginians, the Romans, the Arabs, the Normans, the Knights of Malta, the French, and the English.

Despite these extraneous influences, the Maltese have managed to keep their own culture, traditions, and, most of all, their unique language, which is usually classed as a Semitic one but which also has a strong Romantic influence. In the 1920s and 1930s there was considerable controversy about which language should become the official language of Malta—Maltese, English, or Italian. After many years of hot debate, Maltese and English were chosen as the official languages. Today, Maltese is the native language, essentially spoken by all. English is widely spoken, particularly in academic circles, and most Maltese are also proficient in Italian.

Following independence from Britain in 1964, Malta experienced a rapid growth in industrialization and tourism. This was accompanied by an overall improvement in the standard of living of the general population. As often happens, however, these improvements had their repercussions. Those who could not adequately adjust to these changes found themselves being left behind. Nevertheless, Malta's welfare system, initially established in 1947, offered assistance in the form of distribution of social security benefits. In 1948 the Government had, for the first time, introduced "old age pensions and raised the minimum wage. Slum clearance began, essential products were subsidised, and … schools were built" (Tonna, 1993, p. 24).

Since then the welfare system has been continually improved and updated to reflect current needs. Today, benefits both in cash and in kind have been developed. These include subsidies on housing, unemployment benefits, and children's allowances. The children's allowances are intended to assist parents with the costs of rearing their children until they reach school-leaving age. The state also offers a free health service and free schooling.

With an average of 40 million Maltese liri (approximately U.S. $96 million) a year in government expenditure, education in Malta is one of the highest beneficiaries of government funds. However, though considerable progress has been made, certain sectors of the population are still not benefiting fully from education.

EDUCATION IN MALTA

In Malta, all children are required by law to attend school between the ages of five and 16. Free public-sector school education begins in coeducational primary schools, which cater for children aged five through 10. From the age of 11 to 16+, children attend secondary schools. There are separate secondary schools for girls and for boys. For those who wish to pursue their education further, there are state-run 'sixth forms' in schools for 16- to 18- year- olds that prepare students for formal 'advanced level' examinations that are requirements for further training at university, vocational schools, technical institutes, and other centers of adult learning. There is also an autonomously run but state-financed university. At primary, secondary, and sixth form levels there are also private schools, and there are other schools run by the Roman Catholic Church.

There is a public-sector primary school in practically every town and village in the Maltese islands. There are also kindergartens for the younger children (those aged from about three to five), attendance at which is not obligatory. At around the age of 10, children in most public-sector and private schools take an "11+ examination" before proceeding with their studies. The outcome of this examination determines the type of secondary school that a child will attend. In the public-sector school system, children gaining an examination score of at least 50 percent would be assigned to a Junior Lyceum; they would be assigned to a state secondary school if they obtained between 16 percent and 49 percent of the total marks; students obtaining fewer than 15 percent of the total marks would be assigned a place in an "Opportunity Centre." Private schools in Malta have their own systems for arranging student transfers between primary and secondary levels. Some schools automatically promote children from primary school level to secondary school level, others set a competitive entrance examination.

At the age of 15 or 16, students may take their Secondary Examination Certificate (SEC) examinations. These are academically-based examinations that are essential to a student's progression to sixth form or to any other 16+ school, because they are almost always cited as entrance requirements. Success in SEC examinations is also a prerequisite for many job opportunities, particularly those pertaining to clerical appointments with the government or in private industry.

Given that examinations and certification play an important and significant role in an individual's career progression in Malta, it is inevitable that many parents would opt for what they consider to be the best education for their children. Although opinions do differ on whether public-sector or private education is "best," the general perception appears to be that students at church and private schools fare better than their peers at public-sector schools. Zammit Mangion (1992) says that "although most private schools teach the same subjects as are taught in Government schools and prepare students for the same terminal (external) examinations there are still many parents who see in the education provided by private schools an alternative to, and perhaps a better one, or, one which is more to their liking, than that available in Government/State schools, and an education which they would particularly like to give to their children" (Zammit Mangion, 1992, p. 278).

One possible reason for this could be that in many public-sector schools progression through school is age-related. Students are not required to demonstrate comprehension or competence before being promoted to a higher class.

In private schools, this is not always the case, and students may be obliged to repeat the year if they have failed to demonstrate their understanding of the material covered in class. Public-sector schools are obliged to register all school-age children (starting at age 5 years), unlike some private and church schools where a certain amount of choice remains with the school authority. (Schools run by the Roman Catholic Church are bound to take in a certain percentage of their yearly intake from so-called "problem families").

Undoubtedly, the fact remains that the number and complexity of problems in schools is increasing and that the student support services are insufficiently well-staffed to cope with the volume of problems. An example of this is the very small number of school social workers; presently a total complement of seven for the whole of Malta, to deal with a total school population of 62,764 students. This is an average of around 16 schools and 9,000 students per school social worker. These staffing levels place considerable limitations on Maltese school social workers in the proper performance of their task of ensuring that all school age children between the ages of five and 16 "benefit from the best possible education, in the best possible conditions, and to the best of their abilities" (Education Welfare Division, 1996). Staffing levels in the Education Welfare Section have not been increased since 1996, when two new social worker posts were created, despite numerous subsequent requests for additional staff.

There are a total of 5,922 full-time teachers in public-sector, church, and private schools. The majority of these teachers are qualified to at least bachelor of education level, which is a four-year, full-time university program that offers specializations in the various school subjects.

SPECIAL EDUCATION

During the last few years Malta has been striving to adopt an inclusive education policy that offers a chance for children and the school as a whole to assimilate other students who have intellectual, emotional, sensory, or physical difficulties. For this assimilation to take place adequate professional and intensive support must be given to mainstream schools. Once again, in this sphere, lack of adequate human resources prevails, because the special education section of the Education Division is unable to furnish enough teachers to meet every request.

There are, nevertheless, 9 special schools in Malta providing education for approximately 387 students who have significant learning difficulties, multiple physical or sensory disabilities, or other disabilities that prevent them from learning within a normal school environment.

These schools are divided as follows:

- mental impairment, one school
- emotional and behavioral difficulties, one school
- learning difficulties, three schools
- physical impairment, one school
- visual impairment, one school
- hearing impairment, one school
- multiple impairments, one school.

When children are placed at a special school, they become the responsibility of the Special Education Section. A recommendation to place a child in a special school must be made by the Child Development Advisory Unit (CDAU). This unit is based at St Luke's Hospital, which is the main public-sector hospital in Malta. The CDAU, consisting of a multi-disciplinary team, "offers a diagnostic review and placement service to children with special educational needs, with emphasis on early intervention" (Education Division of the Ministry of Education web site). This unit often requests school social workers to undertake a home assessment. Sometimes, these assessments are carried out in liaison with social workers from the Health Department.

The Education Division also provides a peripatetic, one-to-one teaching service provided at the student's home, typically for a temporary period. Generally, recipients of this service include children with severe learning difficulties, children who have school phobia, or children who have disabilities but who are still able to benefit from this service. The school social worker may, from time to time, be asked to visit the home to determine whether home tuition is serving its purpose or whether it is still needed. The social workers carry out the same tasks with special schools as they do with other schools.

SOCIAL PROBLEMS

The Family

Since the end of World War II, the Maltese family has continued to decrease in size. Whereas in the 19th century large families (with six or more children) were Malta's pride, it is now relatively unusual to find families with more than two or three children (Zammit Mangion, 1992). Many factors have been cited as the cause for this, for example, that more women work outside the home, that education has improved, or that people are more materialistic. Another factor that is frequently cited is that, given all these conditions, it seems preferable to provide a good standard of living to one or two children rather than a lower standard of living to a higher number of children.

Marriage, family life, and children are important milestones in the life of the majority of the Maltese. In 1997 a total number of 2,414 marriages were recorded (Central Office of Statistics, 1998). To this one can add the importance that most people give to the home and to work to provide a good life for the family. In Malta, as in other countries, there are also other types of families, including cohabiting couples with and without children, extended families, and single-parent families. During 1997, a total of 356 births to unmarried parents were registered. This was 7.2 percent of the total births for that year (Central Office of Statistics, 1998).

Drug Abuse

In November 1991, Caritas Malta, a church-run agency for treatment of substance abuse, conducted a survey of adolescent drug use in Malta. The research sample surveyed was 26,519 school children, that is, 78.5 percent of students in Form II and upward (students aged between 12 and 18+). All public-sector, church, private secondary, and post-secondary schools were represented. This survey showed that 4.7 percent of respondents said that they had made use of drugs in the year before the survey. The survey pointed out that the most popular drugs were the so-called "soft" drugs such as cannabis. Much fewer respondents admitted to abusing "harder" drugs such as heroin or cocaine.

Whenever a drug problem is identified at a school, the school policy is for the head teacher (principal) immediately to refer the student concerned for professional help and support. In Malta, Caritas and Sedqa (a government-managed organization) are the agencies that provide social work and other therapeutic help to drug users. There is good cooperation between the two agencies and they operate facilities ranging from therapeutic communities to drug dependence units and day-counseling centers.

Child Employment

The Education Welfare Section monitors school attendance and protects children from the risks associated with illegal employment. The social worker is sometimes called upon to give advice to parents, children, and employers on child employment. In the case of families with financial difficulties, helping the family to find a solution is not an easy task, as there are times when there needs to be a change of priorities within the family itself. At times there are cases when the parents believe that it is better, at times certainly cheaper, to have their son or daughter work in the family business, rather than employing an outsider. Here again the family is urged to consider its priorities, especially long-term, about allowing the child to benefit fully from formal education. In these cases, the child is not only missing school; he or she does not possess the necessary work permit, and is not protected by any national insurance cover and therefore would have no legal entitlement to any benefits for any injuries sustained while at work, for paid sick leave, and so on. In such a situation, and where the child is over 15 years and the work set does not put the child in any particular danger, the parents may request a temporary exemption so that the child is given permission to work after school hours. In all cases, the parents are asked to sign their consent to the understanding under which the temporary exemption for part-time work, after school hours, is granted. Children over the age of 15 are also allowed to work during the summer months, when schooling has stopped for the summer recess. Young Maltese people are legally permitted to start working from the age of 16, provided that their 16th birthday does not fall after the beginning of the academic year. In this case, the following school year would have to be completed before he or she could commence work legally.

The Employment and Training Corporation is a government body that monitors places of employment to ensure compliance with all governmental regulations on employment. It is also entrusted with the training and retraining of workers. According to information supplied to the Education Welfare Section by the Inspectorate Section of the Employment and Training Corporation, a total of 79 school-age children were found by the Corporation's inspectors to be working during school hours, without the necessary work permit during 1999. In these cases, the employer is taken to court.

It has sometimes been the case that the social workers from the Education Welfare Section also refer cases to the Employment and Training Corporation inspectorate for investigation. Following discovery of the illegal employment of children, the Employment and Training Corporation would also insist that proceedings be instituted in the criminal courts against the employer. Sanctions include fines and, in the case of repeated offenses, also prison terms.

Relative Poverty

The welfare benefits introduced in 1948 have been constantly improved and emphasis has been laid on developing more and more progressive means of taxation. Many argue that it is impossible, in any country, for all society to move ahead at the same pace and that there will always be those who, for whatever reason, will be left behind. Brearley (1995) says that it is important that these persons be recognized and assisted to overcome their disadvantage, which may not necessarily be of a strictly financial nature. She argues that social work should be proactive and that social workers should be in a position to advocate for, and thereby be agents of, change. Recognizing this, Maltese social workers have recently established the Malta Association of Social Workers, with a current membership of 85 members, to promote and articulate their point of view. To date, the association has mainly dealt with issues concerning social work in general rather than school social work specifically.

THE DEVELOPMENT OF SCHOOL SOCIAL WORK

In October 1946, when Malta was still a British colony, Governor E.C.A. Schreiber issued a proclamation enforcing compulsory education for children aged six to 14 years for the whole of Malta and Gozo. As a result, school attendance officers were engaged with the sole purpose of enforcing compulsory education.

On 23 August 1974, the Education Act No. XXXIX, gave the Minister of Education the power to "make provision for the appointment, conditions of employment, duties and powers of Education Welfare Officers... including provisions for empowering (them) to visit children at home ... and make other enquiries notwithstanding the objection of their parents." This Act, together with other subsequent amendments, saw to the gradual development from school attendance officers to education welfare officers who were, in fact, now increasingly assuming the role of school social workers.

The years following the 1974 Act saw also a steady increase in the certification of education welfare officers. It was only in February 1993, however, that all welfare officers in Malta, including the education welfare officers, were given the title of social workers. In fact, that year is a very important milestone in generic and school social work services in Malta because a collective agreement was signed between the government and union representatives of social workers.

Through this collective agreement, welfare officers who possessed at minimum, a diploma in social work, were designated as social workers. Furthermore, for this one time only, welfare officers who did not possess any qualifications relevant to social work were given similar status although all newly appointed staff would be required to hold the recognized license to practice, the Diploma in Social Work.

The Education Welfare Section within the Education Division was established in 1989. Previously, the office of the Education Welfare Section was situated at the Centru Hidma Socjali (a generic social work agency) within the Department for Social Services. In this way, school social work was given an important priority and the service was transferred to its modern, state-of-the-art offices at Floriana, on the outskirts of Valletta. Emphasis was made on finding a location that offered easy car parking and was very central and accessible to the public at large.

The Diploma in Social Work is a three-year, part-time qualification awarded by the University of Malta, which consists of 36 academic credit-units covering psychology, sociology, and social work. The course also has four practice placements during which the student is tested in various social work practice skills: observation, assessment, intervention, and evaluation. At the end of the course the student is required to submit a 10,000-word dissertation on a topic relating to social work issues. Each credit-unit consists of 14 hours of lectures, three small-group tutorials, and is usually assessed through both a written test and an assignment. Other qualifications in social work offered by the university include a four-year, full-time bachelor degree.

Under the collective agreement, the following structure was adopted for social workers in Malta:

- principal social worker
- senior social worker
- accredited social worker
- registered social worker II
- registered social worker I.

In accordance with the collective agreement, the main (state) employers of social workers in Malta, the Welfare Department, and the Education Department, are required to organize and deliver training courses for their employees. One such course is the Certificate in Social Work Management organized in liaison with the University of Malta. Completion of this two-year, part-time course is a requirement for progression to the grades of senior social worker and principal social worker.

Perhaps the most important development since the signing of the collective agreement and the change in name from welfare officers to social workers has been the increase in professional awareness. Though social work is not, as yet, formally recognized as a profession (draft legislation to this effect is pending in parliament), its members have progressed by creating and undergoing changes leading to increased professionalism. The school social workers are continually adding to their knowledge through further study and research and through forming contacts and partnerships with other agencies abroad. In-service training is regularly organized and each social worker is encouraged to attend seminars and courses related to social work.

School Social Work Role

In the last few years there has also been a marked change in the role of the school social worker. Whereas, some years ago, the accent of the welfare officer's work was based on trying to ensure that children attend school, school social workers currently use a range of social work methods to help resolve problems leading to absenteeism. In fact, nowadays, absenteeism from school is no longer regarded as the problem itself but rather the result of other issues. It is, therefore, these issues that are being addressed. The school social worker is attempting to adopt a home-school-community focus by being proactive and by proposing and working toward bringing about pertinent changes to families, schools, and other social institutions. School social workers also are actively engaged in meetings with the judiciary, the police, the Employment and Training Corporation, the Medical Association of Malta, local councils, and others. These are part of a planned effort to change systems that are either outdated or not functioning. It is hoped that these changes, when effected, will be beneficial to the education system as a whole.

The school social workers consider that, whereas it will always be important to build helping relationships with individuals and families, they will increasingly have to work in the community if they are to fight injustice and bring about meaningful social change. This is because the child is sometimes unfairly blamed for not participating in schooling, as is very evident in cases when the system does not fit the child. There are cases when students who do not cope at a particular stage will forever find themselves in difficulty because insufficient time is dedicated at school to their particular needs. It is no wonder, therefore, that these students often start missing school, at times even staying away for long periods of time. The school social worker will, in these cases, try to advocate in favor of these students for help to be provided. The school social worker is the link between the student, the student's family, and the school, and as such has to group these and other resources together so that a solution in favor of the student is found.

The last 10 years have seen gradual but very important changes in school social work:

- All school social workers now have to be fully qualified at least to diploma level.
- Awareness of the need for social workers has continued to grow among teachers, medical staff, lawyers, other professionals, and most parents.
- The school social workers have themselves embarked on a continuous phase of changes aimed at providing a more effective service to clients, including staff training, attending talks and seminars, and developing a library with updated and recent publications.
- There is an ongoing interest in research, including supervision of undergraduate students in their theses and undertaking research projects to evaluate service provision.
- A list of rules, regulations, and procedures to ensure that common policies are understood and adopted by all Maltese school social workers have been formulated (Pace, 1995).
- Continuing professional development is encouraged by peer support and by encouraging case discussions among school social workers.

The role of the school social workers in the Education Welfare Section is twofold: first, they prosecute parents who fail to send their children to school; and second, they intervene, as necessary, to assist children through home visits, school visits, and taking up other purposeful engagements to encourage children to take a meaningful interest in their schooling and education. In other words, they adopt what are sometimes classed as both care and control roles.

Current school social work practice puts emphasis on research as a necessary and integral part of its development. One such example consisted of a survey on absenteeism in public-sector secondary schools during 1997 and 1998 to investigate the reasons for poor attendance (Education Welfare Section, 1999). The survey found that several categories of children were especially prone to poor school attendance:

- children in families under stress;
- children in families who do not value the importance of schooling and who therefore do not encourage their children's attendance;
- children living in families who have family-run businesses, particularly small shops and small enterprises;
- children who have a sick family member; and
- children who have a learning difficulty.

As a consequence of this research, "Project Focus" (Education Welfare Section, 1999) was subsequently carried out to identify where the need for school social work services was most acute. Given that the previous research pointed out that one-sixth of all the state secondary schools studied accounted for 53 percent of the total absenteeism rate, the Project Focus research concentrated on these particular schools. It was found that, together with the high rate of absenteeism, these schools also had a high concentration of other social problems, including parents who were drug users, dysfunctional families, and parents who had little respect for the importance of schooling. It was therefore decided that, for one academic year, the seven school social workers would concentrate their efforts primarily on these schools. This would serve as an evaluative framework for the effectiveness of their services.

At the time of writing, the process of evaluating this project is underway. Already there are heartening signs of a good measure of success. After only a few months of social work intervention, this project has led to a very good percentage of former absentee students returning to school. That some of these students previously had a long record of sporadic school attendance seems to point to a continued use of this kind of intervention, especially for the near future.

For the last two years, the Education Welfare Section has run a yearly summer school for children during the summer vacation. Based on promoting the concept that "learning is fun," the school has consisted of a series of activities based on systems of informal learning and creating discussion groups centered on various topics. University students who wish to work at the summer school receive a government grant, and are required to befriend children and to encourage them to take an active interest in schooling. Home visits by a social worker would accompany the summer school project whenever the need was felt or to carry on working with cases that were already open.

Another area of responsibility of the school social worker is that of working with children who display difficult behavior. A very important task here is that of helping the teacher who is in daily contact with these children. Intervention should preferably be preventive in that the school social worker should advise teaching staff about ways of identifying behavior change, and subsequently, ways of dealing with difficult behavior.

Quite a common problem is that some parents are not aware of, or do not fully understand, their responsibility regarding their children's formal education. During their numerous home visits, school social workers are often faced by parents who take their children's school nonattendance very lightly. There have been cases when the reason given for children's nonattendance was that they are not "good for school" because they are "ignorant."

Another issue approached by social workers is that of organizing and delivering talks to teachers. These are intended to raise awareness of social work interventions and are oriented to explaining the different situations that school social workers meet during home visits. During these talks, it is normal practice for case studies to be presented so that real-life material can be used to elicit deeper understanding of the different situations experienced by children. It is hoped that in this way teachers will be in a better position to identify any behavior changes in their students and make appropriate referrals to school social workers. The school social workers keep in close touch with the schools through frequent visits and meetings with the school staff to tackle problems as soon as they crop up.

The policy of improving school attendance levels is advanced by school social workers undertaking the following steps:

- in conjunction with schools, identifying cases of nonattendance that necessitate further action;
- assessing the circumstances that have led to the irregular school attendance, identifying causes, and other significant factors that may assist in resolving the problems;
- planning appropriate action together with the child, the family, the school, or any other agency to resolve the problems;
- implementing a plan of action to support the child and the family in overcoming their difficulties;
- evaluating the outcome and, together with the family and child, reassess the situation; and
- initiating prosecution in cases when it is evident that social work intervention has not been effective in resolving attendance problems and when no reasonable justification for the student's absence from school is provided.

School social workers also participate in various boards and commissions within the Education Division. One of these is the anti-bullying program, which was set up in 1996 to curb bullying in schools. The board responsible for the anti-bullying program believes that bullying can only be fought if the efforts of administrators, teachers, parents, and children are coordinated. It therefore advocates the setting up of a systematic structure to promote appropriate children's behavior and to handle bullying when it occurs. Referrals to school social workers and to school psychologists can be made when the case warrants it. In other instances, it is possible for a child to be prosecuted, on the insistence of the head teacher, should the bullying have serious repercussions on the victim. Usually, however, a special officer chosen from among the teaching staff will deal with the case directly at school. In this way the problem will be dealt with on the spot, in the shortest time possible, and by a person knowledgeable of that school's particular environment. It is suggested that "the school should, and in most cases will, be concerned to deal effectively with this sort of trouble as quickly as possible, before it becomes entrenched" (Lawson, 1994, p. 25).

When a school-aged child perpetrates a criminal act and the act is brought to the attention of the police, they have the discretion, particularly regarding less serious offenses and minor contraventions, not to prosecute. In such cases, it is customary practice for the police to refer the child to the Education Welfare Section to offer social work intervention. During this intervention, the school social worker will periodically report back to the police to provide information about the child's progress.

With more serious offenses, including violence against another person, damage to property, theft, or perjury, the police ordinarily arraign a child before the juvenile court. A school social worker sits on the board within the juvenile court to advise the court on matters concerning the child's education. The school social worker may also intervene in such cases, particularly if the child has a problem with school attendance. The school social worker also may be called on to provide written reports to the court, and to work in cooperation with competent persons (for example, other professionals, schools, and the child's family) to prevent further delinquency.

Furthermore, the school social workers offer support, counsel, and advice to a variety of clients in different circumstances by responding:

- to requests for help from individual children on numerous matters including problems at school, bullying, and relationship difficulties;
- to inquiries from parents who are in need of advice or support; and
- to requests from head teachers and school staff, about matters relating either directly or indirectly to the students in their care, and from other agencies.

Issues for Future Direction

This chapter has considered the structure of education in Malta and how school social work is involved in the system—an involvement that is geared to promoting the success and continued development of education for the benefit of all school-age children.

The rapid economic growth that has occurred in Malta recently has brought about a general improvement in the standard of living of the Maltese. In today's society, more people own their own home, have cars, and own all that is seen as necessary for comfortable living. In order to maintain this style of living people, at times, have to take on extra jobs. The number of women employed outside the home is also on the increase.

However, this development has also had detrimental effects on certain groups in society such as the family, older people, youth, and children (who perhaps have been the hardest hit). School social workers, being in close daily contact with school-age children and their families, are witness to the increasing number of people in need of social work intervention, a demand that is growing faster by far than the increase in school social worker establishment.

The shortage of school social workers is not simply because of the scarcity of supply of skilled workers, but is also a result of recruitment policies. Too often, also, advertisements of vacancies have followed recruitment activities undertaken by other agencies, with the result that either other agencies (even including those subsidized by government) recruit the bulk of qualified social workers or other potential recruits find alternative employment, such as teaching, where posts are often more readily available.

In March 1990, the Ministry for Social Policy published a book entitled *A Caring Society in a Changing World: Proposals for a Social Welfare Strategy for the Nineties and Beyond*. In his foreword to this book, former Minister for Social Policy, Dr. Louis Galea, wrote "I want to emphasise that the best criteria for measuring the quality of service in the social area are not so much the amount of money spent, but rather the competence and dedication of those who give the service to people in need. Therefore, the outcome of this strategy depends on the extent to which society succeeds in encouraging young people to dedicate themselves to the challenges offered by this work - work which gives great satisfaction."

This statement undoubtedly holds true for the new millennium. It is hoped that the human resources issue will be taken up as soon as possible to increase the establishment of school social workers and improve the services currently being provided and enable new services to be set up.

The human resources issue is being stressed very strongly because this is closely linked to other issues in school social work in Malta; issues that have to be addressed in the very near future if our clients are to continue receiving the best possible services that social work can offer.

An area that needs further expansion (but that is dependent on the employment of more school social workers) is preventive work, especially with primary-school-aged children. The school social workers are very much aware of the importance of this work. Although the Project Focus initiative showed that a small number of secondary schools accounted for a large proportion of absenteeism and that social work intervention had to focus primarily on those schools, it has also been decided that priority should be given to intervention at primary level. It is, however, very frustrating to know that while preventive work is of paramount importance, this cannot as yet be fully undertaken because of a shortage of staff. Furthermore, the longer this situation prevails, the more difficult the situation will become, unfortunately to the detriment of our students and society at large.

Another issue that needs to be addressed in the very near future concerns provisions in the Education Act of 1988 relating to penalties in cases of repeated noncompliance with the law regarding parents' duty to ensure that their child attends school regularly. The original scope of the penalties was to serve as a deterrent for those who do not send their children to school without any valid reason. The experiences of school social workers indicate that, in most cases, the fines imposed by the court are not serving the purpose for which they were established. It seems also that, even when these provisions are applied according to "the letter of the law," which states that parents should be fined Lm1 for every school day missed by their child, any improvement in school attendance is minimal. At this stage, one has to ask whether it is time to find alternative measures that would be more effective in combating absenteeism (for example, having an adequate number of school social workers involved in preventive and other social work intervention). Some argue that cases should be referred to court only as a last resort, after all efforts to find the causes are assessed and all possible remedies tried.

It is the aim of the Education Welfare Section to continue to identify those areas that are in need of social work intervention. The Project Focus described in this chapter was precisely one such exercise at pinpointing priority areas, to ensure that school social work services evolve in tandem with clients' needs and that limited resources are deployed most effectively. An advantage of participating in Project Focus has been the detection of a number of students who are regular school attenders, but who nevertheless appear to be experiencing difficulties of various sorts. Instances of disruptive behavior, neglect, problems with learning, and others, have come to the forefront and have been dealt with by the school social workers. Previously, when each school social worker had to deal with an average of 16 schools, these cases were often overlooked because of excessive pressure of work.

Research, such as the Project Focus initiative, has also provided evidence of the need for more group work with teachers, parents, and students. This new service has been started and has been very well-received by all.

Furthermore, research data are being used to advocate for changes with the policy makers at the Education Division. It is hoped that, with the development of increased research and information technology skills, further relevant research will be undertaken.

School social work is a continually changing and evolving profession. The Education Welfare Section started from a very small office at the Welfare Department and then moved on to large and client-friendly offices in the Education Division. Tasks have evolved from being those of basically checking attendance and effecting prosecution to school social work practiced by qualified social workers.

School social workers perform a brokerage role, informing students and parents of the different educational (and other) resources available; an enabler role, to encourage clients to be active participants in their learning; an advocate role, to approach school staff on behalf of parents or children, or to approach parents or children on behalf of school staff; and teacher (or role-model) who speaks to children and their families in the comfort of their own homes. Given that school social work has important roles to play in mediating between parents, teachers, students, and other competent professionals, it is important that it is further developed using the most up-to-date knowledge and skills.

REFERENCES

Brearley, J. (1995). *Counselling and social work*. Buckingham: Open University Press.

Caritas Malta (1991). *Survey on adolescent drug use in Malta*. Malta: Caritas Malta.

Central Office of Statistics (1998). Maltese Government web site. e-mail cos@magnet.com

Central Office of Statistics (1999). Maltese Government web site. e-mail cos@magnet.com

Education Division of the Ministry of Education. http://www.education.gov.mt

Education Welfare Section (1996). *Mission statement of school social workers*. Unpublished report, Education Division, Floriana.

Education Welfare Section (1999). *Project Focus*. Unpublished report, Education Division, Floriana.

Lawson, S. (1994). *Helping children cope with bullying*. London: Sheldon Press.

Ministry for Social Policy (1990). *A caring society in a changing world: Proposals for a social welfare strategy for the nineties and beyond*. Valetta: Interprint.

Pace, G. (1995). *Procedures, rules and regulations governing school social work at the Education Welfare Section*. Unpublished manual, Education Division, Floriana.

Tonna, B. (1993). *Malta Trends*. Valetta: The Signs of the Times-Institute for Research on the Signs of the Times Media Centre.

Zammit Mangion, J. (1992). *Education in Malta*. Valletta: Studia Editions, Social Action Movement.

Author's acknowledgement: I wish to thank my fellow school social workers, Francis Chircop, Rosemary Ellul, Carmen Buttigieg, and Damian Spiteri for their support in compiling this chapter.

10 SCHOOL SOCIAL WORK IN HUNGARY AND OTHER COUNTRIES IN CENTRAL AND EASTERN EUROPE: SUPPORTING CHILDREN IN A PERIOD OF SOCIETAL TRANSFORMATION

Isadora Hare

Social Indicators* — Hungary	
Population	9,917,000
Percentage under age 15 years	17
Percentage urban (2000)	64
Life expectancy at birth	67.8 men, 76.1 women
Fertility rate	1.20 children per woman
Percentage of illiterate adults (2000)	0.5 men, 0.8 women
Per capita GDP in $U.S. (1999)	4,813
Percentage unemployed (1997)	7.0

*Social Indicators. From the Statistics Division of the United Nations. Refer to notes on page 249.
Reference: http://www.un.org/Depts/unsd/indicators/indic2a.htm

In attempting to describe the practice of social work in schools in this large area of the globe, one must remember that there are numerous countries in the region, each with differing characteristics and populations. They are grouped together because they share a history of communist rule characterized by totalitarianism, planned economies, and rigid social structures that collapsed during the last decade, giving way to emerging democratic, free-market systems of political and economic organization. This represents a change of gargantuan proportions; therefore, the region must be described as being in a transitional phase in which social institutions are still in a state of flux. Schools and social support services delivered to children and families in this context are prime examples of institutions still in a state of constant change. This has major implications for social work practice in schools both in Hungary and other countries in the region.

REGIONAL OVERVIEW

Research into this region is greatly facilitated by the work done in recent years by the United Nations Children's Fund (UNICEF) through its International Child Development Center (ICDC). Also known as the Innocenti Center, it was established in 1988 with core funding from the Italian government to serve as a specialized research and training facility. Since 1992 the center, with additional funding from UNICEF and the World Bank, has been engaged in a project that monitors and analyzes social conditions and public policy affecting children and their families in Central and Eastern Europe. The Regional (MONEE) Project has produced a series of regional monitoring reports on health, social, and educational trends affecting children in the region.

DESCRIPTION OF THE REGION

In a major report on children at risk in Central and Eastern Europe, the MONEE Project includes 18 countries in this region, identifying five main geographic sub-regions:

- Central Europe, comprising the Czech Republic and Slovakia (formerly Czechoslovakia), Hungary, Poland, and Slovenia (5 countries);
- South Eastern Europe, comprising Albania, Bulgaria, and Romania (3 countries);
- The Baltic States, comprising Estonia, Latvia, and Lithuania (3 countries);
- The Western Commonwealth of Independent States (CIS) comprising Belarus, Moldova, Russia, and Ukraine (4 countries); and
- The Caucasian countries, comprising Armenia, Azerbaijan, and Georgia (3 countries).

The child population in this region numbers 100 million (United Nations Children's Fund International Child Development Center, 1997b, p. 3).

If nine additional countries are considered, namely the four independent countries formerly comprising Yugoslavia and all five Central Asian countries formerly part of the Soviet Union (Kazakhstan, Kyrgyzstan, Tajikistan, Turkmenistan, and Uzbekistan), the population of children in this vast region rises to 115 million (United Nations Children's Fund International Child Development Center, 1998, p. vii).

After summarizing trends in the region as a whole, this chapter will focus on Hungary, a well-developed country in Central Europe and, more briefly, on six other countries located in Central Europe, South Eastern Europe, the Baltic area, and the Western CIS: Estonia, Lithuania, Poland, Slovakia, Romania, and Russia. However, generalizations based on the wide range of countries and data inevitably involve simplification and some distortion, and interested readers are encouraged to pursue the topics further. These six countries were selected because of the participation of their social workers in international forums and the availability of relevant data.

SOCIOPOLITICAL AND ECONOMIC BACKGROUND

"The communist experiment in Europe, which ended at the beginning of the 1990s after five decades in Central and South-Eastern Europe and the Baltic countries and seven decades in the rest of the former Soviet Union, was perhaps the most grandiose effort in the history of mankind to alter radically social conditions and basic social institutions" (United Nations Children's Fund International Child Development Center, 1997a, p. 16). In its initial years, war, immigration, hunger, and other family and social dislocations produced very negative effects on children. As the authoritarian regimes stabilized and were extended to other parts of the continent, policies such as political repression, collectivization, migration, the disruption of small communities, and a single-minded focus on planned economic growth produced societies that discounted the humanity of their citizens, both adults and children.

Nevertheless, these governments with their rigid and centralized control did create social institutions and systems that in some ways promoted the welfare of children and families. Communist countries were able to reduce several child health risks and to develop education systems whose standards were comparable to those of Western countries. They provided better employment opportunities for women and broader pre-school and child care coverage than most free-market industrialized countries. Under socialism, artificially-maintained full employment made joblessness virtually unknown. Free public health care and compulsory education were provided, as was a wide range of free subsidized benefits such as pre-school care, kindergartens, child care leave, school lunches, and after-school and vacation programs. These made it easier for families to meet both their child care and work responsibilities and helped children to maintain minimally required levels of nutrition and development. Housing was inexpensive, although of low quality. The maintenance of law and order behind the Iron Curtain curbed juvenile crime, substance abuse, homelessness, and child prostitution, though these were never totally eliminated (United Nations Children's Fund International Child Development Center, 1997a, p. 22).

Serious problems remained, such as high abortion and maternal mortality rates, unfavorable male mortality, persistent infant mortality, and environmental degradation. In general, despite an extensive network of centrally controlled institutions, these countries manifested "an inhumane approach to the disabled, deprived, delinquent, and vulnerable, whether children or adults" (United Nations Children's Fund International Child Development Center, 1997a, p. 16).

However, the political and economic revolutions during the 1990s have produced massive and sudden changes, including political fragmentation, economic crises, and, in some countries, vicious warfare resulting from extreme nationalism and ethnic intolerance. Children have been particularly vulnerable to the processes occurring within this transitional phase.

While the market forces operating during this period are empowering individuals and liberating human initiative and energy, balanced development requires support from societal values and social institutions. However, the old societal infrastructure has collapsed to a large extent and values have eroded, and it will take time for new institutions to develop. The shifting emphasis away from state-sponsored income redistribution and job security provisions toward market allocation of resources has increased income inequalities, child poverty, and reduced access to child-care, health, and education services. As the UNICEF Report states:

"For children ... the period known in history as the transition will have meant a childhood with their nutrition, health, education, and emotional needs left unmet, and their development neglected to differing degrees and often put on the wrong track" (United Nations Children's Fund International Child Development Center, 1997a, p. 16).

DEMOGRAPHIC TRENDS

In each of the 18 countries in the region, marriage, remarriage, and fertility rates fell steeply during the period from 1991 to 1996. Marriage and remarriage rates have plunged the most in the Baltic and Caucasian countries (where in some cases the number of marriages has dropped by half). Among the countries in the western part of the CIS the drop in marriage rates has been the greatest in Russia (23 percent) (United Nations Children's Fund International Child Development Center, 1997a, p. 13).

The divorce rate has also increased considerably in Central and Eastern European countries. In Russia, Belarus, Moldova, Slovakia, and Estonia, the increase has been particularly significant; and in Estonia in 1995, more divorces than marriages took place.

Fertility has also decreased by between one-quarter and one-third in most countries, particularly Latvia, Estonia, and Armenia. Reductions have been less in Albania, Hungary, and Slovenia (United Nations Children's Fund International Child Development Center, 1997a, p. 13). However, accompanying the drops in fertility, there have been sharp rises in the proportion of births to teenage and to older unmarried mothers in a number of countries. For example, the figure has risen from approximately 12 percent to 20 percent in both Hungary and Russia, and from 25 percent to nearly 45 percent in Estonia (United Nations Children's Fund International Child Development Center, 1997b, p. 9).

Morbidity and mortality among adults have major implications for the well-being of children. The loss of a parent increases the risk that a young child will be placed in public care. Even older youth who are dependent on family stability and resources face risks (United Nations Children's Fund International Child Development Center, 1997a, p. 39). This region has experienced an overall deterioration in adult health and an unprecedented increase in premature mortality among working-age males, so much so that extensive international attention has been directed toward this phenomenon. The increase in mortality during the 1990s has been so severe that average male life expectancy at birth has dropped below 65 years in seven countries, and below 60 years in Russia and Latvia. "The mortality rate for men aged 40–49 in 1995 was twice that in 1989. The gap between male and female life expectancy in Russia is now larger than in any other country in the world" (United Nations Children's Fund International Child Development Center, 1997b, p. 3).

These demographic trends represent major changes in family formation and maintenance. It seems clear that the "huge pressures of the transition, including those from unemployment and reduced incomes, appear to be splitting families apart" (United Nations Children's Fund International Child Development Center, 1997b, p. 8). Larger numbers of children are being placed at risk physically, economically, and socially.

MAJOR SOCIAL PROBLEMS AFFECTING CHILDREN

During the so-called "golden age" of socialism it was assumed that the state largely provided for the needs of children. The only children considered at risk were those who were orphans or were abused, and the chief method of care for them was placement in large institutions where it was assumed they received adequate care. In fact, it was often considered that institutional care was preferable to life with parents considered neglectful, and therefore contact with parents was discouraged. However, after the Berlin Wall fell in 1989, a different picture of state care emerged, particularly as it was expressed through institutional care. The details of the grim and inhumane conditions exposed, especially in Romanian orphanages, reverberated throughout the world.

A decade after the Velvet Revolutions, however, it is clear that children in most parts of Central and Eastern Europe are at increased risk from a number of factors. These include the following five factors:

1. **Poverty:** During the transition years, poverty has grown considerably in all countries, but most severely in countries of the former Soviet Union. With few exceptions, child poverty has risen more than overall poverty rates, and over time seems to be concentrated among certain groups. Many parents, in the attempt to compensate for sharp drops in income

coming from lower wages and fewer child-related allowances, participate in the "gray economy" (United Nations Children's Fund International Child Development Center, 1997a, p. 8), working at second jobs or even engaging in illegal activities (Ferge, 1996; Hare, 1993, p. 18). This can result in child neglect or maltreatment, and the inappropriate use of child labor to supplement family income, which in turn contributes to truancy and school dropout (United Nations Children's Fund International Child Development Center, 1997a, p. 55).

2. **Environmental Damage and Pollution:** Industrial, agricultural, and energy policies during the communist era ignored the environmental and health risks involved in rapid economic growth. Children are particularly vulnerable to the ill-effects of such environmental degradation.

3. **Morbidity and Mortality Among Children:** While child mortality indicators in the region do not reflect the extent of social and economic dislocation, there has been an increase in undernutrition and in the incidence of diseases of poverty, particularly infectious diseases such as diphtheria and tuberculosis. The prevalence of disabilities has also increased. These include congenital malformations and disabling conditions resulting from accidental injuries.

4. **Risk Behaviors Among Youth:** The increased freedom in the countries of the region has unfortunately brought new risk behaviors to adolescents and young adults that are characteristic of Western societies. These include alcohol and drug abuse, sexually transmitted diseases, and suicide. According to UNICEF: "The heightened profile of these problems among Central and East European youth may be linked not only to new freedoms and risk taking, but to the increased responsibilities and hardships faced by young people and to the inadequate institutional or societal response to these problems. ... Traditional social controls have weakened, and institutions that would enable a measured response to these problems are still relatively underdeveloped" (United Nations Children's Fund International Child Development Center, 1997a, pp. 47–48). Mortality among adolescents resulting from accidents, poisoning, and violence has also increased.

5. **Crime Rates Among Youth:** Historically, crime rates in the region were low. However, the lifting of social and political controls, along with disintegrating public order and the deteriorating economic situation, has led to a rapid increase in criminal activity both among adults and juveniles. A large proportion of reported juvenile crimes are crimes against property, such as theft and burglary, but violent crimes are also increasing in many countries. Murders committed by juveniles have increased dramatically in Russia, Latvia, and Lithuania. Juvenile homicide rates are up to eight times higher in Russia and the Baltic countries than in Central Europe (United Nations Children's Fund International Child Development Center, 1997b, pp. 11–12).

EDUCATIONAL SYSTEMS AND ISSUES

During the communist era, despite differences among individual countries in the region, schools in most countries succeeded in providing universal access to eight years or more of free basic education (primary and lower secondary schooling). This produced widespread literacy in the population and outstanding levels of gender equity (United Nations Children's Fund International Child Development Center, 1998, p. 20).

The quality of education was also ranked high because of the high performance of children from certain countries in the region on international standardized tests, particularly in mathematics and science (TIMSS – Third International Mathematics and Science Study). However, these tests measured only a small part of learning achievement and of educational quality in general. UNICEF's evaluation of the region's school systems at the end of the 1980s was that "children accumulated a lot of knowledge, but were relatively weak (in comparison with children in Western countries) in *applying* this knowledge in new situations....This weakness is a serious problem in the effort to realize a type of economy and society that requires more flexibility from individuals then [*sic*] did the planned system" (United Nations Children's Fund International Child Development Center, 1998, p. 31).

Further, the rigid and authoritarian methods of teaching involving rote-learning and the teacher dominance characteristic of the socialist system fail to stimulate children, meet their overall needs, or equip them with the judgment and decision-making skills necessary in a market economy and democratic system of government. As John Micklewright, Head of ICDC Research, has stated, "schools were far from having the 'child centered' focus envisaged in the UN Convention on the Rights of the Child" (United Nations Children's Fund International Child Development Center, 1998, p. viii).

In general, the structure of the educational system from the preschool to upper secondary level usually comprised the following three types of schools:

1. Preschool education at two levels:
   (a) Crèches or nurseries for infants and children under three, often located at places of work;
   (b) Kindergartens for children from three to approximately six that served both custodial and developmental functions.
2. Compulsory schooling, often called basic or elementary schooling, in general lasted eight years from ages six or seven to 14 or 15. Often this was divided at about age 10 into primary and lower secondary levels.

3. Secondary education (often called upper secondary) was divided into three types of schools:
   (a) General secondary schools, also known as gymnasia or lycées, offering a four-year program of academic study that prepared students for tertiary education
   (b) Technical schools offering three- to five-year programs leading to a diploma and the possibility of further studies in areas such as medicine and engineering
   (c) Vocational schools providing specialized and limited vocational training for specific occupations. Many countries also offered vocational programs combined with academic courses, permitting access to higher education (United Nations Children's Fund International Child Development Center, 1998, p. 21).

Educational reform in the region since the 1990s has had to take place in the context of huge economic and social change. While the economies of most countries are now growing, the total size of the economic pie has shrunk, limiting the ability of governments and families to finance school costs. Further, the pie is divided up in such a way as to increase inequality, and the amount of government revenue available to finance public services such as education has fallen. While in some countries there have been positive changes in the educational system, ranging from curriculum reform to the production of new textbooks, there have also been negative results. Key trends in education reflect the following:

- The general level and quality of education has declined. Teacher pay and morale have fallen, and buildings and equipment in many countries are in disrepair.
- The costs to families of educating children have risen, often sharply. Fees charged for kindergartens have increased, and in some countries fees have been introduced for upper-secondary schools.
- Enrollment and attendance have often dropped, especially in the less-developed parts of the region.
- Educational disparities have increased. The development of elite, better-funded, upper secondary schools and private schools increases choice for children from wealthier families, but places other children at a disadvantage.
- The national examination systems in the region require reform. Currently, the main school-leaving qualifications typically have almost no social, employment, or mobility value (United Nations Children's Fund International Child Development Center, 1998, p. 34).
- While many young people face unemployment on leaving school, there is some evidence that the positive effect of education on earnings has risen.
- Children worst affected by educational developments include ethnic minorities, those in rural areas or small villages, children caught up in wars caused by ethnic strife, and children from low-income families.

Health and Social Issues and Services in Schools, and the Current Status of School Social Work

One of the strongest features of schools during the communist period was the provision of extracurricular activities and social and health-related services in the schools, which at most required nominal financial contributions from parents. These included the provision of subsidized meals at school, health care, and after-school activities. Many kinds of recreational activities were also provided both after school and during vacations. In some school districts subsidized boarding schools existed particularly for children from rural villages and small towns (United Nations Children's Fund International Child Development Center, 1998, pp. 35–36).

Writing particularly about Hungary, Judit Lannert states: "Cultural, sporting, and recreational activities all played an equally important role in the socialist order and were provided at low or no cost to all members of society, but especially to children and youth. Such activities ranged from local community centers offering an enormous variety of cultural recreational activities to specialized camp programs for children and youth..., many of which undeniably had a very strong propaganda component but nonetheless provided a wealth of opportunities for promoting both the mental and psychical health of the nation's youth" (Hungarian National Committee for UNICEF, 1998, p. 271).

The case of Poland illustrates the reduction in access to such "wraparound" services, and other states manifest similar trends. Some of the changes are the result of increased fees for extracurricular services. Access to preventive medical care has dropped. In Poland, schools are no longer the point of contact between children and physicians and dentists. Children are expected to visit medical centers in the areas where they live. This has been associated with a decline in regular checkups. The percentage of children in Poland receiving subsidized meals dropped from 20 percent in 1990 to 6 percent in 1995 (United Nations Children's Fund International Child Development Center, 1998, p. 36).

Hungary was one of the few countries that maintained the percentage of students receiving meals at school at almost 60 percent between 1989 and 1996 (United Nations Children's Fund International Child Development Center, 1997a, p. 37).

As UNICEF comments: "If schools are seen as places where the welfare and development of children are to be nurtured in a variety of ways, then any decline in the social support supplied through the educational system marks a major move in the wrong direction" (United Nations Children's Fund International Child Development Center, 1998, p. 36).

The private sector is assuming some of the functions that formerly were supplied by education ministries. In Poland, Hungary, the Czech Republic, Slovenia, and Slovakia, for example, many private entities now provide recreational activities. However, these are available only to higher-income families, thereby increasing disparities in the society (United Nations Children's Fund International Child Development Center, 1998, p. 55).

What is the place of school social work against this backdrop of societal and educational change and demographic trends? While in certain countries such as the former Czechoslovakia and Hungary, social work practice existed before World War II, after the war the communist regimes terminated the profession and training for practice for ideological and political reasons. As Talyigás and Hegyesi have stated: "According to the ideological explanation, a socialist system is devoid of deprivation, an adequate institutional network can prevent crime and deviance, and illnesses can be reduced. For these reasons, poverty was not to be analyzed and described, and social work as a profession was not to be mentioned" (Talyigás & Hegyesi, 1992, pp. 64–65).

In spite of this ideology, various forms of related activities emerged during the communist period and afterward. These activities are performed by persons with a variety of professional backgrounds, and with a variety of titles. Translated into English, these titles include "social organizer," "curator," and "animator," but the title and concept closest to social work is that of "social pedagogue". Social workers from the United States and Britain in general know little about social pedagogy, but various forms of this concept and practice exist both in Western Europe and in many countries in the former Soviet bloc. As international contacts proliferated during the 1990s, Anglo-Saxon social workers began to learn more about social pedagogy, and began to struggle with defining the relationship between the differing concepts of social pedagogy in different countries, and with the relationship between social pedagogy and social work, as it has developed over the last century in the English-speaking countries around the globe.

Initially, it seemed that social pedagogy might be synonymous with school social work, since the term "pedagogy" in English is closely associated with education and teaching. However, this proved to be an oversimplification, because in different countries in both Western and Eastern Europe the terms "social pedagogy" or "social education" referred to a variety of philosophies and activities practiced in various settings. Problems of understanding arose in the translation of titles and concepts, and were compounded by differing frames of reference and traditions. Over time, for example, it became clear that social pedagogy in the Russian sense was not school social work as such, but rather a type of community-based social work practiced in housing projects and elsewhere, comparable to community center, settlement house, and case management activities (Zlotnik, 1992, p. 14). Other conceptions of social pedagogy embrace work in residential institutional settings such as prisons, children's homes, and mental hospitals (Switzerland) or work done in recreational settings (The Rectors Conference of National Institutes for Social Educators [Denmark], 1995). The latter work is similar to earlier concepts used in the United States, such as "social group work".

The relationship between social work, social pedagogy, and the specialized practice of school social work is complex and needs further study and clarification. As Malcolm Payne has stated, "In different countries, the boundaries of what might be described as social work vary. ... Settings [and methods] overlap" (Payne, 1996, p.162). However, internationally, the ties between social work and social pedagogy are growing closer. For example, many associations of social pedagogues are members of the International Federation of Social Workers, and in many countries of Central and Eastern Europe, social pedagogues do practice in school settings and regard themselves as operating like school social workers (School Social Work Association of America, 1999, summaries from Russia and Latvia).

As school social work evolves and proliferates around the world, including Central and Eastern Europe, practitioners who regard themselves as social workers or social pedagogues will play a greater role in facilitating the overall development—cognitively, emotionally, physically and socially—of children and youth in school settings.

THE EXAMPLE OF HUNGARY

Geographical Features and Historical Highlights: A Brief Sketch

Geographically, the Republic of Hungary, in the Carpathian Basin, situated between the Carpathian Mountains and the Alps, is a land-locked country on the eastern side of Central Europe. Its seven neighbors are Austria on the west, Slovakia (formerly part of Czechoslovakia) in the northeast, Ukraine in the north, Romania to the east, and Slovenia, Croatia, and Serbia (of the former Yugoslavia) in the south. Over many centuries, Hungary has been subjected to waves of conquest and occupation, beginning with the Romans at the start of the Christian era, followed by the Huns, the Mongolian Tartars, the Turks, the Austrian Habsburgs, the Germans (from 1944–1945), and most recently, the Russians. After World War I, during which the Austro-Hungarian Empire allied itself with Germany, the Treaty of Trianon in 1920 allocated approximately two-thirds of Hungary's territory and more than one-half of its population to the neighboring countries of Romania and Yugoslavia. To quote the Hungarian National Committee for UNICEF (1998): "Not only did the country lose its most economically productive territories [including Transylvania], but it was also compelled to pay war reparations as well as the costs associated with resettling its people" (p. 3). Today Hungarians represent 11 percent of the population in Slovakia and nine percent in Romania (United Nations Children's Fund International Child Development Center, 1998, p. 57).

Hungary's capital city, Budapest, was formed by the union of Buda and Pest, situated on either side of the Duna (Danube) river and now has a population of more than 2 million. Additionally, in 1997, there were 3,168 local governments in 19 counties operating throughout the country (Nagy, 1998, p. 37). Hungary's geographical location has placed it at the crossroads of both Eastern and Western Europe, and at the beginning of the 20th century both the economy and academia were on a par with many countries in Western Europe. Hungary also began to modernize and liberalize economically as early as 1968 during the communist period. This laid the groundwork for the transition, making Hungary better prepared for change than other countries in the region. Nevertheless, "the task of transforming a partly reformed planned economy into a Western-style market economy has proven far more difficult than anticipated" (Hungarian National Committee for UNICEF, 1998, p. 15).

Today, Hungary is a parliamentary democracy with a one-chamber Parliament. During the period of the transition since 1989, when the one-party system was abolished, the Hungarian electorate has swung back and forth in its political orientation. After the first election held in 1990, a conservative government coalition was formed with a Christian-Democratic orientation. The stresses of the period led to a reaction in the 1994 elections, which led to the Hungarian Socialist Party forming a socialist-liberal coalition. In 1998, the third free election resulted in victory for the Fidesz-Hungarian Civic Party, which formed a center-right coalition dominated by younger politicians (Nagy, 1998, p. 10). These swings illustrate how the country is struggling to decide what kind of new society it wishes to create.

Demographics

The Hungarian population worldwide numbers approximately 15 million. However, those living outside the country, including those who have immigrated to the United States, number approximately 5 million (of whom some 2.5 million live as an ethnic minority in neighboring countries, primarily Romania and Slovakia). Within Hungary, the population in 1996 was 10.2 million, and declining. This decline has been a steady trend since 1980, primarily because of a reduction in the birth rate from a high of 18.4 live births per thousand population in 1975 to only 10.4 per thousand population in 1996. In that same year, the number of elderly people aged 60 years or older exceeded that of youth under 15 years old, 19.4 percent of the population against 18 percent. Clearly this has major implications for education.

The expansion of the market economy and the economic crises of the 1990s have also resulted in significant changes in income distribution and income disparities (Nagy, 1998, p. 17). There are almost six times as many children living in the poorest 20 percent of households compared to the richest 20 percent. However, the richest 20 percent of households with dependent children tend to spend 4.5 times as much on schooling of their children as the poorest households (Nagy, 1998, pp. 19–20).

Hungary has small minority groups from Germany (2.6 percent), Serbia (2.0 percent), Croatia, Slovakia, and Slovenia, but the largest minority group is the Roma (also known as Gypsies, now regarded as a derogatory term). These Roma or Romanies are estimated to number between approximately one-half million and 700,000, representing 4 percent of the population.

The Hungarian language is of Finno-Ugrian origin, grammatically similar only to Finnish, and incorporating elements from the Turkish, Slav, and German languages, reflecting the different periods in Hungarian history.

Social Problems

With the collapse of the communist system in 1989, major changes occurred in the economy. Macroeconomic measures included changes in the structure of public spending, with radical cuts in producer and consumer subsidies (Hungarian National Committee for UNICEF, 1998, pp. 47–61). The evolution of the new economic system resulted in unemployment, rampant inflation, and cutbacks in support and services to families. Poverty rates rose rapidly. During the 1980s, the annual rate was approximately 10 percent. By 1992, the rate doubled to 20 percent, and by 1995 poverty affected approximately one-third of the population. The country is debating the nature of its poverty—whether it stems from the previous regime or the transition to the new, whether it is deep or shallow, transient or continuing—but in general children are the age group most affected, with the Roma minority in particular suffering the most dramatically.

In general, the health status of Hungarian children is relatively good, especially in very young children whose health is closely monitored in nurseries and kindergartens. Health risks rise with age, as determined by comprehensive school health services. These services, however, tend to be uneven in distribution, and require expansion to serve school dropouts. Areas of concern regarding child and youth morbidity and mortality include nutrition-related problems, low levels of physical activity, and increases in health-compromising behaviors such as smoking and alcohol consumption. Hungary has the highest rate of alcoholism in the world, affecting children as young as 11 through 15, and producing negative effects in families.

Drug abuse is also increasing. In a rapid assessment survey in Hungary in 1996, 12 percent of secondary school students reported that they were regular users, and almost one-quarter (23 percent) reported that they had tried drugs at least once (United Nations Children's Fund International Child Development Center, 1997a, p. 51).

The suicide rate for adult males in Hungary is also the highest in the world. As the Hungarian National Committee of UNICEF reported in 1998: "Stress is exerting a strong effect not only upon adults but children as well, especially upon older youth in general and school dropouts in particular, a growing number of whom, faced with an uncertain future, are developing learning, emotional, and behavioral problems" (p. 233). The report also emphasized that mental health care is severely limited in Hungary, especially for youth.

The Educational System in Hungary

The Hungarian educational system is currently undergoing a major transformation. During the communist period, education was rigidly controlled through the central government, and "the direction, form, and content of educational programs and materials [were] determined by socialist ideology and economic imperatives" (Hungarian National Committee for UNICEF, 1998, p. 269).

A new framework was laid down in 1993 by the Public Education Act, which was amended in 1995 and 1996. However, an earlier act in 1990, the Act on Self Government, which established local governments with greater autonomy, led to the shift in educational administration and funding away from centralized control to the more than 3,000 local governments established across the country. In 1997, 2,400 of these maintained a public educational institution (Nagy, 1998, p. 37). The state continues to provide unrestricted block grants to the local authorities from the central budget; these are of a normative quota type and are based on the number of students per educational level. However, local authorities may spend these amounts in any way they choose. The state also provides earmarked grants for specific projects. In addition, the local governments create their own sources of funding from local taxes and grants from the private sector.

Compulsory schooling in Hungary lasts from six to 16 years of age. Children may start school any time between five and seven years, and those who began in the 1998/99 school year will have to remain in school until they are 18 years old. The educational reform laws of the 1990s have also changed the relationship between the primary schools and the secondary schools, and eliminated the formerly firm division between general and vocational secondary education (Nagy, 1998, p. 55).

In 1995, the Hungarian Parliament adopted the National Core Curriculum (NCC) that defines content required at the ends of the 4th, 6th, 8th, and 10th grades. These requirements were formulated according to 10 "comprehensive cultural domains" or "knowledge areas," not in terms of individual subjects (Nagy, 1998, p. 97).

Since the transition, the prohibition on private schools has been lifted, and increasing numbers of schools run by religious organizations and private foundations are emerging. Churches may now operate their own schools and regain ownership of property seized by the state under the former system; and the renascent Jewish community now sponsors five schools in Budapest alone.

Educating Children with Special Needs

Within the Central and Eastern European region, the education of children with disabilities has been dominated by the Soviet science of "defectology." The term itself implies a negative attitude to the development of such children and is associated with their placement in special schools, isolated from other children, and often housed in large-scale residential institutions under unfortunate conditions. In Hungary, however, there is a long tradition of providing educational opportunities for children with disabilities. These have "yielded some fairly impressive results [including those of] the Pető Institute for motor-impaired children, which is internationally renowned" (Hungarian National Committee for UNICEF, 1998, p. 294).

The education law in Hungary provides for the education of children with disabilities in an independent subsystem within public education (Nagy, 1998, p. 83). In 1996 there were 200 separate centers providing special education. The majority of these are at the primary level. In addition, almost 500 regular primary schools have special education sections, and some initiatives are beginning to integrate children with disabilities into the mainstream. When this occurs, additional funding is provided from the state on a par with the normative grants made to special institutions (Nagy, 1998, p. 83).

According to the Hungarian National Committee for UNICEF, in 1996 more than 43,000 children were involved in special education programs. Ninety percent of those were classified as mentally impaired although a percentage of these are "only marginally impaired or have ended up in special education programs due to socioeconomic or cultural circumstances" (p. 294).

Educational opportunities at secondary level are very limited. There is one school for visually impaired youth and one for those who have severe hearing impairment, and some two-year vocational schools for youth assessed as "mildly retarded".

In Budapest, the Bárczi Gúsztáv College, founded in 1900, is a famous institution training special educators to serve children with a variety of disabilities. When training for social work was introduced, this college became one of the first to offer such training.

THE EDUCATION OF MINORITIES

In general, Hungary has a history of racial and religious tolerance. One exception involves the Hungarian Jews, against whom anti-Semitic laws were passed even before World War II. After the Nazis invaded Hungary in March 1944, the Arrow Cross, an extremist-right-wing party, assisted the Germans in deporting 437,000 Hungarian Jews to Auschwitz (Braham and Miller, 1998, p. 55). The other major exception to the rule is the plight of the Roma people. However, Hungary is not unique in this treatment and shares its discriminatory policies not only with other countries in Central and Eastern Europe, but also with many countries in Western Europe, which deny Romanies political asylum and discriminate in other ways (Dunbar & Slajerova, 2000, p. 1; Erlanger, 2000, p. 14).

In 1993, Hungary enacted the Minority Rights Act that has facilitated the development of multicultural education and bilingual programs, particularly for children from the German minority. However, although there are scattered programs catering to the Roma, this minority "still constitute the most poverty-stricken and socially disadvantaged group in Hungarian society" (Hungarian National Committee for UNICEF, 1998, p. 365).

The Hungarian Roma population can be divided into three groups: 60–70 percent of the total population are the Romungros, whose primary language is Hungarian; 20–30 percent belong to the Olah group and speak Romani, an Indo-European language of Sanskrit origin; and 8 percent constitute the "Bea" or Rumanian branch, speaking an old Rumanian dialect (Hungarian National Committee for UNICEF, 1998, p. 366).

Although data are limited regarding the Roma, it is clear that children comprise the major portion of their population, with the percentage being proportionately double that of the ethnic Hungarian population. Most Roma families live in extremely poor housing, often in urban ghettoes as well as rural areas, and their health and nutritional status are a serious concern (Hungarian National Committee for UNICEF, 1998, p. 380). In summary, Roma children are caught up in a vastly complex, problematic world characterized by poverty, unemployment, unfavorable living conditions, poor health and nutrition, and blatant discrimination (Hungarian National Committee for UNICEF, 1998, p. 386).

Educationally, for many reasons, lack of access to a normal education is one of the greatest barriers preventing Romanies from entering mainstream Hungarian society. Educational discrimination leads to segregation of Roma children, often in remedial education classes or separate "remedial" schools. Very few complete primary education and, of these, only 3 percent gain admission to secondary school. The remainder may end up in short-term vocational training that fails to equip them to enter the labor market.

There is an urgent need for innovative programs for the Roma, which will assist them to lead productive lives and overcome the negative perceptions and attitudes of ethnic Hungarians toward them. These include Head-Start-type programs for preschoolers, and remedial learning programs for primary-school students and youth who have dropped out of school (Hungarian National Committee for UNICEF, 1998, p. 397).

SCHOOL SOCIAL WORK IN HUNGARY

The social sciences and social work existed in Hungary before World War II but were abolished as "imperialist disciplines" during the communist era. As the author stated in 1993: "The prevailing sociopolitical philosophy held that the state socialist system would provide for welfare needs through universal structural provisions, therefore giving minimal attention to personal social services" (Hare, 1993, p. 9). Social policy was characterized chiefly by benefits-in-kind and income supports (Talyigás and Hegyesi, 1992, p. 62). People believed that the state system was meeting all needs.

After the 1956 uprising in Hungary, which produced a more relaxed political climate, an Institute of Sociology was established in 1965 at the Hungarian Academy of Sciences, and training for psychologists was again introduced. In 1968, the Ministry of Education began to establish educational guidance, advisory, or counseling centers, similar to the western concept of a child guidance center. They were designed to deal with behavior and learning problems of children aged three to 18 years, and their families. At first psychologists and teachers made up the staff, but by the 1970s "family caregivers" were added to link home, schools, and clinics. This was a type of social work practice, and after some time, part-time training courses for this work were introduced.

Other precursors of modern social workers included "social organizers," who provided managerial services in institutions, and "cultural animators," who worked in community cultural centers. District nurses provided maternal and child-health counseling. Other developments included the creation of the Poor Relief Foundation in 1979 and LARES, the first nonprofit human service organization. Social scientists such as Dr. Zsuzsa Ferge, Katalin Talyigás and Gábor Hegyesi conducted research on methods of reforming social policy, and concluded that social work education was needed in Hungary.

In 1985, major developments occurred both in practice and in education for social work. After research revealed an increase in social problems, a government directive was issued to establish a network of Family Assistance Centers to provide a variety of therapeutic, case management, and referral services. In the same year, a social policy course was established at ELTE, the Eötvös Loránd University in Budapest, which in time facilitated the beginning of a course in social work education at the university. Today, social work courses are given at colleges and universities throughout the country. There is an Association of Schools of Social Work, formed in 1990, which currently has: 11 Schools of Social Work, eight schools of social pedagogy, and 18 colleges training paraprofessional social assistants. According to the current president of the Association, Dr. István Budai, a lively debate is currently underway on the relationship between social work and social pedagogy (Budai, January 30, 2000, personal communication).

In the early 1990s some of the family assistance centers began to assign some of their workers to schools in their district, thus establishing school social work services. These included dealing with attendance problems and a number of social and emotional problems identified by the school. Various school principals recognized and appreciated how social workers could assist with families who were poor, unemployed, and disorganized. Their work included home visits, social assessments, counseling, and linking home, school, and community (Hare, 1993, p. 21).

However, school social work services did not continue to develop along these lines, but rather have become subsumed under child welfare services. These services were created in terms of Act No. XXX1 of 1997 "on the protection of children and the administration of guardianship affairs," which was adopted by the Hungarian Parliament after 10 years of careful deliberations and debate.

Children who cannot live with their own parents are a particularly vulnerable group in all societies. As UNICEF ICDC has stated: "one of the most serious problem [*sic*] of the socialist legacy was the tremendous reliance on institutional care at the expense of social work services to help families at home" (United Nations Children's Fund International Child Development Center, 1997a, p. 63). Chronically ill and disabled children were especially at risk of institutionalization in large facilities, and the institutional system for juvenile offenders was even more harsh (United Nations Children's Fund International Child Development Center, 1997a, pp. 64–65).

The system is pervasive in Central and Eastern Europe where estimates indicate that there are about one million children in public care. However, Hungary is unique in the region for its strong focus on reducing the number of children in public care. Between 1989 and 1995, the total number of children in infant and children homes, homes for disabled, and foster care dropped from 23,438 to 18,306 (United Nations Children's Fund International Child Development Center, 1997a, p. 67). According to the UNICEF ICDC, three factors contributed to this decline: first, because reforms were started during the 1980s, the transition-related changes may have caused a less dramatic disruption to social values and family coping strategies. Secondly, strong universal family support policies continued into the 1990s and may have helped prevent family breakdown. Finally, the network of family assistance centers established in the mid-1980s provided social work services to support families (p. 66).

Hungarian culture has traditionally placed a high value on children (Hungarian National Committee for UNICEF, 1998, p. 319) and before the socialist era social policy promoted foster care for homeless children and resocialization of young offenders (Hungarian National Committee for UNICEF, 1998, p. 347). Consequently, the first years of the transition were spent in intense debates leading to the reform of the child welfare system, which finally produced the legislation passed in 1997. This law emphasizes prevention and family preservation as the main priority in the promotion of child protection, and places foster care and adoption ahead of institutionalization as desirable options for children needing alternatives to in-home care. A prime advocate for this legislation, Dr. Mária Herczog, is currently President of the Hungarian Association of Social Workers, formed in 1988, and is a leader in the movement to provide training for professional foster parents in Hungary.

The 1997 child protection law established child welfare services at the local government level. Because of the national economic problems and the paucity of resources available to local authorities, many school social workers were incorporated into the child welfare services, which in some cases are housed in the same premises as the family assistance centers (Banyai, personal communication, February 1, 2000). Many child welfare workers have good relations with the schools and work closely with them, but not in terms of fulfilling a school social work role.

Schools appoint teachers to act as child protection officers, who monitor at-risk children and report them to the child welfare authorities when necessary. These child-protection teachers have no social work training, and function primarily in an administrative capacity. However, some attend courses relevant to their child protection responsibilities as part of their mandatory continuing education requirements. Further, child protection teachers in schools within a particular region may meet regularly to discuss their functions (Piroska Zsolnay and Tilda Kecskes, Child Protection Teachers, Ozd, personal communication, January 31, 2000). They have to track the attendance of children receiving family allowances from the local authority because continuation of the benefit is dependent on regular school attendance after the age of six, and absence can result in a termination of benefits.

Some special schools have social workers on staff, such as alternative schools for dropouts run by nongovernmental organizations. However, when social work students request field placements in school social work, these are difficult to find (Banyai, personal communication, February 1, 2000).

In an international study coordinated by the World Health Organization in 1997–1998 that researched health behaviors in school-aged children in 28 countries, Hungarian respondents aged 11, 13, and 15 years were among the fourth lowest who reported that they "liked school a lot". The other countries at the bottom of this scale were Finland, the Czech Republic, and Slovakia. (World Health Organization, 2000, p. 50). In view of this finding, Hungarian schools should strongly consider employing social workers to assist schools in improving school climate and in helping administrators, teachers, students, and parents resolve problems.

SKETCHES OF THREE OTHER COUNTRIES IN THE REGION

These sketches are based primarily on papers presented at the International School Social Work Conference organized in Chicago in April 1999 by the School Social Work Association of America.

Estonia

Estonia, in the Baltic region, is a post-Soviet country that acquired its independence in 1991 after centuries of foreign occupation. According to Tiiu Kadajane and Judit Strömpl, "the most important influence of the totalitarian regime was the process of producing a personal sense of worthlessness. Behind the ideology of liberating people from the yoke of 'capitalist' power, a new, more total, power was used in the Soviet era. In fact, everything was subordinated to the single value - the state, governed by the Communist party. …The goal of pedagogy was to develop individuals who would be useful to the Communist state. Soviet collectivism was created solely to control the individual." (Kadajane and Strömpl, 1999).

Estonian society is in the process of transition from the Soviet system to a free-market economy based on Western values and beliefs. While the people are motivated to adopt this new way of life, they cannot immediately reverse the effects of the totalitarian system on them.

While Estonia has ratified the UN Convention on the Rights of the Child, practical implementation of its terms is far from the reality. Consequently, poverty is rampant and there are many street children whose parents have disappeared, or are drug-addicted and homeless, or who have run away from home for other reasons.

School social work is emerging to deal with the problems of school truants. Truancy is defined in different ways in Estonia. It refers to behavioral problems in the school, violence and anti-social behavior, and learning difficulties, in addition to absence from school. It is also used to indicate conflict between the school and the parents of troubled children. School climate is still based on the authoritarian power relationships characteristic of the previous regime. Rebellious students are often confined in "special schools," similar to reform schools in the western world. After research into school attitudes, parental attitudes, and attitudes of child protection workers and youth police officers, the writers concluded that they (the authors) needed to study social work and other related areas of understanding and intervening in these problems.

Lithuania

Lithuania, the largest of the Baltic Republics, has a population of almost four million, of whom about 927,000 are children (Kondrasoviene, 1999). Like other countries in the region, major social problems have emerged during the period of transformation from communism to democracy. As Kulys and Constable stated in 1994: "Since almost no one in Lithuania has had any real life experience of how a democracy functions or what the elements of a market economy are, democracy and market economy remain primarily theoretical concepts. Thus the transition process is fraught with conflict, mistrust and despair" (p. 81). In terms of social welfare, the country must "decipher what aspects of the old system to keep, what needs to be changed, what needs to be completely eliminated, and what must be added" (Kulys & Constable, 1994, p. 84).

According to Lidija Kondrasoviene (1999), in a paper delivered in 1999, numerous problems have emerged in the schools, reflecting trends in the society as a whole. Poverty affects school attendance, and youngsters who drop out of school often live on the streets, become beggars, or commit crimes. The curriculum is often too difficult for the students, and the schools have an atmosphere of indifference with few links between school and community. Students have negative attitudes toward the school, and manifest anxiety, low self-esteem, and a lack of confidence about their studies. Teachers are concerned about the performance and behavior of students, and about the fact that many come to school hungry, tired, and physically abused. They are also concerned about the fact that many parents exhibit asocial behavior and do not communicate either with their children or with the school. Unemployment, poverty, and alcoholism are major problems, as well as drug addiction, suicide, and homelessness.

Interest in social work was stimulated by contact with the West and the exposure of other professionals such as physicians to social workers in western countries. Additionally, unemployment has propelled professionals from other disciplines, such as engineering and architecture, to seek retraining as social workers (Kulys & Constable, 1994, p. 87). In 1991, the Utena Medical College was the first institution in Lithuania to begin training professional social workers with the help of international exchanges with German, Dutch, and Scandinavian schools, as well as with academics from the United States. Some students are placed for their field instruction in educational institutions, Youth Educational Centers, and day care centers for children with disabilities or other special needs. Social work roles include providing psychological assistance, stress management, linking parents and school, providing legal assistance, assisting parents to adjust to their children's needs, and assessing strengths. Another major center of social work education is the Vytautus Magnus University in Kaunas, and several other centers also offer education in social work.

Poland

Poland enjoys the distinction of having launched the initiative for a United Nations Convention on the Rights of the Child as early as 1978 (United Nations Children's Fund International Child Development Center, 1997a, p. 113). The text of the convention was finally adopted by the UN General Assembly in 1989.

With its population of 38 million (not counting Poles living in neighboring countries), Poland is the most populous country in East Central Europe. Along with Czechoslovakia, Poland had the beginnings of social work and social work education during the period between two world wars. Poland in fact had "a fairly high level of education and theory development that continues in different metamorphoses to the present day" (Constable & Frysztacki, 1994, p. 20).

Polish social welfare and social work are established in the Social Welfare Assistance Law. Professional social work is defined as a major instrument of assessing need and proving social welfare assistance that enables persons and families to overcome difficult life situations. The local community is charged with the major responsibility in providing help and supervision. The social work role involves the development of service systems, assessment of need, delivery of individual and family services, and program development (Constable & Frysztacki, 1994, p. 27).

While social work education programs were closed down during the Stalin era, concepts from social work were seen as an instrument of human collective action and government social policy. Consequently, 35 two-year, post-secondary schools of social work were established. These now collaborate with three university programs at Jagiellonian University in Cracow, Warsaw University, and the University of Lódz. Social work practice is action-oriented, focused on problem solving, involves persons and families, mobilizes natural helping networks, and is strongly rooted in the community (Constable & Frysztacki, 1994, p. 30).

School social work services in Poland are provided by school pedagogists, a professional category established by an education law in 1975 and amended in 1993. School pedagogists were to be employed in schools of 400 students or more at every level of the educational system. The school principal was responsible for employing a school pedagogist to provide pedagogical and psychological support to students, but could also delegate these functions to a trained teacher.

The role of "class teacher" (similar to a homeroom teacher in the United States) involves remaining with a class for four years and having responsibility for the educational problems of the class and for referral to the school pedagogist if necessary. The main problems include learning problems, behavioral disorders (such as aggression or truancy), and financial problems. Research into the role of the social pedagogist in 10 schools in Cracow in 1998 revealed that class teachers lacked knowledge of the family and health problems of their students and that communication and collaboration between class teacher, school pedagogist, and families needed improvement. Functions performed by school pedagogists included casework, parent consultation, therapeutic interventions with students, referral to community resources, and help in organizing learning (Bochenska-Seweryn & Kluzowa, 2000, p. 3).

Poland has an Association of Social Workers that is a member of the International Federation of Social Workers, and in Cracow there is a local association of pedagogist practitioners. One of the challenges facing social work education in Poland is "reconciling the social work and social pedagogy emphasis in the different university programs" (Constable & Frysztacki, 1994, p. 29) and achieving greater integration between the different levels of preparation for social work practice.

ISSUES FOR FUTURE DIRECTION

The countries of Central and Eastern Europe that experienced decades of Soviet-style communist authoritarian dictatorship face gigantic challenges in converting their economies and political structures into free-market and democratic models of societal organization and value systems. As oppressive as the previous system was, the challenges of freedom, choice, individual agency, and social advocacy can be frightening. The educational institutions preparing upcoming generations clearly have a crucial role to play in the process of transformation and in equipping future citizens for civil society. However, they must simultaneously undergo transformation themselves. They must also develop strategies to deal with the children who are victims of the huge changes occurring in the society. School social work and social pedagogy can make a vital contribution to this evolution in Central and Eastern Europe. This is a major challenge for the profession in the region and internationally.

REFERENCES

Beaton, A., Mullis, I.V.S., Martin, M.O., Gonzalez, E.J., Smith, T.A. & Kelly, D.L. (1996a). *Mathematics achievement in the middle school years: IEA's Third International Mathematics and Science Study*. Chestnut Hill, MA: Boston College, Center for the Study of Testing, Evaluation and Educational Policy.

Beaton, A., Martin, M.O., Mullis, I.V.S., Gonzalez, E.J., Smith, T.A. & Kelly, D.L. (1996b). *Science achievement in the middle school years: IEA's Third International Mathematics and Science Study*. Chestnut Hill, MA: Boston College, Center for the Study of Testing, Evaluation and Educational Policy.

Bochénska-Seweryn, M. & Kluzowa, K. (1999). *School social work in Poland*. Unpublished paper. Jagellonian University, Institute of Sociology, Krakow, Poland.

Braham, R. and Miller, S. (Eds.). (1998). *The Nazis' last victims: The Holocaust in Hungary*. Detroit: Wayne State University Press in association with the United States Holocaust Memorial Museum, Washington DC.

Constable, R. & Frysztacki, K. (1994). The context for practice and education in Polish social work: Foundations for the international consultation process. In R. Constable & V. Mehta (Eds.), *Education for social work in Eastern Europe: Changing horizons* (pp. 19-34). Chicago: Lyceum Books, Inc.

Dunbar, E. & Slajerova, L. (2000). Hostility against Europe Roma population transcends national boundaries. *Psychology International, 11*, 1, 4–5.

Erlanger, S. (2000, April 2). Across a new Europe, a people deemed unfit for tolerance: No room for gypsies. *New York Times, Week in Review*, Section 4, pp. 14, 16.

Ferge, Z. (1996). Social citizenship in the new democracies: The difficulties in reviving citizens' rights in Hungary. *International Journal of Urban and Regional Research, 20,* pp. 99–115.

Hare, I. (1993). *New developments in Hungarian social work*. Washington, DC: National Association of Social Workers.

Hungarian National Committee for UNICEF. (1998). *Hope in the midst of hardship: The situation of children and families in Hungary*. Budapest: Hungarian National Committee for UNICEF.

Kadajane, T. & Strömpl, J. (1999). *School truancy as a new phenomenon in Estonia*. Unpublished paper.

Kondrasoviene, L. (1999). *Social work development in Lithuania*. Unpublished paper, Utena Medical College, Social Work Department, Utena, Lithuania.

Kulys, R. & Constable, R. (1994). The emergence of social work in Lithuania. In R. Constable & V. Mehta (Eds.), *Education for social work in Eastern Europe: Changing horizons* (pp. 81–90). Chicago: Lyceum Books, Inc.

Nagy, M. (Ed.). (1998). *Education in Hungary 1997*. Budapest: National Institute of Public Education.

Payne, M. (1996) *What is professional social work?* Birmingham, England: Venture Press.

The Rectors Conference of National Institutes for Social Educators International Committee. (1995). *The training of social educators in Denmark*. Copenhagen: The Rectors Conference of National Institutes for Social Educators International Committee.

School Social Work Association of America. (1999). *The state of school social work around the world*. Unpublished paper, Chicago: *School Social Work Association of America*.

Talyigás, K. & Hegyesi, G. (1992). Social work in Hungary: New opportunities in a changing society. In M. C. Hokenstad, S. K. Khinduka & J. Midgley (Eds.), *Profiles in international social work* (pp. 59–70). Washington, DC: NASW Press.

United Nations Children's Fund International Child Development Center. (1997a). *Children at risk in central and Eastern Europe: Perils and promises. Central and eastern Europe in transition: Public policy and social conditions*. Economies in Transition Studies, Regional Monitoring Report 4. Florence, Italy: United Nations Children's Fund International Child Development Center.

United Nations Children's Fund International Child Development Center (1997b). *Children at risk in central and Eastern Europe: Perils and promises: A Summary*. The MONEE Project, Regional Monitoring Report 4. Florence, Italy: United Nations Children's Fund International Child Development Center.

United Nation Children's Fund International Child Development Center (1998). *Education for all?* The MONEE Project, Regional Monitoring Report 5. Florence, Italy: United Nations Children's Fund International Child Development Center.

World Health Organization. (2000). *Health and health behaviour among young people*. WHO Policy Series: Health Policy for Children and Adolescents (HEPCA) Issue 1, International Report. Copenhagen: WHO Regional Office for Europe.

Zlotnik, J. L. (1992). *Social work for children and families in the Soviet Union*. Washington, DC: National Association of Social Workers.

Acknowledgements

The content of this chapter is solely the responsibility of the author. She wishes to thank the following persons who provided valuable information used in the writing of the chapter:

Emóke Banyai, Video Home Training Association (for family communication), Budapest; lecturer at Eötvös Loránd University (ELTE), Budapest.

Mária Bognár, National Institute of Public Education, Budapest.

Istvàn Budai, Professor, Course Leader, Head of Department of Social Work at Széchenyi István College, Gyor, and President of the Association of Social Work Education in Hungary.

Zsuzsa Ferge, Professor of Sociology and Head of the Department of Social Policy, Eötvös Loránd University (ELTE), Budapest.

Éva Orsós Hegyesi, President of the Office for National and Ethnic Minorities, Budapest.

Mária Herczog, Director of the National Institute for Families and Children, Budapest, and President of the Hungarian Association of Social Workers.

Katalin Talyigás, Director of Social Work Programs, The American Jewish Joint Distribution Committee, Inc., Hungary Program.

Otto Kovacs, Principal of General School, and Eva Benkö Fahèr, Director, Szabò Lörine General and Vocational Schools, and Szèchenyi Istvàn Secondary School on Business, Ozd, Hungary.

Piroska Zsolnay and Tilda Kecskés, Child Protection Teachers, Szabò Lörine and Szèchenyi Istvàn Schools, Ozd, Hungary.

Special thanks go to Bridget Freeman, MSW, for her valuable assistance in the production of this chapter.

11 SCHOOL SOCIAL WORK IN KOREA: CURRENT STATUS AND FUTURE DIRECTIONS

Ki Whan Kim

Social Indicators* — Republic of Korea

Population	47,069,000
Percentage under age 15 years	21
Percentage urban (2000)	82
Life expectancy at birth	71.8 men, 79.1 women
Fertility rate	1.51 children per woman
Percentage of illiterate adults (2000)	0.9 men, 3.6 women
Per capita GDP in $U.S. (1999)	8,871
Percentage unemployed (1999)	6.3

*Social Indicators. From the Statistics Division of the United Nations. Refer to notes on page 249.
Reference: http://www.un.org/Depts/unsd/indicators/indic2a.htm

NATIONAL CONTEXT

The Korean peninsula is located in the far east of southern Asia and shares its northern border with China and Russia. It is 222,154 square kilometers (approximately 85,779 square miles) in size and 1,000 kilometers (621 miles) in length. The size of the Korean peninsula is almost the same as the United Kingdom.

Korea has one of the longest national histories with a single ethnic group in the world. Korean history dates back to 2333 B.C. when King Tangun established the first kingdom called Choson, which means "the land of morning calm". After the founding of this first kingdom, the Korean peninsula was repeatedly divided into several kingdoms until 668 A.D., when it was finally unified into one country. In 1910, the Korean peninsula was occupied by Japan until 1945 when Japan was defeated in World War II. At that time, the Allied Forces divided the peninsula at the 38th parallel into the Republic of Korea in the south and the Democratic People's Republic of Korea in the north. The Republic of Korea, based on capitalism and democracy, is generally referred to as Korea or South Korea. The Democratic People's Republic of Korea, based on communism, is generally referred to as North Korea.

After being divided for five years, North Korea invaded South Korea in 1950 and initiated the Korean War, which lasted until 1953. Owing to different ideologies and a civil war, the two Koreas have not communicated with each other for the last 50 years. Hence, this paper describes the status of school social work in the Republic of Korea (hereinafter referred to as "Korea").

In 1998, the population of Korea was 46 million, with 450 persons per square kilometer (1,165 persons per square mile). In addition to this high population density, the following are recent characteristics of the Korean population: a steady decrease in population growth; a decrease in the proportion of the population below age 15 and an increase in the proportion of the population over 65; and an increase in the size of the urban population.

The first characteristic of the Korean population is the steady decrease in population growth. In the early 1960s when Korea began its consecutive five-year economic developmental plans, rapid population growth was considered to be a serious social problem. In those days, the rate of population growth was 3 percent per year, the death rate was 12.1 per 1,000 people, and the birth rate was 42 per 1,000 people. To slow the rapid population growth, Korea implemented various types of family planning campaigns, such as tax exemption for families with fewer than two children. Following this endeavor, the annual rate of population growth in the 1990s gradually decreased to less than 10 per 1,000 people, and the death rate also decreased to 5.5 per 1,000 people. The current population is expected to grow at a moderate rate to 50 million in 2010 and is expected to remain constant from 2020 (National Statistical Office, 1998).

The second characteristic is the decreasing number of young people and increasing number of older people. During the last three decades, the proportion of the population aged 65 and older increased from 2.9 percent to 5.9 percent, and the percentage between 15 and 64 increased from 54.8 percent to 70.7 percent, whereas those aged under 15 decreased steadily from 42.3 percent to 23.4 percent. Although the percentage of the population below 15 years of age is a little higher than those of other countries, such as Japan (16.3 percent) and the U.S. (22.0 percent), this trend is projected to decline to 17.2 percent in 2020 because of the continued decline in the fertility rate. These general trends are expected to stay the same until 2010.

The third characteristic is migration from rural to urban areas. This is one of Korea's major social problems and results in heavy density of population, a lack of housing and education facilities, and an increase in the crime rate. The proportion of the population living in urban areas increased from

41.2 percent in 1970 to 77.7 percent in 1995, whereas the proportion of the population living in rural areas decreased from 58.8 percent to 22.3 percent during the same period. Currently, one out of every four Koreans lives in Seoul, the capital of Korea. The populations of cities are expected to increase to 80.6 percent in 2000.

Decreasing numbers of young people and the overpopulation of urban areas will be directly or indirectly related to school social work services in the future. Decreased numbers of young people will reduce the number of students, whereas the overpopulation of cities will increase the student problems. Therefore, future school social work services in Korea should reflect these characteristics of the Korean population by preparing to handle the problems of young people growing up in cities.

Since the commencement of a series of successive five-year economic development plans in 1962, Korea has achieved rapid economic growth, averaging 8 percent or more per year for the last 35 years. The gross domestic product (GDP) per capita steadily increased from $87 in 1962 to $10,076 in 1995. With this remarkable economic growth, Korea became widely recognized as one of the modern industrialized countries and became a member of the Organization for Economic Cooperation and Development (OECD) in 1997. The achievement of rapid economic growth during the past three decades can be attributed to three factors: export-oriented government economic policy; a high-quality and low-cost labor force; and cheap foreign capital. These three factors were driven by Korea's strong economic policy, which focused on a development strategy of "economic growth first and fair distribution later." Under this strategy, politicians gave low priority to equity issues and social welfare expenditure in social developmental decision-making.

Rapid economic growth, based on the "economic growth first" policy came to a halt in 1997 as a result of domestic and international financial crises. Korea was placed under the control of the International Monetary Fund (IMF) and experienced previously unimagined economic and social problems. In 1998, Korea recorded a negative economic growth rate (-5.8 percent), an unemployment rate of 8.5 percent, an increase in broken families, and 6,000 people homeless (Cho, 1999). Because of these economic and social crises, Koreans began to realize that building a social welfare system is as important as achieving high economic growth. The social welfare system came to be considered as an essential social institution, providing a social safety net to the people. From the beginning of 1999, Korea gradually began to recover from its economic and social crises and was able to pay back some of its loans to the IMF. However, the discrepancy in income distribution between the rich and the poor continued to grow and distrust of politicians increased.

KOREA'S SOCIAL WELFARE SYSTEM

Even though the concept of a welfare state was included in the first Korean Constitution in 1948, the social welfare system in Korea was not launched until the early 1960s. The first Korean social security law to become effective provided national pensions for civil servants in 1960. Next was public assistance for the poor in 1961; this law, however, did not become effective until 1969.

After the legislature passed these two laws, further social welfare provision was initiated for political motives. In 1961, when General Park gained political power by a coup, he introduced some basic social security laws to justify his seizure of power and to reduce people's resistance to his authority. During this period, Korea enacted various welfare-related laws such as the Medical Insurance Act (1963); the Disaster Relief Act, the Social Security Act, and the Workmen's Industrial Accident Compensation Insurance Act (all in 1963); and the Child Welfare Act (1961). Many of these social welfare laws, however, were statutory orders and remained dormant until the 1980s.

Although some of the basic social welfare laws were enacted during the 1960s, providing social welfare was still considered to be an act of charity and emergency relief only for the poor, not the right of all citizens. In the early 1960s, most allocations of social welfare services were funded by foreign missionary aid. With limited funding and poor coverage, many Koreans suffered during this period from absolute poverty and unemployment.

Along with rapid economic growth that occurred after the late 1960s, the living standards of Koreans improved tremendously, and the percentage of the population living in absolute poverty decreased. The percentage of the population living in absolute poverty decreased from 40.9 percent in 1965 to 14.6 percent in 1976 and to 3.5 percent in 1997 (Ministry of Health and Welfare, 1998). With improved living standards and the growing national economy in the 1970s, Koreans gradually came to recognize human rights and to value quality of life. Koreans began to consider "the welfare state" as an essential human right and expected the prosperous 1980s to improve their quality of life.

From the late 1970s, however, Korea began to face various social problems resulting from rapid industrialization and urbanization, such as unequal income distribution, unemployment of low skilled laborers, broken families, an increasing number of criminals, and increasing levels of juvenile delinquency. It became apparent that Korea needed to establish a more solid social welfare system as a social safety net to prevent and solve these problems. Consequently, in the 1980s, Korea implemented new social welfare laws and activated dormant ones.

In the 1980s, the Korean legislature passed the Welfare Act for the Elderly, Revised Child Welfare Act, and Welfare Act for the Handicapped (all in 1981); the Act on Education of Preschool Children (1982); the Expanded Medical Insurance Act, and the Act for National Pension (both in 1988), among others.

Korea also regulated the qualifications of social workers and classified them into three levels based on academic degrees and work experiences. Under this new regulation, the Korean government hired 3,000 social workers in 1987 and placed them in socioeconomically-deprived residential areas. Their role was to screen the qualifications of social service applicants, provide public assistance to the poor, and participate in local policy making.

In addition to hiring government social workers, from the mid-1980s, Korea started to establish community welfare centers in socioeconomically-deprived residential areas. These are private social welfare agencies that are funded from local government and provide comprehensive social work services such as psychotherapeutic counseling, job training, rehabilitation, and economic support. The number of community welfare centers in Korea rapidly increased. By 1999, there were approximately 300 centers, and the number of social workers working in the centers had grown to about 4,000.

With increasing awareness and need for social services, Korea expanded its social welfare services by enacting social-welfare-related laws in the 1990s. Key pieces of welfare legislation introduced during the 1990s were the Act for Promotion of the Employment of the Handicapped (1990), the Law for Youth (1991), the Law for Children's Daycare (1991), the Revised Social Welfare Service Act (1998), and the Basic Act on Social Security (1999).

Whereas various social welfare systems have been developed during the past two decades, there has always been tension between social welfare policy and economic development policy regarding the allocation of the nation's resources to social welfare beneficiaries. Economists often perceived the social welfare system as an economic burden, whereas social workers and social activists perceived it as an essential social institution (Lee, H., 1999). Korean government expenditure on social welfare was, and still is, much less than that on economic development and is still low by international standards. Compared to other countries at similar developmental stages, Korea spends a much smaller proportion of government expenditure on social welfare. For example, in 1993, 29 percent of total government expenditure was on a broad range of social welfare services such as health, social securities, and education, whereas Brazil and Spain spent 38 percent and 50 percent, respectively, on the same services. In 1995, only 5.6 percent of total Korean government expenditure (0.8 percent of GNP) was allocated to major social security provision such as social insurance, public assistance, and social services (Park, 1997).

Despite the low percentage of government expenditure on social welfare, Korea became a social welfare state in 1995 by legally instituting all major social welfare systems. Currently, Korea's social welfare system consists of three categories—social insurance, public assistance, and social welfare-related services. Social insurance covers all four major social insurance programs—Workmen's Compensation Insurance (1963), Medical Insurance (1978), National Pension Insurance (1988), and Employment Insurance (1995).

By instituting four major social insurance programs, the number of persons covered by each social insurance program increased. For example, beneficiaries of the national pension insurance increased from 4.43 million in 1988 to 16.26 million in 1999 (National Pension Corporation, 2000). In recent years, medical and national pension insurance programs have been revised to cover the entire population.

Public assistance programs involve subsistence, income support, and medical care for the poor living in absolute poverty under the Law on Livelihood Protection (1961). The coverage provided by public assistance programs has expanded gradually to include major living expenses such as expenses associated with childbirth, food, household fuel, funeral, and school fees for middle and high school students from low-income families.

The purpose of other social welfare provision in Korea is to promote the quality of life for the socially disadvantaged, such as families headed by children, persons with mental and physical handicaps, older people, and single working mothers. Although the need for these types of social services has increased recently because of industrialization and urbanization, some of these services are still provided by private agencies with little government financial support.

THE KOREAN EDUCATION SYSTEM

To understand Korean school social work, it is necessary to understand the history and goals of the Korean education system and the problems faced by students. The purpose of school social work is to help students achieve their academic goals by resolving their problems. Hence, this section will first describe the general history and goals of the Korean education system and then describe the problems faced by students.

Koreans have always emphasized the importance of education, and teachers have commanded respect. Although there have been changes in the educational system and goals of education, traditional values respecting education still remain.

Traditionally, Korea had two types of educational institution—a private elementary school called "Sodang" and a public school for higher education. The first public school called "Taehak," meaning National Confucian Academy, was established in 372 A.D. Taehak expanded until Korea opened its door to western countries in the late 19th century. The purpose of traditional education was to prepare young men for future public services; participation was limited to boys of noble classes. In 1886, Korea established the first public elementary school open to citizens of all classes under the influence of Western culture, especially Christianity. Despite such changes, public education was still available to only a small number of Koreans until the mid-20th century. In the early 20th century, only 30 percent of children between the ages of seven and 12 enrolled in primary schools, and only 5 percent of students who graduated from primary schools advanced to secondary schools.

In 1949, Korea, desiring equal education opportunity, established a modern education system on a 6-3-3-4 year basis. This system consists of a six-year elementary school at the primary level, a three-year middle school, a three-year high school at the secondary level, and a four-year college or university at the tertiary level. Under the Korean Constitution, elementary education is free to every child aged between seven and 12 years. Middle and high school education is not compulsory and there is a charge for tuition except for students in some rural areas and from poor families.

Even though only six years of elementary education are compulsory, the tradition of valuing education and a desire for higher education has led to an increased number of schools and students during the last 30 years. The number of secondary schools and students increased from 1,909 schools and 1.16 million students in 1965 to 4,561 schools and 4.5 million students in 1996. The admission rate to advanced education also increased each year. The transfer rate from elementary school to middle school increased from 66.1 percent in 1970 to 99.3 percent in 1995, when that from middle school to high school increased from 70.1 percent to 98.4 percent during the same period (Ministry of Education, 1997). As a result, approximately one-quarter of the total Korean population is students, and Korea has successfully eliminated illiteracy in recent years.

The purpose of modern Korean education is to prepare its citizens in perfecting their individual character, developing the ability for an independent life, and acquiring the qualifications required by citizens in a modern democracy. Despite these objectives, Koreans have faced many unique school problems related to college admissions. Enthusiasm for education and the feverish desire to attend "first-rate" colleges have exposed both students and their parents to stress. For example, high school students in Korea have 1,200 formal classroom hours per year compared to 900 hours in the U.S. and 650 hours in the OECD countries. In addition to longer classroom hours, most Korean students enroll at private tutoring institutes for after-school studies. The nation's total expense for private tutoring is 6 percent of the nation's GDP, which is 1.37 times larger than the government's educational budget for 1998. A Korean family spends on average 18 percent of its living expenditure on its children's studies after school hours (Institute for Education Development, 1998).

Because of long hours of study and substantial expenditure on extracurricular studies, some educators criticize the way that Korean schools focus solely on preparing students for college admission. Most students compete against each other. They suffer from academic pressure and from their parents' high (and sometimes unrealistic) expectations about their academic performance. Hence, students who cannot succeed in a competitive school environment tend to show signs of maladjustment in school, dropping out and engaging in various problematic behaviors. Because of the high value placed on college entrance, most teachers and schools are not concerned about the individual potential of students and ignore the special needs of students with disabilities. Special classes and schools for students with disabilities are so limited that only 42.8 percent of students who need special educational services, for example for learning disabilities or mental handicaps, attended either special classes or special schools in 1998 (Lee, S., 1999).

Recognizing the severity of school problems, Koreans have coined the term, "classroom destruction" to describe the current situation and are currently trying to resolve the problems using educational reforms. Examples of educational reforms were the Ministry of Education's approval of alternative schools for maladjusted students and the expansion of the school counseling system to elementary schools in 1998. The Ministry of Education also realized that social service is necessary in school settings to improve students' academic performance and is considering school social work as a possible way of resolving student problems.

Although student problems can be attributed to various causes, most researchers agree that school itself is the major source of these. According to a national study of 1,650 middle- and high-school students, factors that made school life difficult were: lack of interest in classroom learning (72 percent), rigid school regulation (66 percent), poor school facilities (56 percent), competition among students (52.4 percent), and corporal punishment (51.9 percent) (Institute for Education Development, 1998). This research revealed that most student problems resulted from academic pressure and high competition related to college admission.

Every year, only 1 percent of students who graduate from high school are able to enter "first-rate" colleges, and less than 50 percent of high school graduates enter any four-year colleges. The remaining high-school students either re-study for colleges or involuntarily search for jobs.

In this fierce competition for college admission, most Korean students suffer from academic pressure in their daily school life. This pressure leads to various student problems: school maladjustment resulting in dropping out of school, running away from home, and school violence; emotional problems; lack of communication with teachers/parents; and an increasing number of students on limited incomes.

The most serious sign of school maladjustment is the increasing number of students who drop out of school. More than 3 percent of middle- and high-school students (almost 70,000 students) drop out of school every year. Approximately 5 percent of vocational high school students drop out of school because of the limited likelihood of entering a college and the stigma attached to vocational high schools. The number of students dropping out of school has increased by 50 percent within the last 15 years (Ministry of Education, 1998).

Dropping out of school not only results in loss of educational opportunity but also leads to juvenile delinquency and crime. School dropouts often run away from home and are vulnerable to juvenile delinquency. The Police Office revealed that almost 20,000 children were officially reported as runaways, and 52 percent of runaway girls work in the red-light district or liquor bars. The Korean Office of Prosecution reported that the number of juvenile offenders increased by 42 percent between 1992 and 1996, and juvenile offenders comprised 7 percent of the total number of criminals. Sixty-six percent of juvenile offenders were students (Office of the Prosecutor, 1998).

School violence is another type of school maladjustment that has appeared in recent years. One-third of middle- and high-school students are victimized by actual or threatened school violence such as robbery or physical violence. Although school violence and the threat of violence in Korea are less serious than in the United States because the use of guns is not an issue, violence takes place in all levels of the school system. Ganging up and isolating a certain type of student, generally an underachieving student from a low-income home, is a common problem. This type of school violence happens in and around the school site and is committed by students, dropouts, and even teachers as a form of corporal punishment.

A high level of emotional problems among students related to academic stress is the second most severe type of problem in Korean schools. The number of students hospitalized in psychiatric units has increased during the last 10 years and 79 percent of such hospitalizations are caused by academic stress. The most severe manifestation of academic stress is the increase in the number of student suicides. Twenty-one percent of middle- and high-school students and 43 percent of senior students in high school admit to having seriously considered committing suicide because of poor academic performance. According to wills prepared by students who committed suicide, one-third of student suicides (approximately 100 incidents annually) are caused by academic pressure (Han *et al.*, 1997).

The third most severe student problem is a lack of communication with teachers or parents. One reason for the lack of communication between students and teachers is the high number of students per classroom. In 1998, the average classroom size of Korean schools was 49 students per teacher compared to 31 students in Japan and 23 students in the United States. Students also find it physically difficult to talk to their parents because most Korean students spend more than 12 hours per day in school. According to a national survey, more than 50 percent of students had not communicated with their teachers and more than 10 percent had not had a meaningful conversation with their parents during the year preceding the survey (Institute for Education Development, 1998). Without communication between students and teachers, school is considered to be an institution that is focused only on academic performance.

The final important student problem emerging in recent years is the increasing number of low-income students. Rapid industrialization and changing social structures have resulted in an increasing number of broken and low-income families. The number of households headed by children increased from 8,692 in 1991 to 11,513 in 1996, whereas the number of households headed by mothers increased from 5.7 percent to 6.7 percent during the same period (Ministry of Health and Welfare, 1997). Moreover, during the economic crisis of 1998, the number of students who were unable to bring their own lunch to school increased dramatically from 12,381 in 1996 to 139,280 in 1998, which is almost 2 percent of the total student population (Ministry of Education, 1998). A rise in the number of homeless students living with their family in the street or in shelters also became more evident during this time.

In recent years, teachers and social workers consider that school social work is one possible way of resolving these student problems because of its dual objectives of sustaining students' rights by providing various social services, such as economic support and counseling, and of improving their academic achievement by providing educational support.

SCHOOL SOCIAL WORK IN KOREA

Koreans have historically considered social work as a charity or emergency relief for the poor or orphans. With the establishment of a social work department at a four-year college in 1947, however, social work gradually came to be considered as a professional and scientific endeavor. The increasing number of social problems resulting from rapid industrialization prompted Koreans to consider social work as a professional service for resolving various social ills. In 1998, more than 70 colleges in Korea had a social work department, and approximately 50,000 social workers worked in various social work fields (Korea Council of Social Work Education, 1998).

Despite this increased interest in social work, school social work was not considered to be an important social work service until recently. School social work was first introduced to Korea in college social work textbooks in the 1960s, although it was simply referred to as one specialized social work service in countries with advanced welfare systems. Neither theories nor practical methods of school social work were fully explained.

School social work services first appeared in Korea in the late 1960s. One community social welfare center in Seoul, funded by the Canadian Unitarian Church, provided school social work services for the community's low-income elementary school students and juvenile delinquents. The community welfare center contracted with a local elementary school for a social worker to visit the school on a weekly basis. During those visits, the social worker provided counseling services and material support, and linked students and their families with community resources. The social worker also made home visits. These early services are similar to those that visiting teachers in the United States provided in the early 20th century.

However, it was not until the late 1990s that social work was implemented in school settings. The major reasons for this delay were a lack of understanding by both teachers and social workers that school social work is a necessary service for improving a student's academic performance, and the implementation of a school counseling system in Korean schools.

Until the 1990s, social work services in schools were only perceived as providing emergency relief and economic support to impoverished students. Even with the increase in student problems, neither teachers nor education administrators considered school social work as a possible service for resolving student problems. They did not understand the dual objectives of school social work: to help students to achieve their academic goals and to resolve students' problems by providing social services. Schools were focused on teaching and preparing students for college admission rather than resolving students' problems and protecting students' human rights. Therefore, school social work was considered to be beyond the scope of school functions and was not adopted as a necessary school service, despite the increase in student problems during the 1980s.

The second reason for the lack of development of school social work in Korea is related to changes in the Korean education system. After launching a public education system, Korea instituted school counseling services in middle and high schools to assist maladjusted students. In 1958, the Seoul Education District provided 47 teachers with 240 hours of training and dispatched them to middle and high schools as school counselors. Although these teachers were not professionally trained counselors, they provided academic advice and psychosocial therapy and discussed students' future plans. These roles were similar to those of school social workers in the United States. The school counselor system was widespread throughout the nation and the Act for School Counselors was enacted in 1973. This Act required middle and high schools to hire one licensed school counselor for every 18 classes (approximately 1,000 students). The act was revised in 1985, requiring one licensed school counselor to be hired for every 12 classes in middle schools (approximately 700 students) and for every nine classes in high schools (approximately 500 students).

In addition to this mandatory law for school counselors, the Ministry of Education organized voluntary parent school counselors in 1985. The role of these voluntary counselors was to support the licensed school counselors. In 1996, the number of voluntary school counselors increased to approximately 5,000.

Until the mid-1990s, there were fewer than 10 published articles in Korean social work journals related to basic knowledge of school social work and no college textbook on school social work. Hence, neither teachers nor social workers were familiar with school social work.

In the 1990s, the emerging student problems of the 1980s made teachers and social workers question the effectiveness of the school counseling system and provoked a search for more effective and comprehensive services within schools. As a result, the Ministry of Education and the Seoul Education District each decided to introduce school social work services. In 1996, the Ministry of Education chose four middle and high schools out of the entire nation for a two-year pilot project, and the Seoul Education District chose three middle and high schools in Seoul for a one-year pilot project. Each of the seven sample schools hired either a full- or part-time social worker with a master's degree in social work and titled him or her as "Hakyosahoesaupka," a literal translation of school social worker in the Korean language. In these pilot projects, social workers provided individual and group counseling, home visiting, education to teachers and parents, and welfare benefits. After the initial trial period, which demonstrated the effectiveness of school social work, additional steps were taken to implement school social work more widely in Korean schools.

First, after participating as a school social work project in Seoul, one of the high schools hired one full-time and two part-time school social workers. This was the first time in Korean history that school social workers were hired in a school setting. Second, six of the 13 local education districts of Seoul each hired one school social worker and placed them at their youth counseling centers. Although the roles of these social workers were limited to providing the referred students from district schools with counseling services, their services are expected to be expanded to include visiting district schools, educating parents and teachers, linking community resources, and home visiting, which are services traditionally provided by school social workers.

Third, the Ministry of Education announced plans to implement school social work starting in the year 2000 following evaluation of the pilot project, and the Seoul Education District started its second pilot project of school social work with five middle and high schools in 2000.

In the late 1990s, Korean social workers also became interested in school social work. For example, in 1997, the author obtained sponsorship from the Samsung Welfare Foundation to learn about school social work in the United States and, with the assistance of the School Social Work Association of America, organized a week's visit to Chicago for 10 Korean social workers working at various community welfare centers. After the Chicago visit, the 10 social workers implemented school social work services in their own community welfare centers and began expanding the services to the entire nation. As a result of these efforts, almost 300 community welfare centers in Korea have named their own youth services as school social work services. Despite the name, however, only a very limited number of community welfare centers have officially contracted with schools to provide services in school settings rather than in community welfare centers.

Reflecting the growing interest in school social work, most colleges recently started to teach school social work as an elective course, and two textbooks have been published in 1997. One textbook is *School and Social Welfare: Theories and Practice of School Social Work* (Han et al., 1997) and the other textbook is *School Social Work* (Chun *et al.*, 1997). In addition, the subject of school social work was chosen as an elective course for a national examination for qualified social workers in 1998.

Because of this emerging interest in school social work, social workers organized the Korean Society of School Social Work in 1997. The society has approximately 300 members consisting of social workers, academic members, and social work students. The society publishes the annual *Korean Journal of School Social Work* and bi-monthly newsletters. It also holds bi-annual seminars to share information and knowledge of school social work around the nation.

After the first pilot projects of 1996, school social work has achieved recognition as a professional service. Teachers and education administrators recently realized the effectiveness of school social work for resolving student problems. The social work profession itself has also actively promoted school social work as a new social work specialty. Social work educators and researchers published textbooks and articles related to school social work, and most community welfare centers adopted school social work as one way of providing services to youth. School social work in Korea, however, is still in the beginning stages, and more efforts are required to accomplish its objectives.

To achieve the key objectives of school social work, a school social worker must work with students, teachers, parents, and the community, and link them together based on an ecosystem perspective. School social workers must perform the roles of a psychotherapist, educational counselor, broker, utilizer of community resources, and policy maker (Allen-Meares, 1994; Allen-Meares *et al.*, 1986). The role of school social workers in Korea has, however, been limited to providing psychotherapeutic counseling services for resolving student problems. Such a limited role may lead others to misperceive the school social worker as a school counselor rather than a professional who performs various roles with teachers, students, parents, and the community. To differentiate the role of the school social worker from that of the school counselor, the school social worker needs to be an education reformer. Because most student problems result from the competitive school environment, the school social worker should help the schools change their education systems. By instituting change in the education system, the school social worker is able to sustain an individual student's educational rights and potential. By being an education reformer, the school social worker can be a policy maker, which is urgently needed for the full implementation of school social work in Korea.

Another role that is needed is that of broker between school and community resources. According to Kim's national research, which surveyed 3,823 students, parents, and teachers regarding the need for social services in schools, all three groups expressed a need for community resources, such as leisure facilities and cultural activities in their schools (Kim, 1999). This study indicates that the school social worker should link school and community resources to improve students' daily school life. This role of broker may assist in the development of the community-based, school-linked service model, which is currently considered as one of the most effective school social work service.

ISSUES FOR FUTURE DIRECTION

Even though school social work in Korea is in its beginning stage, implementing school social work is the primary goal of many social workers who are working with children. To achieve this goal, the first step is to promote school social work to teachers and education administrators. Because teachers view students and schools as their own territory, they generally feel responsible for their students' problems. This attitude raised conflicts between teachers and school social workers when school social work pilot projects were introduced in Korea. The conflict between teachers and social workers intensified with the enactment of the new Law for Education in 1997, which expanded the school counseling system to elementary schools and limited the qualification of school counselor to those with the teacher's license, even though the roles of school counselor overlap in some ways with those of school social worker.

To resolve the conflicts between teachers and school social workers, school social workers should emphasize their professional roles, focusing not only on advocacy for students' interests, but also as a mediator between students and teachers.

The second step for implementing school social work in Korea is to prepare school social workers, with appropriate educational qualifications and certification, to deal with various student problems. As mentioned earlier, student problems are very diverse and result from the competitive school environment and rapid social change. To provide an effective service, school social workers must work not only with students but also with teachers, parents, and the communities. Because the objectives of school social work are not limited to resolving student problems, school social work must also improve students' rights and academic achievement by changing the educational environment. To achieve this purpose, qualified school social workers in Korea need to work on reducing the adverse impact on students of the competitive school environment through political action and advocacy for educational reform.

The third step for implementing school social work in Korea is to consider the social and cultural characteristics of Korea. In contrast to the traditional model of school social work in the United States, most school social work services in Korea are currently delivered in private community welfare centers rather than in individual schools. By providing services outside of a school setting, community welfare centers have historically reduced the existing tension between teachers and school social workers. Hence, when school social work is first being implemented, community welfare centers will work to help both teachers and social workers maintain their special function without infringing on each other's roles.

Gradual transition from such a delivery system to a school setting may benefit not only teachers and school social workers but also benefit parents. Traditionally, Koreans show their respect for their children's teachers by totally relying on the teachers' evaluation of their children. Most parents believe that visiting the school to discuss their children's problem may be perceived as a sign of disrespect for the teacher or lack of trust in the teacher's ability. Furthermore, most parents feel uncomfortable when a teacher visits their home to discuss their children's educational progress because of the deeply ingrained belief that they must treat the teacher well by preparing gifts or food as a token of their appreciation. Hence, social workers working at community welfare centers may start to increase communication between home and school by playing the role of a broker or a mediator between teachers and parents. Therefore, it is necessary for school social workers in Korea to consider the most efficient method of using community welfare centers as a unique delivery system and most readily accessible agency until school social work is adopted in the school system.

The final step for implementing school social work in Korea is to consider and adopt international standards of school social work. School social workers in Korea can hasten the development of the profession in Korea by communicating with social workers from other countries to share their experiences and knowledge with their counterparts overseas. In this period of globalization, such sharing would provide political influence in developing and implementing school social work in Korea.

REFERENCES

Allen-Meares, P. (1994). Social work services in schools: A national study of entry-level tasks, *Social Work, 39*, 560–565.

Allen-Meares, P., Washington, R., and Welsh, B. (1986). *Social work services in schools*. Englewood Cliffs, NJ: Prentice-Hall.

Cho, M. (1999). *The urbanization of the IMF crisis in Korea, the IMF crisis and city: The case of South Korea*. Seoul: The Korea Center for City and Environment Research.

Chun, B., Kwon, B., Cho, W., Lee, K., & Lee, S. (1997). *School social work*. Taegu, Korea: Institute of Social Welfare Development.

Han, I., Hong, S., Kim, H., & Kim, K. (1997). *School and social welfare: theories and practice of school social work*. Seoul: Hakmunsa.

Institute for Education Development. (1998). *National survey of students' school life*. Seoul: Institute for Education Development.

Korea Council of Social Work Education. (1998). *Annual report of Council*. Seoul: Korea Council of Social Work Education.

Kim, K. (1999, December). *Needs assessment for school social work services in Korea*. Paper presented at a Seminar at Yonsei Social Welfare Research Center, Seoul.

Lee, H. (1999). Globalization and the emerging welfare state: The experience of South Korea. *International Journal of Social Welfare, 8*, 23–37.

Lee, S. (1999). A study of definition and screening procedures for the learning disabilities. *Journal of Emotional and Learning Disabilities, 15(2)*, 6–15.

Ministry of Education. (1997). *Annual statistical report*. Seoul: Ministry of Education.

Ministry of Education. (1998). *Annual statistical report*. Seoul: Ministry of Education.

Ministry of Health and Welfare. (1997). *Annual statistical report*. Seoul: Ministry of Health and Welfare.

Ministry of Health and Welfare. (1998). *Annual statistical report*. Seoul: Ministry of Health and Welfare.

National Pension Corporation. (2000). *Vision 2010*. Seoul: National Pension Corporation.

National Policy Agency (1999). *The White-Book of 1998*. Seoul, National Policy Agency.

National Statistical Office. (1998). *Yearly report of population*. Seoul: National Statistical Office.

Office of the Prosecutor. (1998). *White book of juvenile*. Seoul: Office of the Prosecutor.

Park, C. (1997). *Social security and economic development in Korea*. Seoul: Korea Institute for Health and Social Affairs.

12

SCHOOL SOCIAL WORK IN JAPAN: A PARTNER FOR EDUCATION IN THE 21ST CENTURY

Eizaburo Yamashita

Social Indicators* — Japan	
Population	127,334,000
Percentage under age 15 years	15
Percentage urban (2000)	79
Life expectancy at birth	77.8 men, 85.0 women
Fertility rate	1.33 children per woman
Percentage of illiterate adults	Not available
Per capita GDP in $U.S. (1999)	34,276
Percentage unemployed (1999)	4.7

*Social Indicators. From the Statistics Division of the United Nations. Refer to notes on page 249.
  Reference: http://www.un.org/Depts/unsd/indicators/indic2a.htm

NATIONAL CONTEXT

Japan is a geographically small, densely populated country. It has a population of 120 million living on four main islands in an area a little smaller than the state of California. Most of the country is too mountainous for habitation, agriculture, or other economic activities, so the population is crowded into narrow coastal plains and valleys. The rural population has been declining even further since the 1960s because of rapid industrialization, much of which is concentrated in a vast continuous urban area between Tokyo and Osaka on the central island of Honshu.

The culture and politics of foreign countries have influenced Japan for centuries. Above all, Buddhism, imported from China in the 6th century, has shaped Japanese religious beliefs, art, literature, and culture. However, indigenous Shinto beliefs, which are closely related to Animism, still shape the spiritual life of many people and their love of nature. Japanese people worship Buddha, the traditional gods, and even the Christian deity at the same time

217

without conflict. There are many other ways, apart from religion, in which Japan has borrowed comfortably from other cultures and yet retained its unique cultural identity. In recent decades, the mass media, trade, and increased travel have promoted greater contact between the Japanese people and different cultures, traditions, and ethnic groups. Japan is no longer an isolated country, as it was for so much of its history. However, there continues to be a psychological separation from the rest of the world based on language, attitudes, and culture. Ethnically it is still a homogeneous country, tending to further reinforce the feeling of separation. The sense of belonging to Asia is diluted by Japanese people's strong inclination to be part of Western culture.

Most Japanese adopt the Western lifestyle in their homes, clothes, food, and music. As a result, there has been a weakening of adherence to Japanese cultural heritage and ethnic identity since World War II, accompanied by inevitable stress to the social fabric of the country.

In the 1600s, the Tokugawa regime enforced a policy of separation from other countries, which resulted in the shielding of Japan's unique culture from external contact. This separation lasted until pressures from the West in the middle of the 19th century encouraged the opening up of the country to the outside world. The Meiji government came to power in 1867, and Japan rapidly entered the modern world with a new constitution and an emphasis on the growth of both military and economic strength. The government's goal was to catch up with Western societies, and education was highly valued as a tool to make this happen. The purpose of education was to be either a good soldier or worker as the "child of the emperor."

Rapid industrialization and universal education were also accompanied by militarization. Japan became a colonial power by invading its neighbors. Militarism ultimately led to conflict with the Western powers and Japan's entry into World War II in 1941. Japan surrendered to the Allies in 1945 and was occupied by the United States. The new democratic constitution drafted under the guidance of the American occupation forces renounced war and introduced a new political system. Educational reform became a significant part of post-war change. With the new constitutional emphasis on individual rights, children were to be taught that they are valuable as individuals, in contrast to the prewar value of sacrifice to the emperor.

Koreans are the only ethnic group of significant size in Japan, constituting less than 0.7 percent of the population, or approximately 800,000 people. Most of the first generation of Koreans in Japan came as laborers between 1910 and 1945, many of them by force. Currently there are first-, second-, and third-generation Koreans in Japan, including both North and South Koreans. South Koreans are mostly integrated into the Japanese school system, but many North Koreans go to schools that they established themselves to help maintain their culture and political ideology. Many Koreans use Japanese names, a practice that was imposed on them in pre-war days, and one that they continue to avoid discrimination. As the relationship between Japan and South Korea has improved in recent years, Japanese attitudes toward Koreans have correspondingly improved. However, there are still obstacles to equality for Koreans, stemming both from prejudice and inequity in Japanese law and social customs. For example, North Korean girls wearing traditional Korean dress (Chima Chogori) are often harassed whenever political controversy occurs between Japan and North Korea.

Before the economic stagnation of recent years, many people of Japanese origin from the Middle East and South America lived in Japan. Children of these groups attended Japanese schools, but often found it difficult to adjust because Japanese society and schools are not adequately prepared for students with different languages and cultures.

Japanese is the only language officially and routinely used in Japan. Students from junior high to high school are, however, required to study English for six years. Previously, the English language was taught largely by rote, with heavy emphasis on grammar. In recent years, the government has stressed the importance of proficiency in spoken English and, since the mid-1980s, has invested in new plans for changing the way English is taught. There are now native English speakers in junior high schools working as assistant English teachers or assistant language teachers. However, because these classes are only offered once or twice a week there is little evidence that students' proficiency in spoken English is improving. Given that university examinations remain focused on grammar and memorization, there is little incentive for students to apply their efforts to spoken English.

Japanese society has seen many changes in the last three decades. The aging of the population and the decrease in the number of births are two of the major factors producing social change. In 1973, 2,092,003 babies were born, compared with 1,210,000 in 1996. Meanwhile the percentage of people over 65 years of age has increased from 7.1 percent in 1970 to 14.5 percent in 1995. The number will grow to 26.9 percent by the year 2020 (Department of Health and Welfare, 1998). This change in the relative proportions of older people and youth is the greatest public policy concern in Japan today. Public policy is preoccupied with the amount of help needed by older people and the shrinking number of young people available to provide services and a tax base to fund services for them.

Since World War II, lifestyles have changed dramatically. Although people strongly maintain the unique internal value system, many aspects of the lifestyle resemble that in the West, and people are more likely to abandon the cultural heritage of their ancestors. The gap between young and old has been a serious issue since the 1960s. It was difficult for people raised after World War II and educated by democratic methods to get along with the older generation, who were schooled in the virtues of endurance, sacrifice for the nation, and worship of the emperor. The older generation criticized the young, and in the late 1960s and early 1970s, college and high-school students reacted through violent rebellion against the political and educational systems. The enormous growth of industry since the 1960s, with the accompanying change from rural, agricultural to industrial, urban life, has been another contributing factor to the drastic changes in Japanese life. Agriculture stagnated and the country went from supplying 98 percent of its food in 1960 to 67 percent in 1990 (Statistics Bureau, 1995). Opening the market to food imports has produced a measure of national anxiety and opposition.

Rapid change has produced new problems in society, leading to the need for a new profession that could deal with social issues that were previously handled by the family. There were few examples of social work activities until the mid-1940s, and the government had paid little attention to the need for social work. The profession started to develop in the 1950s, modeled on the American and European systems. Methods used are still derived from the United States and Europe, although the services provided are not comparable. The focus of social services in Japan has been on implementation of legislation rather than on meeting people's needs. The government has mainly directed its efforts toward providing social services to older people, in response to the urgent needs of the aging population. Out of 827,189 individuals working for social welfare institutions in 1997, 246,918 (29.8 percent) were providing services to older people, and the number is expected to increase in the near future (Department of Health and Welfare, 1999).

There are two laws that provide for child welfare, the Child Welfare Law enacted in 1947 and the Maternal Welfare Law, focused on support for single mothers and widows, enacted in 1964. These laws provide institutional care of children who cannot be cared for at home because of poverty or behavioral problems. Only recently has the focus of child welfare services shifted from institutional care to family preservation.

Children's basic needs and health care are adequately covered in Japan. The rapid growth of the economy has brought about the reduction of poverty and the provision of high-quality medical services, covered either through parents' employment or the local government system. Medical insurance covers from 30 to 80 percent of the cost of medical care. However, although basic needs are well-covered, the social trends described previously have resulted in various problems for children. For example, the nation's excessive focus on economic development has been at the cost of providing a caring network that supports families. In addition, welfare policy in Japan has been heavily focused on caring for the growing population of aging people.

The social cost of modern industrialization has been a decline in the extended family system. Migration from the country to the cities resulted in a loss of close community networks and extended family that previously buffered children from various stresses. Today, children are more likely to live in isolated nuclear families in large cities without close interactions with other people. In 1995, 58.7 percent of Japanese families were nuclear families, 25.3 percent were single households, 10.5 percent were families with grandparents, and 5.2 percent were other types of families (Department of Health and Welfare, 1998). It is no longer typical for Japanese children to be cared for by their grandparents, and this contributes to social isolation. Divorce is gradually increasing, although it remains below the rates in Western nations. Fathers typically are not involved in child rearing, remaining late at work or following their own interests after work hours. The government has become concerned about the lack of involvement by fathers and has recently instituted a campaign to encourage fathers to pay more attention to their children.

Social work services to children have only recently been instituted for the broader population in the community, and they remain inadequate. Although there has been some growth in direct services to children, the government has disregarded the need for social work services to children in the school setting.

Child abuse has become a concern in Japanese society in recent years. Because there is no reporting system, the number of cases of child abuse is not known. However 4,102 child abuse cases were dealt with in 1996 (compared with 1,101 in 1991) at child counseling centers, which are the main referring agencies established by the local government for cases of child abuse (Department of General Affairs Youth Section, 1998). Importantly, the absence of a reporting system means that there are few ways of protecting children or helping families under stress.

EDUCATION IN JAPAN

After the collapse of feudalism in the 1860s, the country placed a heavy emphasis on the effectiveness of education as a means of modernizing Japanese society. The compulsory school system was introduced in 1872 by the Meiji government, and by the 1890s every child was attending school. There is a highly structured school system with six years of compulsory education at elementary school, for children aged six to 12, and three years at junior high school, for children aged between 13 and 15. Although attendance at high school is not compulsory, 96 percent of all children enter and complete three years of high school. In 1997, 47.3 percent of high-school graduates chose to attend college courses of between two and four years' duration. Eighty-five percent (2,400,000) of students went to academically-oriented colleges, and 15 percent (440,000) went to junior colleges. In 1998, there were 788,547 students studying in technical colleges (Department of Education, 1998b). In addition, most children go to either public or private nursery schools or kindergarten for some years before entering elementary school.

There are approximately 220 school days each year, with the school year starting in April and ending in March. The government has been trying to reduce the number of school days since the early 1990s to secure more free time for students and for teachers, who are likely to feel burdened because of the long working hours. This trend is related to pressure from labor organizations overseas, such as the International Labor Organization (ILO), to reduce the working hours of Japanese workers. Now every other Saturday is free and Saturday school will be abolished by 2002. The maximum class size is now 35 students. All students follow the same national curriculum, which is set by the Department of Education. Teachers, therefore, have limited freedom in their teaching and are not allowed to deviate from the prescribed curriculum.

Children with physical and developmental disabilities are generally educated in separate schools. Although integrated education is the current trend, prompted by pressure from parents and civil liberties groups, and some children with disabilities wish to study in a regular school, there are still many schools that refuse to accept disabled students. Some regular schools do have classes for children with minor disabilities, but the number of such classes is very small, so that 70 percent of students in special education must commute to a school that offers special education classes. There were 12,259 students enrolled in special education classes in 1993, 78.8 percent of whom were in speech therapy classes (Japan Welfare Union of Mentally Retarded, 1995). There is still little collaboration and interaction between these classes and the regular classes within a school. Teaching children with disabilities in separate schools is still the norm, and it remains very difficult for disabled children to enter public high schools. Although 23 percent of high-school students and 6 percent of junior-high-school students attend private schools, these schools usually do not accept disabled students. The right of disabled children to receive a regular education is still not recognized, and legislation is needed to guarantee integrated education for them.

Junior-high and high-school students usually wear school uniforms and their behavior is strictly regulated by school rules. There is, consequently, little sense of freedom at the junior-high and high-school level, in sharp contrast to the more relaxed atmosphere of elementary schools. There is little freedom for students even to determine their hairstyle. Until the early 1990s many junior high schools required the heads of male students to be closely shaved, and skirt lengths of female students were measured. Typically, junior high school students are checked at the school gate in the morning to ensure that they are wearing their uniforms correctly and do not have in their possession anything that is prohibited.

Many school rules disregard the rights and the individual value of the students. Much of the teachers' time is spent making students follow the school rules. This teaching role, called "Seikatsu Shido," which means "student's life guidance," is regarded as important. Teachers interpret this guidance role mostly in directive and authoritarian ways in junior high schools, which might be one cause of student disaffection, as evidenced by increased bullying and nonattendance. Many parents support such strict school policies, including the way they are enforced, even supporting the use of corporal punishment.

Japan has undertaken several reforms in the educational system. The first was the institution of universal education in 1872, which was designed to help modernize the country to catch up with Western countries. After World War II, the educational system was again reformed, based on the democratic goals of treating the individual child as a person with dignity. A third educational reform was begun in the 1980s to respond to rapid social changes and help prepare the country for future change. In particular, the government was looking for ways to deal with problems such as bullying, school refusal, and increased violence in schools. The Central Education Reform Committee (Department of Education, 1998b) recommended empowering children, stressed the importance of education in the home, and encouraged the teaching of morals. However, the current reforms have not made adequate provisions for addressing problems such as bullying and the conditions that lead children to refuse to attend school.

Excessive stress, experienced by many Japanese school children, is closely related to the high value the Japanese public places on education. Most people believe that a child's success in school guarantees future security and a good life. For this reason children are sent to school early and experience intense competition starting in early childhood. Given that admission to a prestigious university is seen as extremely important, both schools and students are exposed to an excessively competitive atmosphere.

One result of this competition is the prevalence of private tutoring schools, called "Juku". Fifty-nine percent of junior-high-school students (rising to more than 80 percent of ninth graders) and 24 percent of elementary school students attended these institutions after regular school hours in 1993 (The Jiji Press, 1998). It is not unusual to see 10-year-old children at train stations after 9 p.m. on their way home from Jukus. These children will then have to complete homework and may not go to bed until after midnight.

Some Jukus are "cram schools" where students are taught far beyond their grade level so that they can keep ahead of the rest of their class. In other Jukus, students are given remedial teaching so that they do not fall behind their peers. There are even Jukus for kindergarten students to prepare for elite, private elementary schools. Cramming for the entrance exams for admission to the "right" high school and university assumes an overwhelming importance and is a source of serious psychological pressure that contributes to school refusal, bullying, acting out, and even suicide.

According to one of the major daily newspapers in Japan, *Asahi Shimbun* (1998), more than 100,000 school children from first through ninth grade missed more than 30 school days in 1997, mostly resulting from psychological stress. Approximately 2 percent of junior high school students and 0.3 percent of elementary school students were in this category of students who were avoiding school. The number of school children who are not attending school has been continuously increasing since the 1970s, leading the government to initiate various programs to deal with the problem. School nurses and special education teachers have been coping with the problem within the school setting. Since the 1980s, there have also been educational counseling centers in each school district, which play a major role in coping with nonattendance. Since 1993, a new program called the "adaptation guidance class," established outside of the school system, has been used as an alternative method to help children make the transition back to school. A program to introduce school counselors was initiated in 1985 and has been growing since then. Despite the plethora of new programs, the number of children who refuse to attend school has continued to rise. These programs have primarily focused on making the child adapt to the school environment, rather than considering the needs of the individual child and modifying the school environment to fit the child. There are still very limited choices for children who refuse to go to school. For example, all schools have the same curriculum, structure, and strict rules.

Students who attend school regularly also live stressful school lives and many discharge their anxiety or anger in unhealthy or antisocial ways. During the 1980s and early 1990s, there was an increase in the incidence of junior high school students involved in school violence, such as assaulting teachers, fighting, bullying, and vandalism as a way of discharging frustration stemming from excessive expectations. It was not unusual for junior high schools to call for police on graduation day to prevent students from attacking teachers, as many students expressed their anger and dissatisfaction on the last day of school. Schools responded to violence by strengthening control over students. Tough physical education teachers were assigned as the "life guidance teachers" and were assisted by police. However, bullying increased in schools and cases of suicide by students who were overwhelmed by the stress of school also were increasing. In 1986, a 14-year-old junior high school student hanged himself in a railway station toilet, after a long period of bullying by a group of peers. His death signaled a trend, with bullying and suicides resulting from bullying spreading enormously among school children throughout Japan.

The latest phenomenon occupying the front page of national newspapers is the "chaotic classroom," also dubbed the "collapsed classroom," in which learning has stopped because of student disruption (*Asahi Shimbun*, 1999). In these classes, most notably in elementary schools, many students do not participate, but leave class without permission or engage in disruptive or violent behavior.

School personnel have attempted various methods of dealing with these problems, but without much success. Schools have focused their efforts on understanding the "pathology" of the children, rather than on the reactions of the children to the system, and have consequently failed to understand the issues and meet the students' needs. The problems experienced by students are related to educational issues, and can only be solved by examining the educational environment and by looking for a way to change the excesses of the educational system. Approaches focused on the potential and value of the individual child, such as are used in social work, would be more appropriate means of resolving these new educational problems.

Classroom teachers have traditionally dealt with students' problems, including contacting parents. Whereas handling students' problems is still a significant role for teachers today, students are increasingly turning to the school nurse for help. School nurses have started to play a larger role in coping with problems among students. Because these services were inadequate for solving the problems, the Department of Education introduced school counselors with professional clinical experience in 1995. The counseling program has been introduced gradually, and therefore the number of schools that currently have school counselors is limited. However, some local governments have launched a school counseling system, employing people without professional training. As this service is extended into more schools, counseling is likely to be seen as a panacea for resolving youth problems in school, although it will not be possible to judge the effectiveness of the program until is has been operating for some years.

School social work as practiced in various countries provides a different approach to dealing with students' problems from the methods used by counselors, nurses, and teachers. The following sections illustrate the potential for using social work methods in the Japanese school system.

HISTORY OF SCHOOL SOCIAL WORK

Because school social work has not yet been formally introduced into Japan, this section gives information about a model project that the author introduced and operated between 1986 and 1998, and discusses the potential role for social work in the Japanese school system.

The author was employed on a part-time basis by the Tokorozawa Board of Education (near metropolitan Tokyo) as an educational counselor, and had conducted a survey of parents and teachers in the Tokorozawa school district regarding school social work for his MSW thesis. The superintendent of schools in Tokorozawa became interested in the information generated by this research and offered the author a position in the school district as a liaison between students, parents, and schools. At that time, schools in Tokorozawa, as in other parts of the country, were in a state of turmoil because of violent behavior of junior high school students. Teachers were confused about the changes in students' behavior and were unable to respond effectively.

Although hired under the title of "educational counselor," the author used the title "school social worker" and provided services to families and the community. This was the first use of the term school social worker in Japan. School social work's potential for solving school problems attracted the attention of the media, which had been reporting extensively on nonattendance and violence in the schools. The opportunity was taken to publish articles and books and deliver speeches in various parts of the country to further publicize the potential of school social work to address the problems experienced by school children (Yamashita, 1989; 1993; 1998a-c; 1999).

Services were provided to students with behavioral problems and those students who refused to attend school. As school violence decreased in the mid-1990s by increasing control over students using tough physical education teachers and police, these services became centered on nonattendance.

Most students who refuse to attend school also isolate themselves from everyone except their families and do not leave their home for long periods of time. Teachers usually make home visits for such children but mostly fail to establish contact with them. Therefore, in most cases parents handle the situation themselves. There are self-help groups around the country for parents of children who refuse to attend school, and these groups provide a chance for parents to support each other. The students themselves need a place other than school where they can go to meet people when they are ready to leave their homes. There are few alternative meeting places for these young people. In 1987, together with people from the local community, a club was established where children could get together regardless of the difficulties they were experiencing, whether they were refusing to attend school or had disabilities of varying conditions. The club, which was called "Free Space", has been run completely by volunteers and has received no financial support from any organization. Between 1987 and 1999, more than 1,000 children and 1,500 parents have visited the club. On weekends more than 60 people, including staff, attend the club to play games, soccer, or table tennis, play guitars, and chat. The club has been an obvious resource for children who are phobic about school. However, there are very few of these clubs because of the lack of financial resources. These kinds of alternatives are crucial for Japanese school children who cannot handle the pressure of the school system as it is currently organized.

In spite of the attention given to this pilot project in the media, no new school social work positions have been created either in Tokorozawa or in other districts, and it is unclear whether anyone else in Japan is working in a school setting performing a similar role. However, few social workers appear interested in working in school settings, and the school system has been slow to open up to specialists from fields outside of teaching. Although counselors have been recruited to schools, this has not yet extended to school social workers.

There are several reasons for this. First, the social work profession is not well-known in Japan, whereas the counseling profession is better recognized by the public and is a popular profession that young people aspire to join. Second, neither educators nor social workers (who tend to limit their services to certain areas such as work with older people, disabled people, and institutional care) recognize the relevance of social work to the school setting. Third, there are obstacles to collaboration between the Department of Education and the Department of Health that have not been adequately addressed.

Despite the lack of support for school social work in Japan, an informal organization was established in 1989 to promote the profession. Volunteers have organized monthly meetings and symposia, and a book was published to stimulate interest in school social work (Kizashi, 1994). In 1997, the organization hosted an international meeting in Tokyo, inviting school social work leaders from the United States to speak to professionals and to members of the public. The School Social Work Association of Japan was established in January 1999 to promote increased awareness of the potential of school social work among the public and the social work and teaching professions.

The professional literature regarding school social work remains sparse, although a few authors have published articles about school social work (see, for example, Kadota, 1997; Sato, 1995; Shibuya, 1998). Selected articles from *Social Work in Education*, the American journal, have been translated into Japanese and published as a book, which is the only volume of translated school social work literature to date (Yamashita, 1998d).

ISSUES FOR FUTURE DIRECTION

There is an urgent need for school social work in Japan, considering the problems of school children and the increasing isolation of both children and families. As previously stated, expectations for educational achievement are very strong, and children are forced into a competitive educational atmosphere throughout their school lives. Great numbers of school children are suffering from the pressures caused by excessive expectations. There are few resources like social work and counseling that could help young people deal with their emotional difficulties.

The pioneering work in school social work reported here has demonstrated both the feasibility of school social work as an effective means of coping with the problems faced by school children, families, schools, and the community as a whole, and that such services will be accepted. However, much more publicity is needed before the public can be expected to recognize the need for, and value of, such programs. Other preparatory work also needs to be carried out in anticipation of starting school social work services. Social work professionals need to be trained to provide services in schools, and more collaboration with other agencies is also needed to prepare for the delivery of comprehensive services to schoolchildren.

Within the school system there are barriers to the introduction of school social work. The education system is closed to outside influence, and it has been slow to accept other professionals and new ideas because teachers have managed the schools alone for many years. In addition, there is neither a legal mandate nor any financial basis for providing a new service. There is also the question of the appropriate aegis for the program. Schools are under the Department of Education, and social work is under the Department of Health and Welfare. These two departments have been highly independent and reluctant to collaborate with other agencies. This separation may also be a factor that has inhibited social work from reaching out into the educational field.

There are two issues to be resolved in this respect. One is whether the Department of Education would be sufficiently flexible to accept different values that bring broader perspective to education. There is a need for the school system to consider the influence of the environment on children and to understand and respect children as individuals. The other issue is whether the Department of Health and Welfare will see the placement of social workers in schools as an effective way of coping with youth problems. Although there has been a recent trend toward collaboration between the two departments, the tendency of each to remain within its own domain would need to be reversed if school social work is to be implemented.

The question of which department would employ school social workers is a crucial issue for the future. Given that the Board of Education has a tremendous impact on educational services and policy, it is highly likely that it would be the agency responsible for employing and placing social workers in schools. However, if social workers worked under the strong control of the school and the Board of Education they would find it difficult to deliver services using social work methods and values. Social workers employed by local government or local social service agencies are more likely to be able to maintain independence and neutrality in dealing with school problems.

To date, there is no college that prepares social workers to work in schools. General social work is taught in both junior colleges and at the college level. However, many people are currently employed in a social work capacity without formal social work training or qualifications. It is crucial to raise the status of social work as a profession and to establish professional standards to avoid the problems that would arise if people without adequate preparation were employed as social workers in schools. Although no specialist school social work training is currently available, the Japan College of Social Work offers some teaching on school social work that has been well-received by social work students. After a training program is available and school social workers have been employed in schools, the need for certification and a legal mandate would need to be addressed.

School social workers are needed to deal with nonattendance, bullying, and behavioral problems, which are the current major concerns of the school system. There will also be an opportunity for involvement in special education. Now that the lack of flexible interaction between regular education and special education is apparent, the education of students with special needs should promote both integration and student self-determination.

Although school social workers are needed to deal primarily with urgent existing problems, school problems will become more complex and diverse as society changes in the next few years. Increasingly, there will be a need for school social workers to collaborate with other professionals in schools and agencies to maximize effectiveness in resolving a wide range of student problems.

Schools have traditionally been places where children were educated to meet the country's needs. Before World War II they were trained to be soldiers or laborers to promote the modernization of the nation. Students were not treated as persons with values and dignity, but as servants of the emperor. Since the war, students have been taught the same virtues of hard work, endurance, persistence, and obedience, but they have been afforded little freedom of expression. Teachers continue to be authoritarian and to discriminate against students with special needs. They value the "good students" who are obedient and high academic achievers. Corporal punishment is still used, and strict school rules are used to keep students under control. The rights of children have not been fully respected and those with special needs experience discrimination.

This lack of attention to students' rights has been costly. Schools and teachers have been challenged by students since the late 1970s through various problems such as violent behavior, school refusal, and bullying. These problems are symptomatic of deep problems in the education system. However, there has been little effort toward change and schools have continued to try to force students to conform, although neither coercive attempts to change the behavior of students who challenge the system nor alternative programs, which are little more than "Band-Aid" solutions, have succeeded in solving these problems.

Schools influence parents as well as children. However parents, mostly mothers (who play the central role in their children's education), refrain from expressing their opinion regarding school matters for fear that the teacher would maltreat their child. Japanese mothers believe that both their child's and their own happiness depends on the child's academic success, so they are unlikely to express opinions that might jeopardize their child's chances. There is a common saying among mothers: "I can't say anything against the school because my child is hostage to the teacher." Although there is a Parents' and Teachers' Association (PTA) in every school, parents are very reluctant to be involved in the activities of PTAs. There are also class meetings that provide an opportunity for parents and teachers to communicate, but teachers usually guide these, and parents are reluctant to speak. So, in spite of the existence of PTAs and school meetings, the relationship between school and home is a distant one.

To change these undesirable relationships between students, schools, and families, schools need to establish a partnership with students and families. Schools also need to relinquish the authoritarian approach. More flexibility is needed in school policies and in the curriculum to promote student involvement in school. Furthermore, there should be alternatives to meet the needs of students, in particular, alternative schools and charter schools such as are offered in the United States. It is true that the Japanese educational system has been successful in many ways. However, the present needs of children are not the same as they were immediately following the war, and students have challenged the system—as evidenced by the current problems in schools.

A school social work program could deal with some of the existing problems by applying social work methods in schools. School social workers would be able to communicate with children with respect and sincere attitudes, help the school system understand the individual needs of the student, and treat the student as a partner in problem-solving. School social workers could also act as a liaison between schools and families, mediating conflicts and coordinating services. When relationships between schools and families are distant, parents need, and would appreciate, such a liaison. School social workers could contribute to remodeling the school system by applying the ecological system of social work. Although, realistically, school social work cannot solve every problem, it could introduce significant knowledge and skills that are currently nonexistent in the school system. It is anticipated that parents and the public would accept a new approach to coping with the increasing problems in school, and would respond positively to the introduction of school social work after they understand its purpose and methods.

REFERENCES

(1998, August 7). Nonattendants over 100,000. *Asahi Shimbun,* p.1.

(1999). Collapsed classroom. *Asahi Shimbun.*

Department of Education (1998). *Report of the Central Education Reform Committee.* Tokyo: Department of Education.

Department of Education (1998). *Statistics on education.* Tokyo: The Printing Office of the Department of Treasury.

Department of General Affairs Youth Section (1998). *White paper on youth.* Tokyo: The Printing Office of the Department of Treasury.

Department of Health and Welfare (1998). *White paper on health and welfare.* Tokyo: Gyousei.

Department of Health and Welfare (1999). *Statistics of health and welfare, 1998.* Tokyo: Statistics Association on Health and Welfare.

Japan Welfare Union of Mentally Retarded (1995). *White paper on developmental disabilities.* Tokyo: Nihon Bunka Sha.

The Jiji Press (1998). *Education data land '98-'99.* Tokyo: The Jiji Press.

Kadota, K. (1997). Is school social work necessary in Japan? *Science of Social Welfare.* (Shakai fukushi gaku). 38, 2, 67–80.

Kizashi (1994). *A new way of life: the path to traditional folk art craftsman.* Tokyo: Gakuen Sha.

Sato, A. (1995). School social work as a community resource: Focusing on the Tokorozawa model and the clinical psychologist. *International Social Work Information, 19,* 20-26.

Shibuya, M. (1998). About the credential system of school social workers in the United States. *Social Work Research, 4,* 30-40.

Statistics Bureau (1995). *Statistics of Japan.* Tokyo: Printing Office of Department of Treasury.

Yamashita, E. (1989). *To see a rainbow: As an accompanying runner for non-attendants.* Nagoya: Reimei Shobo.

Yamashita, E. (1993). *The scenery of the time: Trying to be a true partner of the children.* Tokyo: Gakuen Sha.

Yamashita, E. (1998a). *Keep resisting forever, children!: A report of a school social worker's challenge.* Tokyo: Tokuma Shoten.

Yamashita, E. (1998b). *Songs for the loved ones: Keep walking with non-attendants.* Nagoya: Reimei Shobo.

Yamashita, E. (1998c). Potential of social work services based on schools. *International Social Work Information, 22,* 5-58.

Yamashita, E. (1998d). *What is school social work? Its theory and practice.* Tokyo: Gendai Shokan.

Yamashita, E. (1999). *Ecological perspectives on child issues: From education to cohabitation.* Tokyo: Gakuen Sha.

CONCLUSION

Marion Huxtable and Eric Blyth

Social work and education have much in common. Both professions have a dual goal of developing the potential of the individual and improving society as a result. Children who do not progress academically and socially are likely to live in poverty and dependence; similarly, differences in educational ranking between countries perpetuate the gap between rich and poor countries. Progress for both the individual and the country depends on successful education. School, therefore, provides an optimal setting where social workers can carry out their mission of supporting children's personal development, and in doing so, raise the quality of life for all.

THE NEED FOR SCHOOL SOCIAL WORK

School social work developed following the introduction of universal education, with the goals of bringing poor children into schools, and helping them make full use of educational opportunity and complete their schooling. Although the world has made rapid progress in the last half-century toward universal education, 130 million children of primary school age are still not in school (United Nations Children's Fund, 1999). The Millennium Report of the Secretary-General of the United Nations stated that "education is the key to the new global economy" and urged the Millennium Summit to "endorse the objectives of demonstratably narrowing the gender gap in primary and secondary education by 2005 and of ensuring that, by 2015, all children complete a full course of primary education" (Annan, 2000, p 5). School social work is still needed for its traditional role in promoting school enrollment, improving attendance, and making universal education a reality in developing countries.

Contributors to this book document factors interfering with students' success that are similar the world over: children with disabilities are often excluded from regular schools; children from ethnic or other minority groups are still marginalized; poor children still do not reach their potential; family problems such as divorce affect children's adjustment; violence of various kinds affects students both in and out of school; inter-ethnic conflicts develop within schools; and schools have not adapted sufficiently to meet students' changing needs. After universal enrollment has been achieved, the goals of school social work are to promote inclusion of all students, remove obstacles to success in school, and support students' social and emotional development.

COMMON THEMES IN SCHOOL SOCIAL WORK AROUND THE WORLD

Although different methods are suited to different countries, reflecting the need to adapt social work to the cultural characteristics of each society, the chapters in this book reveal common values, goals, and principles in school social work that transcend cultural and historical differences and unite the profession. The rights of children (especially the right to appropriate education and equal opportunity) and the goal of helping all children reach their potential are the guiding principles for all school social workers. School social workers see themselves as advocates for children, by helping schools respond flexibly to the differing needs of students. School social workers in different countries have much in common regarding the methods used, in spite of the great variation in culture between these countries. Home-school communication, direct counseling for students, consultation with teachers, advocacy for students, and collaboration with community agencies have been the mainstays of school social work.

DIFFERENT PATHS IN SCHOOL SOCIAL WORK

While school social work programs have much in common, there are some significant differences between countries, and even within countries. The differences, however, appear to be secondary compared with the common values, goals, and principles that unite the profession. Some of the major differences relate to:

- the professional titles used and the significance of these titles;
- the relationship in Europe between school social work and the traditional profession of social pedagogy; and
- the differing aegis under which school social work programs operate.

Professional Title

Differing approaches to school social work in different countries are revealed by the professional titles used. Titles and the meaning they carry for the individual holding the title are important to the identity of a profession. It is also important for the title to have a positive meaning for the clients who use the service. In addition, if school social work is to have a significant international role in advocating for children, it needs a stable title that carries a positive image and a clear meaning to the international community, as do other well-established professions. The following summary of the titles currently used is important to the discussion of professional identity and image.

In the Nordic countries the title of *school curator* (from the Latin root *cura* meaning care) carries the sense of concern for the development of individuals and groups.

In the United Kingdom, two titles are used: *education welfare officer* and, less frequently, *education social worker.* The term "welfare" means "wellbeing"; however, it also carries the sense of government intervention, especially when paired with the term "officer." Although the term "welfare" in the United Kingdom did not previously have negative connotations, there has been an ideological shift since the 1980s away from the social contract, in which welfare is seen as a right, toward individual initiative and the market economy, resulting in new perceptions of the term "welfare." The two titles currently in use (*education welfare officer* and *education social worker*) point to questions of divergent training, philosophy, and roles that continue to trouble education social work in the United Kingdom. Most practitioners use the title education welfare officer, and the main role performed under this name continues to be attendance enforcement, with less emphasis on the broader activities of advocacy, mental health work, and prevention that are the signature of social work.

Malta uses the title *education welfare* and Ghana has used both *education welfare* and *school welfare,* reflecting these two countries' historical connections with Britain.

In Canada, the usual title is *school social worker*, although many practitioners hold the dual title *school social worker/attendance counselor* and continue to perform attendance work using social work methods. In the United States, the title *school social worker* is widely used, although, as opportunities open up for school social workers to participate in a wide range of programs in schools, many social workers in schools hold other titles that reflect their current program or role. Some countries that have recently developed school social work service have adopted the title *school social work,* translated into their own language (for example *Schulsozialarbeit* in Germany).

In Argentina, the recent change of title from *school social worker* to *social assistant*, and the accompanying reduction in professional requirements for holding the positions, represent a significant downgrading of the profession. This example illustrates the significance of professional titles and the importance of establishing a stable identity for the profession both within nations and internationally.

School Social Work and Social Pedagogy in Europe

In several European countries, school social work has been influenced by a tradition that exists in neither North America nor the United Kingdom. *Social pedagogy* in Belgium, Denmark, France, Germany, Italy, Luxembourg, the Netherlands, and Spain is a distinct profession that usually requires several years of training (Jones, 1994). The *social pedagog* works with individuals, groups, communities, and social organizations using human relations skills to assist in the human development of client groups in various settings including schools. It is a profession that has become well established since the 1940s with its own professional associations, journals, and conferences. *Social pedagogy* has much in common with social work; for example, both are concerned with helping clients maximize their potential in the areas of social skills, emotional development, and independent functioning. *Social pedagogy* in schools similarly has much in common with school social work. Both professions have also faced problems in their professional identity, status, and recognition, due in part to working with vulnerable populations that often have little clout in the political arena.

In Germany, *school social work* (a direct translation of the term used in the United States) was added to *social pedagogy* in the schools, and there is some blending of roles. This blending of roles is paralleled by the establishment of shared professional training for social workers and social pedagogs in some higher education institutions. In some Eastern European countries the school social worker is not seen as distinct from the *social pedagog*. In fact the terms used are *pedagog skolny* in Poland and *socialais pedagogs* in Latvia (personal communication with Maria Bochenska-Seweryn and Krystina Kluz, Jagiellonian University, Krakow, Poland, 1999; Ludmilla Smirnova and Oleg Denisov, Latvia Association of Social Workers, Riga, Latvia, 1999). In Hungary, where both social pedagogy and social work are new professions, training programs in higher education institutions have been in existence since 1980 for both, with somewhat similar course content. Both professions also have started to practice in schools (Hare, 1993). In contrast to the blending of the two roles in some European countries, they continue to be seen as distinct in others, such as Finland.

The question of whether to blend the two professions together or to keep them separate with different roles and training is another issue for the future of school social work as an internationally recognized profession.

The Aegis of School Social Work

In the development of school social work in different countries, there is significant difference in the aegis and location of the program. It is variously provided by the school system itself, other government agencies, by private agencies with government funding, or by social agencies with mixed funding.

In Hong Kong, the service has typically been provided by nongovernmental agencies using government funding. In Korea, the pilot program has placed school social workers in schools with funding from the Ministry of Education. In the Nordic countries, the school social worker is an integral part of the school. In Ghana, the Ministry of Education provides the service but has located it in a separate department, the Welfare Unit, rather than under the Learning and Teaching Department. In Germany, school social work is the result of collaboration between youth welfare agencies and the school system. In the United States, there is a long tradition of school social workers being employed by the school system. School social workers in the United States are strongly committed to maintaining their position in the school system, believing that it allows them more influence in educational decisions. As roles and methods have changed over the years, the model in the United States has increasingly emphasized teamwork with practitioners of all the other disciplines that work in the school and especially with teachers. The teamwork is enhanced by the close working relationships established when professionals work for the same employer.

In recent years, there has also been a movement toward school-linked services in the United States, in which social work services are provided by a separate agency in collaboration with the school. As the needs of children have increased and the fragmentation of services in most communities produced increased frustration for professionals who serve children, it became apparent that the school is the logical location for extensive social services. Many communities across the country have now established formal relationships between schools and social and health services, locating those services close to schools or in schools. These services are usually provided in addition to school social work services, and ideally there is a close working relationship between the school social worker and workers who staff the school-linked service (Aguirre, 1995; Briar-Lawson, Lawson, Collier, & Joseph, 1997; Corrigan & Bishop, 1997; Cousins, Jackson, & Till, 1997; Tapper, Kleinman, & Nakashian, 1997).

There are advantages and disadvantages to working within the school system. In some countries, it is considered that working outside the system makes the school social worker better able to advocate for the student without being unduly influenced by the school as the employer. On the other hand, working within the school enables the school social worker to develop working relationships with all the staff of the school including administrators, teachers, and others, and to work with this network of adults to provide support for students and improve the school culture. This approach is most effective if school social workers (and other professional support staff) have parity with teachers in professional standards, training, salary, and working conditions. Under these circumstances, school social workers are able to keep their professional integrity and, at the same time, foster collegial relationships necessary for good teamwork.

Where school social workers are based within schools, there is also a need for additional social services for children and families outside of school, such as those provided by school-linked services in close collaboration with schools and located in schools or nearby for easy access by families.

In countries where school social work is less well-accepted it seems to be more productive to provide the service from an outside agency. Such an arrangement may be beneficial if the salary or training of social workers in general or school social workers in particular are not equal to that of teachers, because inequality may interfere with well-functioning partnerships. In this approach, school social workers retain their independence to determine their own goals and methods, and to provide an outside perspective without pressure from the school system.

THE SCHOOL SOCIAL WORK ROLE AND ITS FUTURE DEVELOPMENT

Schools in every country need a team of professionals, including school social workers, working in partnership with teachers to help children with problems that interfere with their education and to ensure that all children are included in the mainstream of school. The value of multidisciplinary teamwork is increasingly recognized in schools today as in many other human service locations. Accounts from various countries in this book indicate that a range of professionals including teachers, school social workers, and other specialists can contribute knowledge from their individual disciplines to develop preventive programs and resolve social and psychological problems. In interdisciplinary teams, school social workers contribute specialized knowledge of family issues, community resources, and how to work with complex systems.

The school social work role has evolved over several decades, and there is constant debate over its direction. Studies of the role in the United States have repeatedly shown that many school social workers spend most of their time in direct work with students and families (Costin, 1975; Allen-Meares, 1977, 1994), rather than on advocacy, leadership roles, and prevention. As schools in different parts of the world struggle with adapting to the fast-changing needs of students, school social workers have the opportunity to take a leadership role in developing programs to meet new challenges. They have knowledge and skills in evaluating problems, understanding behavior, and involving community organizations to help schools make the transition to more democratic institutions.

Poor attendance, bullying, low achievement, substance abuse, and other common social problems affect large numbers of students. School social workers can influence many more students by implementing programs designed to prevent these problems for the entire student body, rather than for the few who are referred directly. School social workers must take the initiative to demonstrate to employers that preventive activities deliver better results than piecemeal interventions with single students.

It is clear that school social workers everywhere often feel hindered by the conditions of their work and the expectations of their employers from acting as reformers, advocates, and leaders in developing new programs. However, every profession must take control of its own destiny. School social workers must use their knowledge of how social change is best implemented within local conditions and cultures to effect change in both schools and in managing their own profession.

STRENGTHENING SCHOOL SOCIAL WORK

School social work has various obstacles to overcome before it can realize its potential. The profession's ability to act as a leader in education is limited by the interrelated problems of inadequate funding, perceived low status, and inadequate recognition in the education hierarchy. The school social work profession's response to these challenges will determine its future development and influence in schools.

Several of the authors raise the issue that provision of services is limited by inadequate funding, particularly government funding. Improving the funding hinges on convincing legislators and policy-makers both of the need for social work services in schools and of the effectiveness of these services. Social work is rooted in idealism and humanitarian goals, but while these are necessary conditions, they are unlikely to be sufficient to influence either administrators in the education system (who determine funding priorities) or legislatures (that pass laws that fund education). When school social workers lobby for their profession, their effectiveness is reduced both by their relatively low standing in the hierarchy of education professions and by the difficulty of proving the value of their services to children. Social work has an uncertain status in many countries, variously associated with its origin in charitable work and its work with poor people; however, it must also accept responsibility for the way it continues to be seen. School social workers must take steps to advance the standing of their profession, by improving and controlling professional standards and training, conducting, and publishing more stringent research, and clarifying its role to administrators, legislators, other professionals, and the public. School social work must also take the initiative to define its role, rather than allow itself to be driven by the agendas of others.

ARTICULATING SCHOOL SOCIAL WORK'S UNIQUE ROLE IN SCHOOLS

School social workers must be able to articulate to policy-makers why the profession is needed and should be funded. Demonstrating the uniqueness of school social work's contribution to the education of children is the key to interpreting the school social work role. The ecological nature of school social work, which focuses attention on all aspects of the child and the child's environment, distinguishes it from other disciplines that care for a more limited aspect of the student's development and are less involved with the relationship of the child to the whole community. The traditional roles of school social work in improving attendance and providing a liaison with the student's family are also a unique contribution to school systems. The connection that school social work offers between school and the wider community is also of growing importance because schools now recognize that they are no longer self-contained environments that function in isolation. School social work is ideally suited to developing collaborative efforts with community agencies and other organizations that broaden students' experience of the world outside of school.

Lastly, social work's traditional emphasis on strengths, rather than on diagnosing problems, as in the medical model, is increasingly recognized by other disciplines. Social work should lay claim to this paradigm and embrace methods that use it, such as those that flow from the resiliency research of recent years (Werner & Smith, 1989). Developing students' strengths is the key to proactive strategies that prevent students developing problems in school.

DEMONSTRATING EFFECTIVENESS

Interpreting school social work to administrators, legislators, and the public that ultimately pays for the service must be backed up by evidence of effectiveness. The countries described in this book are concerned with academic success and school social workers must demonstrate how social work services contribute to students' success in school. School social workers are also closely involved with some of the most complex and recalcitrant problems that affect schools, such as violence, and must not only show their willingness to tackle these problems but also to measure the results of their interventions.

School social work's idealism and humanitarian achievements are still needed in schools and some segments of the public, such as parents, appreciate this aspect of school social work. Numerical results are not always as effective in showing the value of school social work as sharing the story of helping a child overcome seemingly insurmountable odds to become successful.

However, the profession can no longer rely solely on such emotional appeals, but must provide empirical evidence that shows how school social work can improve outcomes, especially educational outcomes, for students. For example, studies that show statistically significant improvement in attendance rates for school populations, cuts in dropout rates, or reduction in incidents of bullying address issues that are important to today's schools. A further step is to demonstrate how psychosocial variables, such as bullying and poor attendance, affect academic outcome. This type of research is particularly complex because it is difficult to isolate factors such as bullying and poor attendance from embedded factors, including academic ability, family problems, social and emotional concerns, and problems of the school itself. This makes demonstrating causative relationships between psychosocial factors and achievement especially complex. Nevertheless, it is important for the profession to be able to demonstrate that social work programs can influence academic success.

The profession needs demonstration projects that show novel approaches to specific problems. Their value can be multiplied if the results are given in measurable terms and if the results show that the intervention has produced significant improvement. In addition to demonstrating measurable improvement, it is important to show that the work can be replicated. Ideally, such research would be conducted through collaboration between researchers and practitioners.

The results of such exemplary practices must be disseminated and school social workers must be encouraged to use protocols of effective programs. Developing effective programs and disseminating results will help reveal the relationship between social conditions and educational success that has been largely overlooked in ongoing educational reform designed to improve academic standards.

HALLMARKS OF A PROFESSION

In addition to demonstrating the uniqueness and effectiveness of social work interventions, school social work must continue the process of professionalizing its discipline. Textbooks, research, journals, specialized coursework, and certification are some of the hallmarks of a discipline that is a profession. School social work has not reached this stage of professionalism in many of the countries described in this book. These are issues to be addressed by schools of social work and school social work associations.

Textbooks on school social work (Allen-Meares, Washington, and Walsh, 2000; Vyslouzil and Weissensteiner, 2001) provide a baseline of information about the field, but have been published in only a few countries. Few journals are available specifically for school social workers, and some of these publish articles written primarily by social work educators rather than by school social workers. Practitioners consequently question the relevance of journals, especially when their content rarely deals with typical problems in school social work. Practitioners should be encouraged to publish their work in national and international journals. This book is an example of the value of publications by school social workers working together with social work educators and others: 11 out of 24 contributors are currently school social workers, and four others have practiced school social work earlier in their careers (see list of contributors).

INTERNATIONAL DEVELOPMENT IN SCHOOL SOCIAL WORK

In today's global environment, school social work will be a more effective, credible, and influential agent in education if school social workers around the world recognize the commonalities of their role and unite to upgrade the profession. A parochial outlook hinders the transformation of school social work into a global profession with unified goals and activities, while international contact can expand knowledge and strengthen the profession through this cross-fertilization of ideas.

School social workers deal with local problems, often with little contact outside of their own school or community, and seldom see themselves in an international role. The problems of the school children they serve are resolved within the school, family, and local community. School social workers come closest to dealing directly with international problems when they work with immigrant children, especially refugee children who have been traumatized by wars or dislocation. However, as this book shows, children's problems are similar in all countries, and children are increasingly influenced by global forces that affect not only the economy but also the local culture and even intimate family problems. School social workers, teachers, and others who work with children at the beginning of the 21st century are preparing them for a life in a global community.

The world of children growing up in the 21st century is compressed into the metaphorical "global village" by increased migration and international travel, together with the revolution in telecommunications and information technology. Cultural influences spread rapidly (albeit mostly from the developed world) to children. The *Pokémon* phenomenon exemplifies how quickly children's activities travel around the world. *Pocket Monsters* (*Pokémon* in English) originated in Japan in 1998 and its toys, cards, videogames, and thousands of web sites became the most popular fad among 6- to 11-year-olds around the world in a matter of months. It will quickly fade just as parents and teachers are starting to understand the complex rules of the game.

In less than 10 years, the Internet has become a part of daily life in many countries. In the United States, for example, 95 percent of schools are connected to the Internet (Kiefer, 2000, p. 2). E-mail is a vital way of communicating with their friends for many teenagers, adults, and, increasingly, for younger children. This revolution in how people communicate highlights the "digital divide" not only between rich and poor families but also between rich and poor nations, and amplifies the problem of social exclusion for segments of the population in developed countries and for whole populations. Access to information via the Internet has the potential to transform the lives of poor children, in both developed and developing countries, and improve their chance of equal opportunity. The proposal to subsidize phone services to Native American reservations in the United States is an example of bridging the "digital divide" in remote or impoverished areas (Kiefer, 2000. p. 2). The goal is to help poor communities leapfrog intervening steps of development to become part of the information age.

Technology makes it possible for school social workers to bridge their own "digital divide" to access information, link up with colleagues, and become a global entity. Social workers in countries where school social work is a new field can quickly find information and make contacts around the world.

Locating and sharing information about effective interventions has rapidly become much simpler with technology, and offers opportunities for international cooperation. School social workers anywhere in the world can now find information about children's problems or technical assistance for implementing prevention programs from various databases. For example, the ERIC database includes vast numbers of documents relevant to school social work (http://ericcass.uncg.edu/), and Medscape provides research on children's health and disabilities (http://pediatrics.medscape.com).

Using technology, school social workers can develop a network with their colleagues overseas to transform the profession into an international community. The International Network for School Social Work (http://internationalnetwork-schoolsocialwork.htmlplanet.com) is a first step in linking school social work associations around the world. Telecommunications, electronic newsletters, linked web sites and "listservs," can help stimulate international job exchanges, assist research, and provide international training opportunities.

Developing appropriate training and conducting research into effective interventions are areas in which international collaboration can improve the profession. An international network of schools of social work that offer specialty coursework in school social work could provide a global resource for social work training and extend training in school social work to areas that so far have no specialized courses. Virtual universities could offer university courses to students in countries that do not have access to social work courses at a university. Specialized courses in school social work, for example, at Michigan State University (http://www.ssc.msu.edu/~sw) are already available via both distance learning using interactive television and by the Internet in the United States. Social work students could receive a degree from a foreign university using modest equipment and without leaving home. For example the African Virtual University (http://www.avu.org/) sponsored by various countries, the World Bank, and Intelsat, currently provides courses, although none in social work, to 22 sub-Saharan countries.

Schools of social work are starting to include international content in their curricula. For example, the accrediting body for schools of social work in the United States, the Council on Social Work Education (Council on Social Work Education, 2001), includes references to international policies in the Educational Policy and Accreditation Standards (EPAS). In the European Union the possibility already exists for joint development of curricula, student and teacher exchanges, and international projects. Erasmus, the European Community Action Scheme for the Mobility of University Students, was introduced in 1987 to facilitate mobility of students and teachers (Socrates-Erasmus, 2000). It has been extended to include countries in the European Economic Area that are not part of the European Union. In South America, the Mercado Común del Sur (Mercosur) carries similar potential for student exchange and transfer of credits, as mentioned in the chapter on Argentina. These trends will help the profession of social work, including school social work, develop its influence in international policies that affect children.

The new millennium and the process of globalization focus attention on the potential for school social work to become an international advocate for children's rights, especially the right to education. The new ease of international contact makes it possible for school social workers to extend their influence beyond their local sphere of action to advocate worldwide for children and their education. It is an opportunity that has been little used thus far. School social workers often limit their function to solving the problems of an individual child, sensing that their low status limits their ability to take on larger issues related to children's rights. Currently the International Federation of Social Workers is one of the few international social work organizations that is active in advocating for human rights and contributing social work knowledge to international social movements. The lack of an international organization representing school social workers impedes their involvement in such advocacy. The first step is to strengthen national professional organizations for school social workers and then bring the national groups together into an international association that can provide input on international children's issues.

THE FUTURE OF CHILDREN

In the last decade of the 20th century, there were developments in science, medicine, and technology that caught most people by surprise. A baby was born from an embryo that had been conceived and frozen seven years before, a human spent over a year in space, monkeys were cloned from embryo cells, and the introduction of the World Wide Web started a revolution in communications (Williams, 1999, p. 934). The rapid pace of scientific progress offers the promise of better health, nutrition, and opportunity for the world's children. Meanwhile, the combined effects of globalization and technology have increased awareness of the vital role of human and intellectual capital in overcoming the problems that face the world. The future of humanity depends not only on technology but also on educating children and solving problems in human relationships. However, the amazing advance in science and technology has not been matched by progress in children's rights, reducing poverty, peaceful conflict resolution, and equal opportunity. School social workers have a unique role to play in promoting these human issues to ensure a brighter future for all children.

REFERENCES

Aguirre, L. (1995). California's efforts towards school-linked, integrated, comprehensive services. *Social Work in Education, 17*, 217–225.

Allen-Meares, P. (1977). Analysis of tasks in school social work. *Social Work, 22*, 196–201.

Allen-Meares, P. (1994). Social work services in schools: A national study. *Social Work, 39,* 560–567.

Allen-Meares, P., Washington, R. & Walsh, B. (2000). Social Work Services in Schools. Needham Heights, MA: Allyn and Bacon.

Annan, K. (2000). *We the peoples: The role of the United Nations in the 21st century* (Millennium Report of the Secretary-General of the United Nations). [Online]. Available: http://www.un.org/millennium/sg/report/full.htm

Briar-Lawson, K., Lawson, H., Collier, C. & Joseph, A. (1997). School-linked comprehensive services: Promising beginnings, lessons learned, and future challenges. *Social Work in Education, 19*, 136–148.

Corrigan, D. & Bishop, K. (1997). Creating family-centered integrated service systems and interprofessional educational programs to implement them. *Social Work in Education, 19*, 149–163.

Costin, L. (1975). School social work practice: A new model. *Social Work, 20*, 135–139.

Council on Social Work Education. (2001). Proposed Educational Policy and Accreditation Standards. [Online]. Available: http://www.cswe.org/accreditation/EPAS/EPAS_start.htm

Cousins, L., Jackson, K. & Till, M. (1997). Portrait of a school-based health center: An ecosystems perspective. *Social Work in Education, 19*, 189–202.

Hare, I. (1993). *New developments in Hungarian social work.* (Report funded by United States Department of Health and Human Services Grant #90-PD0172). Washington, DC: National Association of Social Work.

Jones, H. (1994). Social workers, or social educators? The international context for developing social care. National Institute for Social Work International Centre Paper No. 2.

Kiefer, F. (2000, April 19). Political tangles in hardwiring a nation. *The Christian Science Monitor*, pp. 2,3.

Socrates-Erasmus: the European Community programme in the field of higher education. (2000). [Online]. Available: http://europa.eu.Int/comm/education/socrates/erasmus/home.html

Tapper, D., Kleinman, P. & Nakashian, M. (1997). An inter-agency collaboration strategy for linking schools with social and criminal justice services. *Social Work in Education, 19,* 176–188.

United Nations Children's Fund. (1999). *The state of the world's children.* [Online]. Available: http://www.unicef.org/sowc99/

Vyslouzil, M. and Weissensteiner. M. (2001). Schulsozialarbeit in Österreich. Wien: ÖGB.

Werner, E. & Smith, R. (1989). *Vulnerable but invincible*. New York: Adams, Bannister, Cox.

Williams, N. (1999). *Hutchinson chronology of world history: The modern world*. Oxford: Helicon.

NOTES

SOCIAL INDICATORS
FROM THE STATISTICS DIVISION OF THE UNITED NATIONS
AS OF 1999

REFERENCE:
HTTP://WWW.UN.ORG/DEPTS/UNSD/INDICATORS/INDIC2A.HTM

All statistics for social indicators are taken from the Statistics Division of the United Nations.
"Social indicators covering a wide range of subject-matter fields are compiled by the Statistics Division, Department of Economic and Social Affairs of the United Nations Secretariat, from many national and international sources in the global statistical system. These indicators are issued in general and special print or machine-readable publications of the Division."

Statistics Division
Social and Housing Statistics Section
United Nations, Room DC2-1584
New York, NY 10017, U.S.A.

INDICATORS ON POPULATION
Source: Population Division and Statistics Division of the United Nations Secretariat

INDICATORS ON YOUTH AND ELDERLY POPULATIONS
Source: Statistics Division and Population Division of the United Nations Secretariat

INDICATORS ON HUMAN SETTLEMENTS

Source: Population Division of the United Nations Secretariat

"These estimates and projections are based on national census or survey data that have been evaluated and, whenever necessary, adjusted for deficiencies and inconsistencies. Urban-rural classification of population in internationally published statistics follows the national census definition, which differs from one country or area to another."

INDICATORS ON HEALTH

Source: Population Division and Statistics Division of the United Nations Secretariat

"Life expectancy at birth is an estimate of the expected number of years to be lived by a female or male newborn, based on current age-specific mortality rates."

INDICATORS ON CHILD-BEARING (1995–2000)

Source: United Nations Population Division and World Health Organization

"Total fertility rate estimates the total number of children a girl will bear if her child-bearing follows the current fertility patterns and she lives through her child-bearing years. Total fertility rate is estimated by the Population Division of the United Nations Secretariat using the latest available demographic data from countries and given as five-year averages."

INDICATORS ON LITERACY

Source: United Nations Educational, Scientific and Cultural Organization (UNESCO)

"The United Nations Educational, Scientific and Cultural Organization recommends defining an illiterate person as someone who cannot, with understanding, both read and write a short, simple statement on his or her everyday life."

"For many countries or areas, illiteracy rates are not available from UNESCO for one or more of the following reasons: (a) illiteracy is believed to have been reduced to minimal levels through several decades of universal primary education, (b) it has not been possible to establish revised estimates following recent mass literacy campaigns, (c) not even a minimal database is available for making rough estimates, or (d) countries have preferred that no estimate be published."

INDICATORS ON INCOME AND ECONOMIC ACTIVITY

Source: Statistics Division of the United Nations Secretariat and International Labour Office

"Gross domestic product (GDP) per capita in U.S. dollars is calculated by the Statistics Division of the United Nations Secretariat primarily from official national accounts statistics in national currencies provided by national statistical services."

INDICATORS ON UNEMPLOYMENT

Source: International Labour Office

"The International Conference on Labour Statisticians adopted the following definition of the unemployed as an international recommendation in 1982:

All persons who during the reference period were: (1) "without work", that is, were not in paid employment or self-employment as specified by the international definition of employment; (2) "currently available for work", that is, were available for paid employment or self-employment during the reference period; or (3) "seeking work", that is, had taken steps in a specified recent period to seek paid employment or self-employment."

(Note: Age groups vary from country to country.)

INDEX

LOOK FOR THESE RELATED TITLES FROM NASW PRESS!

School Social Work Worldwide, *Marion Huxtable and Eric Blyth, Editors.* Children of the 21st century live in a world linked by technology, trade, and travel. They share a global classroom in which their ability to learn is shaped by common influences and hindered by common obstacles. *School Social Work Worldwide* opens the boundaries of international school social work as never before. Leaders in the field from 12 countries provide eye-opening perspectives and innovative interventions that make a compelling statement about the value of learning from one another to ensure that the world's children reach their full potential through education. Sequentially arranged chapters follow the expansion of school social work around the world and then look ahead to policy and practice issues for the future.

ISBN: 0-87101-348-7. January 2002. Item #3487. $44.99.

Risk and Resilience in Childhood: *An Ecological Perspective, Mark W. Fraser, Editor.* How is it that some children face enormous odds but prevail over adversity to become successful? How can you develop practice models that foster resilience and build exciting new knowledge about risk and protection in childhood? You'll find answers to these questions and more in *Risk and Resilience in Childhood,* a unique text that introduces and explores the concepts of protection and resilience in the face of adversity.

ISBN: 0-87101-274-X. 1997. Item #274X. $44.99.

Peace Power for Adolescents: *Strategies for a Culture of Nonviolence, Mark A. Mattaini with the PEACE POWER Working Group.* This groundbreaking book looks at the wide range of risk factors and indicators for violence among our children and translates the findings into an effective prevention and intervention system. The *PEACE POWER* method recognizes that we can find peaceful solutions to strengthen our communities and takes a positive and practical approach that respects the divergent cultures and values in our society.

ISBN: 0-87101-329-0. July 2001. Item #3290. $39.99.

Resiliency: *An Integrated Approach to Practice, Policy, and Research, Roberta R. Greene, Editor.* What makes one person more resilient than another? In this well-timed and invaluable new book, faculty across the curriculum, students, and practitioners will find a comprehensive and practical framework that integrates social work theory, policy, research, and method to promote resilience-based practice and facilitate its application. *Resiliency* educates the reader on successful stress and trauma coping strategies and equips them to build client strengths, adaptation, healing, and self-efficacy.

ISBN: 0-87101-350-9. January 2002. Item #3509. $44.99.

Making Choices: *Social Problem-Solving Skills for Children, Mark W. Fraser, James K. Nash, Maeda J. Galinsky, and Kathleen M. Darwin.* Based on a cognitive problem-solving approach, *Making Choices* addresses the urgent need for children to acquire competence in meeting the demands of childhood within social, school, and family parameters. The book is designed for children from kindergarten through middle school whose behavior is impulsive, oppositional, or aggressive. Recognizing that a great deal of children's behavior is tied to problem solving, the volume focuses on how children solve instrumental and relational issues in differing social settings.

ISBN: 0-87101-323-1. October 2000. Item #3231. $33.99.

Multisystem Skills and Interventions in School Social Work Practice, *Edith M. Freeman, Cynthia G. Franklin, Rowena Fong, Gary L. Shaffer, and Elizabeth M. Timberlake, Editors. Multisystem Skills* is a practical guide that covers interventions that work on all levels, from school to family to community agencies to the policy level. Using case examples, this practice-oriented text investigates difficult challenges such as curbing aggressive behavior, improving attendance in at-risk children, empowering families, preventing youth suicide, participating in post-traumatic event debriefing, and developing new strategies for emerging areas of concern.

ISBN: 0-87101-295-2. 1998. Item #2952. $39.99.

(Order form and information on reverse side)

ORDER FORM

Qty.	Title	Item #	Price	Total
__	School Social Work Worldwide	3487	$44.99	_____
__	Risk and Resilience in Childhood	274X	$44.99	_____
__	Peace Power for Adolescents	3290	$39.99	_____
__	Resiliency	3509	$44.99	_____
__	Making Choices	3231	$33.99	_____
__	Multisystem Skills and Interventions in School Social Work Practice	2952	$39.99	_____

Subtotal	_____
Postage and Handling	_____
DC residents add 6% sales tax	_____
MD residents add 5% sales tax	_____
Total	_____

POSTAGE AND HANDLING
Minimum postage and handling fee is $4.95.
Orders that do not include appropriate
postage and handling will be returned.

DOMESTIC: Please add 12% to orders under
$100 for postage and handling. For orders
over $100 add 7% of order.

CANADA: Please add 17% postage and
handling.

OTHER INTERNATIONAL: Please add 22%
postage and handling.

❒ **Check** or **money order** (payable to NASW Press) for $ _____.

❒ **Credit card**
    ❒ NASW Visa* | ❒ Visa | ❒ NASW MasterCard* | ❒ MasterCard | ❒ Amex

_____   _____

Credit Card Number   Expiration Date

Signature _____

Use of these cards generates funds in support of the social work profession.

Name _____

Address _____

City _____ State/Province _____

Country _____ Zip _____

Phone _____ E-mail _____

NASW Member # (if applicable) _____

(Please make checks payable to NASW Press. Prices are subject to change.)

NASW PRESS
P. O. Box 431
Annapolis JCT, MD 20701
USA

Credit card orders call
1-800-227-3590
(In the Metro Wash., DC, area, call 301-317-8688)
Or fax your order to 301-206-7989
Or order online at http://www.naswpress.org

Visit our Web site at http://www.naswpress.org.   CPSS02